Redemption from Tyranny

EARLY AMERICAN HISTORIES

Douglas Bradburn, John C. Coombs, and S. Max Edelson, Editors

Redemption from Tyranny
Herman Husband's American Revolution

BRUCE E. STEWART

UNIVERSITY OF VIRGINIA PRESS   *Charlottesville and London*

University of Virginia Press
© 2020 by the Rector and Visitors of the University of Virginia
All rights reserved
Printed in the United States of America on acid-free paper

First published 2020

9 8 7 6 5 4 3 2 1

Library of Congress Cataloging-in-Publication Data
Names: Stewart, Bruce E., author.
Title: Redemption from tyranny: Herman Husband's American Revolution / Bruce E. Stewart.
Other titles: Herman Husband's American Revolution
Description: Charlottesville; London: University of Virginia Press, 2020. | Series: Early American histories | Includes bibliographical references and index.
Identifiers: LCCN 2019037149 (print) | LCCN 2019037150 (ebook) | ISBN 9780813943701 (cloth) | ISBN 9780813943718 (ebook)
Subjects: LCSH: Husbands, Hermon, 1724–1795. | Whiskey Rebellion, Pa., 1794. | United States—Politics and government—1789–1815. | Pennsylvania—Politics and government—1775–1865. | Taxation—Pennsylvania. | North Carolina—History—Regulator Insurrection, 1766–1771. | United States—History—1783–1815. | Revolutionaries—United States—Biography. | Bedford County (Pa.)—Biography.
Classification: LCC E302.6.H93 S74 2020 (print) | LCC E302.6.H93 (ebook) | DDC 974.8/03092 [B]—dc23
LC record available at https://lccn.loc.gov/2019037149
LC ebook record available at https://lccn.loc.gov/2019037150

Cover art: Citizens capturing tax collectors during the Whiskey Rebellion, 1790s (*inset*; North Wind Picture Archives); "The State of Pennsylvania" from Heads of Families First Census of the United States—State of Pennsylvania, 1908 (*background*; Perry-Castañeda Library Map Collection, University of Texas Libraries)

For Bub and Linda

Contents

List of Illustrations   ix

Acknowledgments   xi

Prologue   1

ONE   "Like the Sun Breaking Out of Darkness": Husband's New Birth   7

TWO   "A New Government of Liberty": The Politicization of Husband   28

THREE   "Shew Yourselves to Be Freemen": Husband and the North Carolina Regulation   50

FOUR   "Perfecting a Free Government": Husband and the American Revolution   74

FIVE   "The New Jerusalem": Husband and the Early Republic   101

Conclusion: Making Sense of Husband's World   131

Notes   145

Bibliography   187

Index   215

Illustrations

1. Historical marker commemorating Husband   2
2. Cecil County, Maryland, 1795   19
3. George Whitefield   21
4. William Tryon   41
5. Edmund Fanning   44
6. Tryon's Palace   52
7. Southwestern Pennsylvania, 1754   78
8. Title page of David Rittenhouse's *The Continental Almanac*   99
9. Husband's New Jerusalem in America   104
10. Title page of Husband's *XIV Sermons on the Characters of Jacob's Fourteen Sons*   110
11. Alexander Hamilton   119
12. Braddock's Field   125

Acknowledgments

OVER THE PAST SIX YEARS, many people have helped make this book a reality. I would first like to thank the staff at the University of Virginia Press, especially Dick Holway and Helen Chandler, both of whom provided me with invaluable assistance throughout the entire process. Woody Holton's and John Brooke's perceptive suggestions greatly improved the final manuscript. I also appreciate the excellent copyediting skills of Margaret Hogan. Moreover, I am grateful to John Inscoe, Daniel Pierce, and Richard Starnes. All took time out of their busy schedules to review my book proposal and provided me with encouragement when I doubted myself. Steven Nash and Judkin Browning have also been there for me.

Other individuals have contributed to this book in a variety of ways. I owe a debt of gratitude to the archivists at the following institutions: the American Philosophical Society, William Paterson University, Guilford College, Maryland Historical Society, Historical Society of Pennsylvania, Historical Society of Western Pennsylvania, University of Pittsburgh, Maryland State Archives, New-York Historical Society, State Archives of North Carolina, Pennsylvania State Archives, Bedford County Historical Society, University of North Carolina at Chapel Hill, and Carnegie Library. I would further like to thank my colleagues at Appalachian State University for their support. Furthermore, the research for this book would not have been possible without the financial aid of Appalachian State University's Humanities Scholars Fellowship and University Research Council Grant. I would also like to thank those scholars whose previous research on Herman Husband greatly assisted me, most notably Mark Jones, Wythe Holt, Carole Troxler, Marjoleine Kars, George Hatchett, Dorothy Fennell, William Hogeland, and Mary Lazenby.

Above all, thanks to my family. Unfortunately, my dad and eldest brother passed away before I finished this book. I will always wonder what they would have thought about it. My father-in-law and mother-in-law, to whom this book is dedicated, are two of the kindest people I have met. Finally, I would like to thank my editor-in-chief and soulmate, Sunny.

Redemption from Tyranny

Prologue

> In the last days, the labouring, industrious people, the militia of freemen, shall prevail over the standing armies of kings and tyrants, that only rob them, and live upon their labour, in idleness and luxury; which is the whole ground and foundation of the contest. Without government, the strong and robust in body tyrannise; and property is not secured. With government, we have to guard against the crafty, designing, and lazy.
>
> —Herman Husband, *XIV Sermons on the Characters of Jacob's Fourteen Sons*

ON JUNE 18, 1795, seventy-year-old Herman Husband took his last breaths in a tavern on the outskirts of Philadelphia.[1] Just two weeks before, the Bedford County farmer had been released from a Philadelphia jail after being acquitted of charges of sedition for participating in an upheaval that would become known as the Whiskey Rebellion. Although Husband had condemned the use of violence during the protest movement, he—like the other whiskey rebels—was an outspoken critic of the 1788 U.S. Constitution and the new federal government, claiming that both benefited the wealthy few at the expense of the common people. Consequently, the Washington administration singled him out as a troublemaker, a reputation that had led to his imprisonment in October 1794. Upon his release eight months later, the old farmer began the journey back to Bedford County but collapsed from his horse just outside of Philadelphia and was taken to a nearby tavern. As he lay dying, Husband must have bemoaned the fact that his vision of the New Jerusalem in America—where every white farmer owned land, participated in government, and enjoyed the fruits of his labor—would never become a reality. The spirit of tyranny had proven too strong to vanquish.

Husband's career as a rabble-rouser began several decades before the Whiskey Rebellion. Born in Maryland in 1724, he was the son of a prominent planter and spent his childhood training to become a member of the colony's Anglican elite. That would change in 1739, when he first heard the famous evangelist George Whitefield preach. The teenager had already begun to question his Anglican upbringing, and Whitefield's exhortation to rely on individual conscience, rather than church officials, to achieve salvation inspired Husband to abandon Anglicanism for the burgeoning evangelical counterculture. This antiauthoritarian rhetoric would also eventually influence his political activism, as he would insist that all white men—not just the elite—had the ability and a moral obligation to participate in government.

In the early 1750s, Husband moved to the North Carolina Piedmont, where he prospered as a farmer, acquiring over ten thousand acres of land in Orange and Rowan Counties. However, in the 1760s, he found himself at odds with the colony's elite and became a spokesman for a group of farmers opposed to the backcountry's political and economic inequalities. Calling themselves Regulators, these agitators sought to challenge the status quo, condemning and on occasion accosting local officials who they believed exploited the common people by depriving them of the fruits of their labor. As a pamphleteer and elected assemblyman, Husband proved an invaluable ally of the Regulators, portraying their cause as a noble attempt to restore honesty and virtue to government and supporting legislation that limited the concentration of wealth in the hands of a few. After North Carolina militiamen suppressed the protest movement at the Battle of Alamance in 1771, he fled the colony with a bounty on his head.

By 1772, Husband had settled in southwestern Pennsylvania. He rebuilt his fortune and soon embraced a new rebellion: the American Revolution.

FIGURE 1. Located near Sandy Creek in present-day Randolph County, this historical marker commemorates Husband's role in the North Carolina Regulation. (Photograph by the author)

Husband believed that Britain was allied with the Antichrist, having passed legislation in recent years that deprived colonists of their God-given civil and religious freedoms, and that independence would enable common men to achieve political and economic equality. Taking solace in the Old Testament, Husband remained confident that the spirit of liberty would ultimately prevail over Satan's kingdom. With God on their side, he believed, American patriots would fulfill biblical prophecy and form a government that would derive its authority from the common people, break the curse of arbitrary power, and usher in the millennium.

As the new nation slid into an economic recession in the 1780s, however, Husband's optimism faded. He blamed national and state leaders for the fiscal crisis, accusing them of betraying the Revolution by passing legislation that perpetuated the status quo, promoted the concentration of wealth in the hands of a few, and threatened the livelihoods of small farmers. Husband also opposed the ratification of the U.S. Constitution, convinced that it would deprive people of their liberty. He offered his own plan for "perfecting a new government" that called for the creation of a multilayered government in which smaller election districts would allow ordinary men to regain their voice in government, attain political office, and peacefully redeem the republic from tyranny.[2]

By the 1790s, Husband had lost faith in the young republic, believing that its leaders had subverted the American Revolution by embracing a federal Constitution that "proceeded from the spirit of the serpent."[3] Now convinced that the nation was not destined to usher in the millennium, as he had once hoped, Husband increasingly looked to the trans-Appalachian backcountry for economic and political salvation. There, he predicted, the common people would stand up against corrupt leaders and fulfill the biblical Ezekiel's vision of the New Jerusalem by creating a government that worked on behalf of farmers, artisans, and other ordinary white laborers. In a final attempt to save the Revolution from itself, he joined the Whiskey Rebellion, a decision that ultimately landed him in an unknown grave on the outskirts of Philadelphia, several hundred miles from his home.

Husband was not alone in his frustration with the new nation. Countless other Americans also felt betrayed by the outcomes of the Revolution, which for them had meant more than simply gaining independence from Great Britain. To these revolutionaries, the republic was—as Thomas Paine wrote—an opportunity "to begin the world over again." The "contagion of liberty" that swept across the American colonies in the 1760s and 1770s inspired marginalized groups, reinforcing slaves' desire to become free and encouraging women to continue their fight for equality. It also emboldened ordinary white men—farmers, artisans, and wage earners—to denounce the political and economic inequalities that prevented them from attaining a stronger voice in government and earning a decent living. While often at odds with one another, these groups all believed that the lofty principles of the Declaration of Independence signified the birth of a new, more radical government deriving its power from the people.[4]

Such expectations proved shortsighted, especially for African Americans and women. The Declaration's pronouncement that "all men are created equal" would not apply to them, at least in the immediate decades to come. Slavery, protected by the U.S. Constitution, remained entrenched in the southern states until the 1860s, at which point nearly 4 million African Americans labored in bondage. The victims of institutional racism, free blacks in both the North and South would also continue to live as second-class citizens.[5] Nor did the status of women significantly change in the wake of the American Revolution. Most men were not ready to—as John Adams put it—"repeal our Masculine systems."[6] Although some benefited from their new role as republican mothers, women for the most part could not vote, hold office, or own property. The young republic would remain a patriarchal society.[7]

Ordinary white men had much more to celebrate about the new nation. After all, they emerged from the Revolution with increased political power and prestige. But they quickly realized that the expansion of white male suffrage meant little without economic reform. For them, the republic they envisioned would survive only if there existed a degree of wealth equality among white men. Drawing on experience, Western political thought, and Christianity, they feared that the affluent would inevitably use their economic power to control the political system and manipulate the marketplace in their favor. Non-elites subsequently championed the creation of a government that protected their interests by limiting concentrations of wealth and property. In their eyes, the U.S. Constitution was far too conservative to accomplish this goal, as it favored the concerns of a corrupt elite whose fiscal policies threatened to subjugate the entire population. Their discontent ultimately led to a series of protest movements throughout the United States during the 1780s and 1790s, including the Whiskey Rebellion in southwestern Pennsylvania and other parts of the backcountry.[8]

The following story is about one of these ordinary men and the world in which he lived. A farmer, evangelical, and political activist, Herman Husband participated in some of the most important events in eighteenth-century America—the Great Awakening, the North Carolina Regulation, the American Revolution, and the Whiskey Rebellion—during which he earned a reputation as a radical, advocating for the reduction of economic inequality among white men. Through his story, this book explores how common people shaped—and were shaped by—the American Revolution, and highlights the varied reasons behind the rise of radicalism and its impact on society during the long American Revolution. Perhaps more importantly, it reveals that equality and democracy have always been contested concepts in American political discourse.

ONE

"Like the Sun Breaking Out of Darkness"
Husband's New Birth

> I began to feel the Wrath of God to kindle in my Bosom, and I cried O Lord Jesus! Convince me of a Truth that it is thee, and I will go at thy Command; and I can in Truth declare it, in a Moment's time he appeared like a Blaze of Light, enlightening the whole Room and said, It is, I, be not afraid. I had shut my Eyes from seeing the Glory of that Light, for it so resembled a real outward Light, that I had no Question of it; and being told to be not afraid, I opened my Eyes and had to behold, that Light was wholly within my Soul.
> —Herman Husband, *Some Remarks on Religion*

Patriarchs

One warm morning in late July 1670, a young Englishman and soon-to-be indentured servant named William Husband awoke to the news that his long journey was nearing its end. For nearly three months, he had been on a ship bound for Maryland, where he hoped to start a new life.[1] Although Europeans had been crossing the Atlantic for nearly two centuries, this was still a dangerous trip, with countless vessels succumbing to foul weather and their passengers to disease. Husband must have been relieved when he spotted a black streak on the western horizon, his first glimpse of the Virginia shore, described by a later traveler as looking "like a forest standing in the water" as the ship approached.[2]

After rounding Cape Henry, Husband's ship would have entered the Chesapeake Bay, continuing northward past the James River to the Potomac

River, the natural boundary line separating the British colonies of Virginia and Maryland. Sailing upstream on the Potomac, the vessel veered onto St. Mary's River, where it finally set anchor near St. Mary's City, Maryland, on August 2.[3] Stepping onto his new homeland for the first time, the ambitious Husband must have welcomed the possibilities of the future.

By 1670, Maryland had gained the reputation as being a "good small-man's country."[4] For decades, land speculators had published promotional pamphlets extolling the colony's rich soils, cheap lands, and abundant employment opportunities.[5] Husband was likely inspired by these popular tracts, such as George Alsop's *A Character of the Province of Maryland*, published in 1666. Alsop, a former indentured servant, proclaimed that the colony was a newfound Eden. "I think there is [no other] place under the Heavenly altitude," he wrote, "or that has footing or room upon the circular Globe of this world, that can parallel this fertile and pleasant piece of ground in its multiplicity, or rather Natures extravagancy of a super-abounding plenty." Alsop insisted that the greatest opportunities for economic advancement were reserved for indentured servants, who, after finishing their terms of service, could quickly purchase land, build farms, and grow tobacco. "They whose abilities cannot extend to purchase their own transportation over into Maryland... I say they may for the debarment of a four years forbid liberty, go over into this Province and there live plenteously well," he declared. "And what's a four years Servitude to advantage a man all the remainder of his dayes, making his predecessors happy in his sufficient abilities, which he attained to partly by the refrainment of so small a time?"[6]

Faced with the realities of seventeenth-century England's declining rural, agricultural economy, such promotional literature struck a chord among thousands of Englishmen. Population increases and rising land prices in the British countryside had led many people, especially young men and women, to seek jobs in London and other towns. But employment opportunities and living and working conditions in these urban manufacturing centers rapidly declined as more migrants flooded their streets in search of work. These dire economic circumstances in England and the promise of cheap land in the American colonies made the dangerous journey and four years of indentured servitude appealing to men like Husband.[7]

But the new world that greeted young Husband was not the paradise that Alsop and other promoters had portrayed. New immigrants faced a dangerous and foreign environment, and many of them would perish from malaria or dysentery during their first year in America.[8] These Englishmen also often found the American climate and cuisine unpalatable; summers were hotter and winters much colder in Maryland than in England, and the wheat- and barley-based diet with which they had been familiar was replaced by one of corn, beans, and other exotic foods.[9] Furthermore, the landscape proved daunting to new arrivals. Unlike in England, vegetation blanketed Maryland's countryside, making the region seem like a wilderness. One immigrant wrote that the white oak, black walnut, and hickory trees, "the Trunks of which are often Thirty, Forty, Fifty, some Sixty or Seventy Foot high, without a Branch of Limb," grew so thick that it was difficult for many people "to travale without molestation."[10]

However, while life in Maryland was not without its challenges, the colony offered Husband and others what England increasingly failed to provide: access to cheap and abundant land. But before the dream of landownership could become a reality, Husband had to complete his term of servitude. It is unclear exactly for whom Husband labored during his first three years in Maryland. It might have been Thomas Notley, the colony's future governor, who paid for Husband's and five other migrants' passage to Maryland in exchange for three hundred acres of land. It could have also been John Griggs, a farmer and tavern keeper who purchased Husband's fifty-acre headright in 1673.[11] Regardless, Husband, like most other indentured servants, probably spent his days cultivating tobacco, the colony's most important and lucrative crop.

Maryland farmers had depended on tobacco production since the colony's founding in 1634, with the explosion of European demand for the smooth, higher-quality Chesapeake tobacco.[12] Witnessing the success of Virginia farmers, Maryland settlers recognized that tobacco was more lucrative than other local crops. By 1639, Maryland was exporting 100,000 pounds of tobacco annually, an average of more than 600 pounds for each adult male in the colony.[13] Only thirty years later, Maryland and Virginia planters together were producing 15 million pounds of tobacco a year.[14]

The cash crop was the backbone of the Chesapeake economy. In addition to selling it at market, farmers in Virginia and Maryland used tobacco as currency well into the eighteenth century. It also connected them to England and the global economy, as merchants exchanged the popular crop for manufactured goods unavailable in the colonies. "We have [no] trade at home and abroad, but that of Tobacco," one farmer declared in the late seventeenth century. "[It] is our meat, drink, clothes, and monies."[15]

Initially, Maryland planters largely relied on the labor of white indentured servants, most of whom—like Husband—were young, single, and male.[16] Growing tobacco was hard work, and servants routinely labored fourteen hours a day, six days a week. Their work began in January, when they cleared the land by girdling and burning trees, a Native American practice that quickly removed vegetation and increased the soil's fertility.[17] The second step was to plant a tobacco bed, covering it with cloth or leaves to protect the seedlings from frost once they sprouted. With that task completed, servants would have worked to prepare the main fields by mounding "the soil into small hills arranged in rows" with a heavy hoe.[18] When the weather was warm enough—usually by late May—the workers would remove the tobacco seedlings from the bed and place them in the main field. The plants would continue to mature until the end of summer and, once harvested in the fall, cure for a month before being shipped to market in November. Servants spent the rest of the year cutting firewood, constructing fences, and repairing buildings.[19]

In addition to the hard work and long hours, indentured servants like Husband were often at the mercy of their owners. Most contracts required masters to provide servants with the basic necessities of life, including clothing, food, medical care, and shelter, and servants could seek redress from the courts to protect themselves from abuse or neglect. But servitude was often harsh. Servants endured poor living conditions, even by seventeenth-century standards, as frugal masters crammed laborers into small, one-room wooden structures with earthen floors and flimsy clapboard roofs. With a diet highly dependent on corn, many indentures also suffered from pellagra, a vitamin deficiency that causes skin lesions and gastrointestinal problems. Punishments for running away were severe, and masters sometimes sold their servants to the highest bidder. More often than not, however, most indentured servants tolerated their circumstances, knowing that freedom as landowners would be their reward.[20]

When Husband completed his term of service in 1673, the young man did not leave his master's farm empty-handed. His former owner was required by law to give him basic provisions to assist him in his first year of freedom: three barrels of corn, a new set of clothes, and a hoe and axe.[21] Husband also received rights to fifty acres of land, but the acquisition of this land proved impractical. In order to obtain it, he would have had to pay clerk's and surveyor's fees for a patent, which required either capital or credit, neither of which Husband possessed.[22] Opting to sell his claim to John Griggs, who might have been his former master, Husband packed up his few belongings, bid servitude farewell, and began his life as a freedman.[23]

Although Husband's next move is unknown, like most new freedmen, he had two choices. He may have worked as a wage laborer on a farm, signing either a short- or long-term contract with a landholder. His experience cultivating tobacco and maintaining a farm would have made Husband a desirable employee, and this could have proved a lucrative option, as the colony's continued labor shortage kept wages high in the mid-seventeenth century.[24] He might also have decided to lease land, paying his rent with a portion of his crop or labor. This would have allowed him to quickly set up a household and begin farming for himself. Either option provided an aspiring planter with the opportunity to build enough capital to purchase his own land, build a farm, and grow tobacco.[25]

Husband did eventually become a landowner, aided in part by the timing of his arrival to Maryland. Until the turn of the eighteenth century, short life expectancies and low birthrates ensured that the colony's population remained relatively small, which led to a continued supply of abundant and cheap land.[26] And though increased production caused the price of tobacco to decline, farmers were mostly able to maintain profits through expanding production during the 1600s.[27] Before the rise of African slavery in the Chesapeake at the end of the seventeenth century, these demographic and market forces enabled many former servants like Husband to accumulate enough capital to buy land within a few of years of earning their freedom.[28]

Husband's path to land ownership may have been accelerated by matrimony. Around 1684, he married a young widow named Mary Bowen.[29] With men outnumbering women in Maryland three to one, and as the owner of her late husband's estate—estimated at slightly over £57, a small but not insignificant amount—Bowen did not have to wait long to find another mate.[30] Husband may have used her inheritance to purchase two hundred acres of land and establish a farm in 1686 in St. Mary's County (modern-day Charles County), the first written record detailing his ascent to the ranks of the small planter class.[31]

While Husband was, in many ways, an average freedman, one characteristic both set him apart and gave him a distinct advantage: literacy. In addition to providing him with the means to supplement his income by finding employment as a scrivener, appraiser, and legal advisor, Husband's literacy also allowed him to participate in the region's political arena.[32] Here again he was aided by good timing. Maryland's low population meant that there were often not enough people to fill bureaucratic positions, especially at the county level, and the elite found it necessary to appoint common men as constables, highway overseers, and other posts.[33] The fact that Husband could read made him an attractive option, and, in 1691, he became a justice of the peace, a position he held for the next eight years.[34]

By 1700, Husband was a man on the make, a budding member of Maryland's yeomanry. Having arrived in America with nothing, in only twenty years he had acclimated to his new country, survived his indenture, acquired land, built a farm, and obtained political office. Despite these successes, Husband abruptly moved from St. Mary's County to Cecil County, located in the northeastern corner of the colony, and he would not buy land again until 1716.[35] The reasons for this move are unclear. Perhaps a bad harvest wiped out his savings, forcing him to leave his farm. Or maybe he was reacting to the emergence of a native-born elite that had begun to dominate St. Mary's County and other older, more established parts of Maryland's Lower Western Shore, diminishing opportunities for small farmers.[36] Whatever Husband's motivation, his decision to relocate to Cecil County was wise for a number of reasons. Founded in 1674, the county's fertile black soils made it optimal for growing tobacco and corn.[37] Sparsely settled, land remained plentiful and affordable. Moreover, the county's vast river network allowed farmers to quickly ship their crops to Baltimore, Annapolis, and other commercial centers.[38]

Husband eventually made his way to St. Stephen's Parish, located in southern Cecil County, where he probably rented a tract of land. By April 1716, he had again accumulated enough capital to purchase 250 acres near the Elk and Bohemia Rivers and a 225-acre plantation north of the Sassafras River, which ran along the border of Cecil and Kent Counties.[39] Records indicate that Husband found success as a Cecil County farmer, enjoying fine earthenware plates and other luxuries that most colonists could not afford.[40]

Husband's five children would come of age on their father's Cecil County plantation.[41] Their days likely revolved around the maintenance of the farm, rising at dawn to milk the cows and feed the chickens and working alongside their father in the tobacco field, weeding and picking worms off the plants. The older boys would have also been responsible for occasionally venturing into the woods to capture one of their father's hogs, the family's main source of meat. Husband's children were not the only source of labor on the estate. The responsibilities of cooking, cleaning, and sewing rested with a white, female servant whose duties likely intensified after the death of Mary sometime before 1717, and at least five slaves worked in the fields, helping to increase the farm's productivity.[42]

By purchasing slaves, Husband was following the lead of other established planters. Initially, Maryland farmers viewed slave ownership as a risky venture. Slaves were more expensive than indentured servants and often died within a few years, making them a poor long-term investment. However, such pessimistic attitudes about the profitability of slavery did not last long. By 1700, the price of slaves had dropped below that of indentured servants and life expectancies were rising among blacks in the Chesapeake, causing slavery to eventually replace indentured servitude as the region's leading source of labor and capital accumulation.[43] In fact, between 1660 and 1710, the percentage of slaves in the Chesapeake increased from 4.8 to 25.6 percent of the total population.[44]

When he died in 1717, William Husband was one of the last of his kind, a former indentured servant who had managed to escape the cycle of debt and tenancy and become an independent, landholding planter. Opportunities for men like Husband had begun to diminish at the turn of the eighteenth century, fueled in part by the rise of slavery, which drove up the price of labor and concentrated unfree workers on large plantations.[45] Demographic changes also worked against aspiring planters. As more people migrated to the colony at the end of the century, land prices steadily rose, forcing recent white settlers to remain wage earners or tenant farmers. Unable to afford land, many of these men and women moved out of the Chesapeake region, which in turn deepened planters' dependence on slave labor. Despite this outmigration, the colony's white population continued to increase, hampering the chances of non-landholding farmers to participate in government as well. With more qualified men to choose from, the colony's burgeoning elite no longer relied on less prestigious whites to serve in political office.[46]

Husband's third son and namesake, William Jr.—father of Herman—would thrive in this hierarchical, slave-based society.[47] By the early eighteenth century, native-born Marylanders like William Jr. made up the majority of the colony's population, and they often enjoyed a number of advantages over earlier generations, particularly those who had arrived as indentured servants. The younger Husband entered adulthood already possessing land and capital, having inherited part of one of the largest estates in Maryland.[48] The colony's rising native-born population also allowed him to marry and start a family at an early age. In 1720, he married Mary, the daughter of Herman Kinkey, a German farmer and ferry keeper who owned a six-hundred-acre plantation in northwestern Cecil County.[49] William Jr. would continue to use marriage to strategically develop and maintain kinship ties to enhance his family's socioeconomic standing. Two of his daughters, for instance, married into the Hollingsworth and Gilpin families, both of which had grown wealthy from Cecil County's burgeoning wheat industry.[50]

During the 1720s, William Husband Jr. prospered as a tobacco farmer, expanding his late father's plantation, buying slaves, and earning the title of gentleman.[51] Dependent on tobacco for his success, however, the young man likely struggled when the price of that cash crop declined sharply during a depression in the 1730s. Historically, economic downturns had failed to encourage most Chesapeake farmers into curtailing their tobacco production. Having already invested in land and labor, planters found this option impractical and continued to grow tobacco, which often further weakened the economy. Tobacco prices would eventually rebound but not before the fortunes of many farmers had vanished. In the 1730s, some farmers began to respond to economic troubles by eschewing tobacco in favor of wheat, a crop whose demand had recently skyrocketed throughout Europe and the West Indies, and thus promised to bring better returns than tobacco.[52] This may have been why William Jr. sold his family's farm around 1737 and moved to his wife's family estate in St. Mary Ann's Parish in northwestern Cecil County, where Quaker settlers had already established wheat-marketing networks with Philadelphia merchants.[53] Herman Kinkey had left to his daughter's family a tract of land situated along a busy road connecting the region to the commercial center of Lancaster, Pennsylvania.[54] Knowing an opportunity when he saw it, William Jr. became a wheat farmer and began acquiring surrounding property, building an estate that eventually encompassed nearly 1,300 acres.[55] Further capitalizing on the region's booming wheat industry, he constructed a gristmill, where he converted locally produced wheat into flour to be shipped to Philadelphia and other markets.[56] Ever the entrepreneur, William Jr. expanded his enterprises to nonagricultural pursuits, building a sawmill—where slaves processed trees into boards—and investing in an iron mine and -works in nearby Baltimore County in 1740.[57]

William Jr. never amassed a fortune comparable to the region's upper elite, but with an estate valued at nearly £1,000, he belonged to a prominent group of planter-merchants that lower-class Marylanders envied. He certainly viewed himself as a gentleman and acted accordingly. He entertained guests in the parlor of his two-story brick house, where they gossiped, danced, and drank alcohol throughout the night.[58] He may have sometimes journeyed to Baltimore or Annapolis to attend elaborate balls in which wealthy people showcased their good manners, grace, and wit, characteristics that they believed separated them from the lower sort.[59] Like other eighteenth-century Chesapeake gentlemen, William Jr. had a passion for gambling. Whether playing cards, nine-pins, dice, or other popular games of chance, he jumped at the opportunity to place a wager. These forms of entertainment, often carryovers from England, held deep cultural meanings for their participants. They allowed the gentry to prove their manliness, maintain their honor, and flaunt their wealth.[60] While William Jr. appears to have flourished in this social world, his eldest son, Herman, would ultimately rebel against it.

An Early Religious Crisis

Born on October 3, 1724, Herman was the second of William and Mary's twelve children.[61] His early life probably resembled that of other children belonging to Chesapeake planter households. Wanting to raise a hardy and virtuous son who would someday inherit the family plantation, William and Mary would have encouraged the boy to develop traits considered manly: a strong will and stoic disposition. Often free from adult supervision, Herman engaged in activities such as racing, wrestling, hunting, and fishing that promoted strength and self-reliance.[62] But he was also expected to control the passions and competiveness that these pastimes engendered. Popular child-rearing books like John Garretson's *The School of Manners* (1701) taught children to practice self-restraint, a virtue that only men of quality possessed; "submit to thy Superiors"; "be not among Equals forward or fretful but gentle and affable"; and "boast not in discourse of thy wit or doings," among other etiquettes.[63]

When Herman was seven years old, he spent several months living with his maternal grandfather, Herman Kinkey. Probably born in Germany, Kinkey had migrated to New Castle County, Delaware, in the late seventeenth century.[64] In 1717, he moved to Cecil County, Maryland, where he purchased a six-hundred-acre farm along the Elk River near Bohemia Manor, the former plantation of explorer and cartographer Augustine Herman.[65] Husband would later write that his grandfather was a man of devout faith and strict discipline who demanded respect from the younger generation. Perhaps that is why William Jr. sent his son to live with him in early 1732. Herman's father may have thought that his son, who was a mischievous child, needed Kinkey's stern guidance to learn how to control his passions and obey his elders.[66] This would come in the form of religious instruction, something that Husband's parents had thus far minimized.

William Husband Jr. raised his family—as his father had—in the Anglican tradition. Although Maryland had been known for its religious tolerance in the seventeenth century, by the 1690s the Church of England had established itself in the colony, rescinding many of the privileges that Catholics, Quakers, and other dissenting sects had once enjoyed. Before moving to St. Mary Ann's Parish in the mid-1730s, William Jr. worshiped at St. Stephen's Anglican Church, where his father served as a vestryman.[67] While Herman would have regularly attended church, it appears that religion did not dominate the boy's upbringing. By his own account, religion was a matter of small concern to his father, who—like many other Anglican gentlemen—viewed church services more as an opportunity to display his status in the social hierarchy than to attain salvation.[68]

While his father did not encourage extreme religious devotion, Herman's grandfather proved far more devout. Kinkey was likely influenced by German Pietism, which stressed individual piety and the following of a rigorous Christian life. This so-called religion of the heart emerged in the middle colonies during the 1720s, largely due to the prophesizing of Theodorus Frelinghuysen, a Dutch Reformed minister who migrated from Holland to New Jersey in 1720.[69] Kinkey certainly adhered to the belief that piety was the means to salvation, requiring his family and servants to read the Bible, pray, and abstain from self-indulgence. Under Kinkey's roof, Herman began to question his Anglican upbringing for the first time and pondered the fate of his soul. "I . . . heard his Servants Lads . . . say the Lord's Prayer and Creed, when they went to Bed, and as I lay with them, I heard them say these by Heart, before they went to Sleep," he recalled. "This, I thought, was what God required of me, and what I must do to go to Heaven, which Place I was not willing to miss of."[70] Husband's short sojourn with Kinkey, who died in late 1732, sparked the beginning of his quest to obtain God's grace and achieve true salvation.

This journey proved difficult, especially for a boy expected to participate in Maryland's secular genteel society. Back home, Husband resumed his training as a gentleman, again filling his days with hunting, fishing, and wrestling. He was particularly adept at gambling—like his father—and dancing. By the eighteenth century, dancing had emerged as an important social activity for most Chesapeake residents, performed during times of celebration in homes, taverns, churches, and other communal spaces. For young men, the ability to dance was of great significance, providing them with an opportunity to display their prowess and court the opposite sex.[71] Husband was no stranger to the pastime. He often participated in dance frolics and even won a monetary prize at one event. Gambling, however, became Husband's favorite activity. "Playing at Cards had . . . newly become very frequent in our Neighborhood among us to both old Men as well as Young in which, for a great while, I had took great Delight," he remembered. "I us'd to play before both Father and Mother, my Father playing sometimes himself, especially when there were any Strangers."[72] Gambling bonded father and son, allowing them to channel their competiveness into nonviolent activities.[73] William must have been pleased; his son was well on his way to becoming a member of the Chesapeake gentry.

Yet young Herman found himself uneasy with the genteel lifestyle. Its emphasis on self-indulgence and luxury took a heavy toll on his conscience, sparking a religious crisis. Whenever he danced or gambled, Husband would hear his grandfather's voice warning him to abstain from such worldly pleasures. "When I laid down to Sleep," he later recalled, "this inward Manifestation would appear, and give me great Uneasiness for my Misbehaviour the Day before, and I had a perfect Knowledge of what it wanted of me, (to wit) to be sober and watchful, which I would in no wise content to, till my youthful Days were over." Unable to find resolution, he prayed to God and asked for forgiveness, repeatedly promising to give up "Lying, Quarrelling, and to stay at Home a Sundays." He began to read the Bible on a regular basis, but the temptation to please the Devil, often at the encouragement of his father, proved too great. On one occasion, William bet a half pint of rum that his son, who was thirteen at the time, could defeat a houseguest at cards. Not wanting to disobey his father, Husband agreed to play and beat his opponent. However, the teenager did not take pride in his victory. "I found no

Pleasure in it, that was not turned into Sorrow, for Christ looked angry at me, even before the Game was done," he remembered. "I was exceedingly troubled whilst in the Game and wish'd, I had not touch'd the Cards, promising never more to play on any Score."[74]

Searching for the New Birth

Husband's growing piety was reinforced by the rise of the Great Awakening, a series of local revivals led by charismatic evangelists that swept across the American colonies during the 1730s and 1740s. This religious and cultural movement, combined with his short time with Kinkey, led the teenager to eventually reject his father's secular culture and fully embrace evangelicalism. New England theologians like Solomon Stoddard had laid the foundation of the Great Awakening a generation earlier, increasingly bemoaning the perceived lack of religiosity in their congregations. Stoddard, in particular, blamed ministers for failing to stress to worshippers the eternal peril of sin. As such, pastors had to awaken sinners through the use of "vivid language and compelling metaphors," reminding them of both God's vengeance and mercy.[75] It was revivals, Stoddard concluded, that would allow preachers, especially in times of moral decline, to restore piety and provide God with a vehicle to shower grace on the repented.

Stoddard proved an effective revivalist, but it was his grandson Jonathan Edwards who—along with Theodorus Frelinghuysen and the Tennent family—truly helped usher in the Great Awakening. In 1729, Edwards assumed his grandfather's pastorate in Northampton, Massachusetts. Although the town had already hosted several revivals, the last occurring in 1727 under Stoddard's watch, Edwards continued to fear that sin persisted, especially among the youth. By the early 1730s, he proclaimed that Northampton again needed a revival, and he targeted young people to initiate one, believing that if these sinners came back into the church, adults would follow. From the pulpit, he crafted a message that centered on his young listeners' emotions by reminding them about the eternal damnation that awaited those who rejected God's grace. The strategy worked. By 1734, Edwards claimed that the town's youth had become "convinced by what they had heard" and "were willing of themselves to comply with the Counsel that had been given."[76] "A concern about the great things of religion began among old and young [and] all [became] seized with a deep concern about their eternal salvation," he recalled. "This town never was so full of love, nor so full of joy, nor so full of distress as it has lately been."[77] The Northampton revival soon instigated similar outbreaks of religious fervor throughout the Connecticut River Valley.[78]

Fears about the decline of religion also encouraged clerics in the middle colonies to take action. The first to do so was Frelinghuysen, whose writings may well have influenced Husband's grandfather Herman Kinkey. After migrating from Holland to New Jersey in 1720, Frelinghuysen immediately lashed out at the religious establishment. He believed that ministers, like their congregations, had grown spiritually dull, having themselves never "truly experienced the converting work of the Holy Spirit."[79] "The outward performance of religious duties," he explained, was meaningless unless an individual had already developed a relationship with God through personal conversion. Sinners could find salvation by laying "aside all pride, haughtiness, and ideas of inherent worthliness, and humble themselves before the Lord," and only then could they open their hearts to God's grace, undergo spiritual regeneration, and partake in religious ceremony.[80] Frelinghuysen's message struck a chord among Germans and Scots-Irish Presbyterians, thousands of whom had recently arrived in Pennsylvania, New Jersey, and Delaware, bringing with them a commitment to piety and an anticipation of revivals.[81]

Throughout the early eighteenth century, other preachers, most notably William Tennent and his two sons, Gilbert and William Jr., also emphasized the importance of personal conversion "over the external observance of liturgical rites."[82] Like Frelinghuysen, they employed evangelical preaching as the means to awaken sinners, delivering highly emotional, soul-searching sermons that caused many of the unrepentant to cry out in despair. By the 1730s, these pastors had begun to make headway, especially in the Raritan Valley of East Jersey, the scene of several local revivals during that decade.[83]

Living in Cecil County, Maryland, Husband was certainly aware of the evangelical movement spreading across the middle colonies. Culturally and demographically, the county was more like Pennsylvania and Delaware than the rest of Maryland.[84] In its northern section, where Husband and his family moved in the mid-1730s, Welsh Baptists, German Protestants, Quakers, and Scots-Irish Presbyterians, having migrated from the middle colonies, had begun to compete with the Anglican Church for converts.[85] "You are no strangers to the cunning and diligence of these people in perverting their neighbors," Anglican minister Hugh Jones of St. Stephen's Parish complained in 1739, pointing out that "Pennsylvania Deists, Quakers, Presbyterians, &c." now surrounded his followers. "I need only to mention that I am obliged to be continually on my guard to defend my weak (but large) flocks against their daily attacks in one quarter or other."[86] The poor quality of some Anglican clergymen did not help the situation, turning many potential members away from the church.[87] In fact, Jones, at the bequest of parishioners, had replaced John Urmstrom, an alcoholic who would later die in a house fire while passed out drunk, as rector of St. Stephen's Church in 1732.[88]

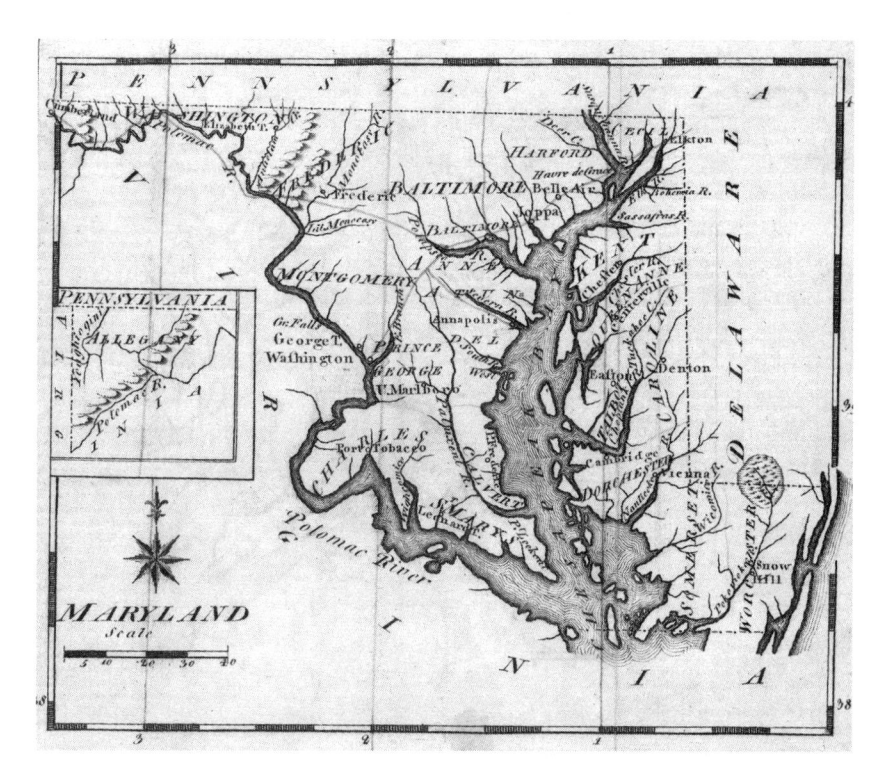

FIGURE 2. Located in the northeastern corner of Maryland, Cecil County became a popular destination for Presbyterians and Quakers, who would heavily influence Husband as the teenager developed his religious beliefs and sought to the experience the New Birth. (Joseph Scott, *Maryland*, Philadelphia, F. and R. Bailey, 1795; Library of Congress, Geography and Map Division)

Although his father viewed these evangelical groups with suspicion, Herman was intrigued by his religiously diverse neighbors. Scots-Irish Presbyterians, in particular, heavily influenced Husband, at least during his teenage years. Situated a few miles west of the major Delaware port of New Castle, Cecil County quickly became home to thousands of Scots-Irish migrants in the early eighteenth century.[89] Most eventually settled in the northwestern part of the county, organizing the West Nottingham Presbyterian Church in 1724 near Rising Sun, just miles from the Husband family's plantation.[90] Husband likely had frequent contact with Presbyterian settlers, who by 1740 had become the largest dissenting religious sect in the region, especially when they converged around West Nottingham Church during communion season. During these meetings, they spent several days listening to hellfire-and-brimstone sermons that evoked emotional responses—crying, moaning, and fainting—from many in the audience.[91] It was perhaps here that Husband first learned about the New Birth, a term increasingly used by revivalists to describe the moment when God's spirit entered into one's soul, which they believed was the prerequisite for salvation. While the details of his spiritual development are unclear, Husband certainly resided in a region ripe for a religious awakening, one that soon welcomed the arrival of the greatest evangelical of the eighteenth century: George Whitefield.

Born in Gloucester, England, in 1714, Whitefield's background made him an unlikely candidate to one day become "Anglo-America's first religious celebrity."[92] A member of the Church of England, Whitefield worked in his parents' inn as a boy. He initially wanted to become an actor, having a talent for public speaking and a love for performance. As a teenager, however, Whitefield heard God speak to him in his dreams, inspiring him to become a preacher instead. Enrolling at Pembroke College, Oxford, in 1732, he immersed himself in religious studies and made friends with Methodist schoolmates Charles and John Wesley. Whitefield also desperately sought to experience the New Birth by fasting "for weeks until his weakened body succumbed to illness."[93] Lying sick in bed, thirsty from dehydration, he suddenly "remembered that on the cross Christ had been thirsty just before his death," and God's spirit then flowed into his body. "I cast myself on the bed, crying out, 'I thirst! I thirst!'" Whitefield wrote years later. "Soon after this, I found and felt to myself that I was delivered from the burden that had so heavily oppressed me.... Now did the Spirit of God take possession of my soul, and, as I humbly hope, seal me unto the day of redemption."[94]

Ordained as an Anglican priest in 1736, Whitefield traveled throughout England, delivering powerful sermons that quickly gained him notoriety. People seemed to be naturally drawn to the young minister. He had a thunderous voice, a flair for the dramatic, and a simple message—"Be born again in Christ"—that crossed denominational lines.[95] With the encouragement of the Wesleys, he journeyed to the colony of Georgia in 1738, where he spent several months establishing an orphanage. Upon returning to England, Whitefield developed a new strategy that enabled him to reach thousands of potential converts: the field meeting. In February 1739, he conducted his first open-air sermon near Bristol, where nearly ten thousand people converged to hear him preach. One month later, he went to London and addressed a crowd of nearly sixty thousand. That November, Whitefield decided to return to the colonies, knowing that American revivalists had already laid the foundation for his touring ministry. Thousands came to hear him speak in Pennsylvania, New York, and New Jersey, many leaving his sermons deeply moved, "awakened to see that religion does not consist in outward things, but in righteousness, peace, and joy in the Holy Ghost."[96]

FIGURE 3. George Whitefield inspired thousands of American colonists, including Herman Husband, to rely on their own consciences when seeking religious guidance. (Elisha Gallaudet, *George Whitefield, M.A./Elisha Gallaudet sculp.*, N. York, 1774; Library of Congress, Prints and Photographs Division)

In early December 1739, Whitefield journeyed to Cecil County, the first stop on his tour of the southern colonies. Residents were curious to hear the famous minister, and even William and Mary Husband made the short trek to North East, where Whitefield preached on December 3.[97] Their son Herman accompanied them, not knowing what to expect. "I imagined he spake as a Prophet of some strange Time at hand," Husband remembered. "May be he tells us when the Day of Judgment is to be." The family arrived to the field early that morning, where a crowd had already gathered, asking each other, "What does this Man preach? any Thing that is New? who answered, No; nothing but what you may read every Day in your Bible: For what is this great Cry then? who was answered after this Manner, stay, you will hear him by and by, you never heard the like before." When Whitefield appeared, the 1,500 people stood in silence. Utilizing his flair for the dramatic, he delivered a powerful sermon on Matthew 25:1–13, the parable of five virgins who missed the opportunity to get married because they could not find the bridegroom at night, having failed to fill their lamps with oil. Whitefield warned the crowd not to follow the example of these women when it came to attaining salvation. They had to always keep their lamps lighted, that is, to keep "Grace in [their] Hearts," he pontificated, never knowing when Jesus would arrive to take them to heaven.[98]

Herman Husband was thrilled. Before him stood a man whose words bore "a Testimony to the Truth" that made perfect sense to the fifteen-year-old Marylander. "We must come to Christ, if ever we attain'd Happiness," he now believed. "We must be born again of the Spirit." Husband later recalled that it was Whitefield's sermon that woke him from his spiritual slumber. He believed that the spirit of God had visited him that day, inspiring him to "take up the Cross" once and for all. From that point forward, Husband rejected his former life and strove—as Whitefield instructed—to keep oil in his lamp with the hope of someday experiencing the New Birth. "A fear was in me that I had rejected him so long," Husband remembered. "I was now ashamed to think how I would not believe in him for all his Strivings with me, and thus I returned wishing, I had hearkened to his Reproofs in Day of my Visitation, lest I were now too late."[99]

Whitefield's visit was a catalyst for the Great Awakening in Cecil County, encouraging Husband and other residents to embrace revivalism and seek out the New Birth. But not all were swayed by his evangelical message. By 1738, Protestants in the middle colonies had become divided over the burgeoning religious movement. Presbyterians, in particular, struggled with how to address these new ideas. Old Side Presbyterians opposed revivalism, fearing the "effects of unrestrained itinerancy and enthusiasm," and applauded the Synod of Philadelphia's recent ruling making "a university degree the prerequisite for licensure." They maintained a "rationalist approach to faith" that emphasized adherence to traditional worship. New Side Presbyterians supported revivalism, although they disagreed on how to best nurture it. Moderates championed the religious awakening but wished to contain its excesses. Others held more radical views, praising the intense emotionalism ignited by evangelical preaching and questioning the religious sincerity of anti-revivalists, who they claimed were ignorant of the New Birth. Despite their differences, moderate and radical New Side Presbyterians were united on several important issues. Both called for greater local autonomy from ruling synods, emphasized the importance of piety, and favored religion of the heart over "an empty, ceremonial way of worship."[100]

This Old Side–New Side split was prominent in Cecil County's Presbyterian population, due in part to the county's close proximity to Nottingham Presbyterian Church, just across the Pennsylvania border. There, the moderate Samuel Blair, founder of a New Side seminary in nearby Fagg's Manor, had labored to get Nottingham Church a revivalist minister following the death of its pastor in 1739.[101] Conflict between revivalists and anti-revivalists ensued, enticing the radical Gilbert Tennent to visit the church in 1740, where he delivered his famous anti–Old Side sermon *The Danger of an Unconverted Ministry*, which only deepened tensions within the congregation.[102] The controversy spread to Cecil County, where West Nottingham Church members also proved unable or unwilling to compromise. In 1741, the New Side faction there separated from the congregation and established a new church across the road.[103]

Herman Husband's spiritual journey would initially lead him to New Side Presbyterianism. At his father's request, the young man continued to attend services at nearby St. Mary Ann's Church through 1740. But he quickly grew dissatisfied with the Anglican minister, who seemed to know nothing about the New Birth.[104] Since Whitefield's sojourn to Cecil County, Husband had heard several Presbyterian itinerants preach in the region, one of whom, perhaps Gilbert Tennent, made an everlasting impression on Husband.[105] "We had News of a Presbyterian Minister, who was said to be of the same doctrine as Whitefield," Herman recollected years later. "He thundered out against Sin, and pronounc'd Death, Damnation, &c. to Sinners, and there was no Salvation but by Christ." Husband liked "him much for thundering out against Sin and Sinners," and began to believe that the New Side Presbyterians could help him "learn how to come to Christ." He soon contemplated visiting the "New Presbyterian Meeting House." However, he was hesitant to join the congregation, fearing that such a move would disappoint his father. One evening in 1741, Husband, confused as to what course to take, walked to a field, knelt down, and prayed to God for guidance. "I [became] filled with Thanksgivings, with Praises, with Joy unspeakable, and full of Glory, with Peace and Joy in the Holy Ghost," he remembered. "Yea it was so far from proceeding from any Thing I attributed to my own Actions, that I could hardly accept the blessed Favour, and went away praising and adoring that God, who had taken Notice of so unworthy a creature." Husband, at last, had experienced the New Birth and, thereafter, went "wholy to the New Presbyterian Meeting."[106]

For the next two years, Husband remained a "constant Adherent to the new Presbyterians or Whitefieldians." He sought to live in accordance with the spirit of God and continued to reject the secular world of his father, abstaining from vices—especially gambling and dancing—and beginning to eat and drink in moderation, believing that gluttony was a sin. "I became [the] entire Master of my Appetite, as any other Passion: So that I eat only to live, and not live to eat," he wrote in 1750. Husband became a fervent proponent of the principles of New Side evangelicalism. He lashed out at Old Side adherents and other anti-revivalists, comparing them to the Pharisees who had persecuted Christ. "I was according to my Age zealous against them, in contending . . . the Authority and Necessity of the inward and sensible Inspirations of the Holy Spirit," he explained. "The Scriptures proved this in the Apostles Days." Crediting New Side preachers with helping to spark the recent revivals by telling "us the Marks . . . of a Christian, and that we must be born again of the Spirit," Husband believed that they were the true agents of God.[107]

Husband was among countless other colonists who embraced the Great Awakening. Most converts came from the lower and middle ranks of society:

wage laborers, artisans, small farmers, servants, and slaves.[108] The populist tone of many evangelical preachers attracted these people to the revival movement, especially in Maryland and other southern colonies. There, evangelicals' call for frugality, self-control, and spiritual equality posed a direct challenge to the secular world of the Anglican elite.[109] Such a critique of hierarchical society appealed mostly to the lower sort, but it also resonated with many genteel men and women who, like Husband, were searching for "meaning in their lives through revivalism."[110] Young and defiant, Husband embraced the burgeoning evangelical counterculture, believing that the Anglican Church had become morally bankrupt.[111] However, he would soon grow dissatisfied with New Side Presbyterians for the same reason and rebel once again.

From Presbyterianism to Quakerism

Husband's religious journey would next lead him to the Society of Friends, whose looming presence in northwestern Cecil County made it difficult for the young man to escape their influence. By the 1730s, the Quakers had established a thriving community on Nottingham Lots, a 48,000-acre tract of land situated near the Husband family's plantation.[112] Most local Protestants— including Herman's father, William—viewed their Quaker neighbors with disdain. Husband initially concurred, believing that Friends "knew nothing of the inward Inspirations of the Spirit." However, his attitude changed in 1742 when he read William Sewel's *History of the Rise, Increase, and Progress of the Christian People Called Quakers* (1717), which chronicles the trials and tribulations of George Fox and other seventeenth-century Quakers in England and New England. For Husband, Sewel's book identified commonalities between the Society of Friends and New Side evangelicals and opened up new horizons in Husband's spiritual quest, "like the Sun breaking out of Darkness into Noon-day."[113] Both the Quakers and New Side Presbyterians, he now discovered, rejected the hierarchy of the Anglican Church; spurned outward ceremony as the means of achieving salvation; and emphasized the importance of the inner light, or spirit within, maintaining that the "central truth of religion was the indwelling Spirit of God, the immanent Word of Light and Life in the hearts of men."[114] He no longer believed that Quakers were "degenerate and fallen from the real Life." Instead, he became convinced that they were truly inspired by God.[115]

When Husband shared his revelation with several New Side friends, they were, to put it mildly, unmoved. One demanded that the young man stop reading Sewel's book immediately, insisting "it was the Works of the Devil, Delusions, and Witchcraft." Others maintained that the Society of Friends "denied the Scriptures and ... Christ's Coming in the Flesh," and that the Quakers were troublemakers who walked "Naked about the Streets . . . daubing themselves with Filth, and going into [New Side Presbyterian] meetings" to disturb them. Finding little proof in such slanders, Husband lashed out at his religious compatriots. "I began to dispute with [the elders and others] concerning the Quakers, in order that they might rightly understand the Quakers Belief," he recalled, "for I was sure it was the Spirit of Christ that brought us from Darkness to Light, by an inward Work, that was sensible to him in whom it was wrought, and not because of our own Works, or outward Performance, or Ceremonies." Known for being stubborn—a trait that he would carry with him to the grave—Husband remained certain that the Quakers' "belief concerning the Spirit was wholly agreeable to our New Presbyterians."[116]

The New Side Presbyterians' dismissal of Quakers only deepened Husband's resolve to learn more about the religious sect, and he set out to find evidence refuting the charge that the Friends "denied the Scriptures to be the Word of God." He began to speak with his Quaker neighbors, one of whom recommended that he consult Robert Barclay's *An Apology for the True Christian Divinity*, which the Scottish Quaker theologian had written in 1676 to defend the Society against its numerous detractors.[117] Most Quakers owned a copy of the treatise, and a local Friend lent his copy to Husband.[118] Reading the book removed any lingering doubts that Husband may have held about the Society of Friends' stance on the Bible. In the section "Of Scriptures," Barclay explained that Quakers had always acknowledged the Scriptures "to be very heavenly and divine writings" and accepted the validity of the Bible, believing that it was "a full and ample account of all the chief principles of the doctrine of Christ."[119] What led to conflict with other Protestants, he argued, was that Quakers did not view the scriptures as "the principle fountain of all truth and knowledge." Instead, Friends maintained that the Bible, although inspired by the Holy Spirit, was secondary to the light of God within. Barclay insisted that it was the "inward testimony of the Spirit," not scriptures alone, that provided believers with a guide to attaining salvation. "The letter of the Scripture is outward, of itself a dead thing, a mere declaration of good things," he wrote. "The principal rule of Christians under the Gospel is not an outward letter, nor law outwardly written and delivered, but an inward spiritual law, engraven in the heart, the law of the Spirit of life, the Word that is nigh in the heart and in the mouth."[120]

Barclay's powerful defense of Quaker doctrine moved Husband, making him even more sympathetic with the Society of Friends and reinforcing his faith in the power of the spirit within. He came to believe that the Bible—like ecclesiastical ceremonies—was of little use unless applied to the "inward Word and Spirit of God." "When I obey'd the Voice of God," he explained, "it opened my Understanding to see the Bible, speaking the same Things, and holy Men of old experiencing the same, then they afforded me Comfort; then, and till then, I reap'd the Advantage of the Scriptures."[121] This line of thought ultimately reinforced Husband's evangelical inclination to rely on his own conscience, rather than church officials, when seeking religious guidance. He would continue to be influenced by these ideas throughout his life. "I am persuaded," he wrote years later, "[that] the Way to preserve from Error, is to receive nothing from Man nor Men, but to try all Doctrine in our own Hearts by that Light and Standard of Truth which he or she knows of a Truth stands in Opposition to Sin, and the natural Inclinations of our evil Passions."[122]

Convinced that the Society of Friends shared his religious beliefs, Husband began to secretly visit the local Quaker meetinghouse in 1742. However, the teenager did not abandon his belief that the New Side Presbyterian Church constituted the "best reformed society," a reflection of his growing interest in postmillennialism.[123] Based on the idea that Christ would return following a thousand-year period of "heavenly perfection on earth," which would be created by "human action and Christian agency," postmillennial thought emerged first in New England and spread throughout the American colonies during the Great Awakening.[124] Many New Side evangelicals viewed revivals as a sign of the millennium's beginning.[125] "That there has been a great religious Commotion in the World in our present Day, is so evident, that it cannot be deny'd," Samuel Finley proclaimed in 1741, arguing that the preparatory stage of the millennium (as told in the book of Revelation) had arrived.[126] Husband shared this conviction, later recalling that as a young man, he became convinced that the apocalyptic prophesies and visions found in the Bible would occur in his lifetime. He believed the revivals signaled the dawning of a new era in which Christianity would prevail over the Devil, and that the New Side Presbyterian Church would play the leading role in making this a reality, being "the one Particular Relegeous Society . . . whose outward order and discipline the Rest [other denominations] was in time to conform to as the object and fulfillment of the Scriptures and the Prophesies."[127] Despite his growing appreciation for the Society of Friends, Husband maintained that New Side Presbyterians were at the forefront of a divine crusade to rid the world of Satan; by adopting the true principles of the ancient Christian church, these enlightened reformers would lead by example. "They seem'd to cry against a dead and carnal Ministry, against the Diversion of the Times, Gaming, Racing, Tipling, [and] Dancing," he explained. "And I soon expected for them to testify against Wars and Fighting; for I was sure it was contrary to the Lamb like Nature of a Christian."[128]

But Husband's enthusiasm for New Side Presbyterianism eventually turned to despair. By 1743, he had grown alarmed at the apparent decline of evangelical zeal within the congregation. Church leaders, he bemoaned, continued to practice old ceremonies and customs that hampered spiritual growth, including a mandate prohibiting members under the age of twenty-four from becoming ordained ministers. Believing that all who had experienced the New Birth, regardless of their age, should be allowed to preach, Husband considered such a rule unholy. He also feared that members no longer viewed the inner light as constituting the highest spiritual authority. "My Friends would begin to mock at a spiritual Worship of God," he recalled. "They began to grow worse than better, and began not to stick at the mentioning so much of the Spirit." Disheartened that New Side Presbyterians had begun to reject the spirit within, Husband concluded that they were "turning back to Old Presbyterianism, and a State of dead Forms."[129] Thus, in 1743, he severed his ties with the New Side church and joined the Society of Friends.

Nearly twenty years old, Husband believed that his religious journey had reached its completion. Like it did for other colonists, the Great Awakening engendered within the young man an intense desire for spiritual independence, emboldening him to reject the Anglican establishment and embrace the evangelical counterculture. But it also ultimately led him to question the validity of New Side revivalists. Despite their rhetoric, they too had begun to deny the importance of the spirit within in the advancement of Christianity. Such was Husband's mindset when he entered into fellowship with the Quakers, certain that they would teach him "the Way of God more perfectly."[130] However, unwilling to betray his own conscience and submit to church authority, he would soon find himself at odds with the Society of Friends and eventually abandon his faith in organized religion altogether.

TWO
"A New Government of Liberty"
The Politicization of Husband

> Should we now through Fear or Favour act as we have done, contrary to Duty and Interest; so far as we do this, we contribute to all the Mischief consequent upon it. Where then is that moving Principle Self-preservation? Will you, can you, voluntarily submit yourselves to Ignominy and Want? These will aggrandize themselves and swim in Opulence.
> —Herman Husband, *An Impartial Relation*

The Young Entrepreneur

Husband found in the Society of Friends a religion that represented not only his moral convictions but also his economic aspirations. While he critiqued the decadence and secularization of genteel society, he did not totally condemn material wealth and shared his father's desire to accumulate capital and move up the socioeconomic ladder. Such ambition did not run counter to Quaker ideology, which remained heavily influenced by Calvinism and mercantile capitalism. Quaker leadership had long encouraged followers to participate in the material world. "True Godliness," William Penn explained in 1669, "don't turn Men out of the World, but enables them to live better in it, and excites their Endeavours to mend it."[1] Friends also celebrated economic success, viewing it as evidence that one was living in the light. By adhering to the virtues of frugality, industry, prudence, and honesty, they believed they could achieve earthly prosperity without compromising their relationship with God. This economic ethic encouraged many Quakers, especially those engaged in trade and commerce, to increase their wealth and political influence throughout the middle colonies during the early eighteenth century.[2] In addition to affirming his aspirations, Husband likely realized that Quaker membership provided him with opportunities to network and partner with brethren in business pursuits, which he could use to build his fortune as a merchant and land speculator.

In his early twenties, Husband worked as a supervisor at his father's iron mine and -works in nearby Baltimore County.[3] There, he married the daughter of Phoebe Cox, and they quickly started a family. When his wife died sometime before 1750, she left Husband a young widower with at least two children.[4] He eventually tired of working for his father's mining operations, perhaps wanting to achieve greater economic independence, and set his sights on becoming a merchant.

As a Quaker, Husband would have known brethren who had capitalized on British America's booming trade with the West Indies, where sugar plantation owners desperately needed foodstuffs to maintain their large slave labor force. Beginning in the late seventeenth century, Quaker merchants in the middle colonies met this demand by shipping countless tons of crops, livestock, and lumber to Barbados, Jamaica, and other Caribbean islands. The presence of Quaker entrepreneurs (and slaveholders) living in the West Indies further enabled Friends to maintain trading and religious networks between the two regions well into the eighteenth century.[5]

Husband sought to tap into this market. In 1750, he, along with four other Quakers, purchased the *Charles Town*, a forty-five-ton schooner.[6] That same year, the twenty-six-year-old Husband, perhaps on board the *Charles Town*, sailed to Barbados for the purposes of "Trade & Curiosity."[7] His ultimate destination was Bridgetown, the island's largest town and one of the busiest ports in the West Indies.[8] Although there is no written record of his experiences there, later writings indicate that the slavery and poverty he encountered on his travels reinforced his racial and class views.

Stepping off the ship, Husband would have certainly encountered slaves, recently captured from Africa, lined up on the wharf and "pent up together like so many sheep in a fold," as former slave Olaudah Equiano recalled.[9] The docks were also home to scores of homeless white men, mostly broken-down sailors who, weakened by malaria and other tropical diseases, had been forced off their ships and now survived by begging for money.[10] Husband's first destination was likely Cheapside, the town's commercial district, where he could have conducted business with local merchants before exploring the city and surrounding community. If he made his way to the outskirts of Bridgetown, he might have walked the streets that housed more of the island's poor whites, who, according to a late eighteenth-century traveler, obtained "a scanty livelihood by cultivating a small patch of earth, and breeding-up poultry, or what they term stock for the markets."[11]

While the sight of Africans being sold like cattle in Barbados (as well as in Maryland) might have repulsed Husband, it was slavery's degrading influence on white society that alarmed him the most. By his own account, Husband had been opposed to slavery since childhood, but not necessarily for reasons of human rights. He recalled that he had foreseen "the Ruin of our [white] Posterity" and feared the institution would "corrupt the European Colour." This "consideration lessened my Pleasure in the increase of them [slaves]," he wrote in 1768, "that when my Father's Estate increased therein, either by Birth or Purchase, it was a Matter of Sorrow on my Mind."[12] The sight of poor, white Barbadians living in squalor and begging for food only confirmed what Husband already believed: that slavery prevented industrious white men from obtaining land and securing employment. In 1755, using the West Indies as an example, he lamented that such a fate would soon befall white farmers in the North Carolina backcountry, a region not yet dependent on slave labor. "The white people cannot nither encrease nor thrive where the treasure of a country is carried from them to purchase those blacks," he warned. "Whereas if this custom was prevented there would not be only a white person employed and encouraged to settle for every black so bought, but that money which goes to purchase those blacks would be put into their hands for their labour, wherewith they soon would become able to procure a farm [and] employ more poor." To make matters worse, he concluded, slaveholding would eventually lead white colonists to turn away from God for money, as it had already done to those in Barbados and other Caribbean islands.[13]

Husband's critique of slavery reflected that of a growing number of American Quakers by the mid-eighteenth century. Quakers had not always denounced the institution; during the seventeenth and early eighteenth centuries, many Friends, especially those residing in southern colonies like Maryland, had no moral qualms about slavery and often relied on enslaved workers to build their fortunes. Throughout the Delaware Valley, slave owners held most of the leadership positions within Quaker meetings, which made many other Friends hesitant to criticize human bondage. Those who did often found themselves reprimanded by church authorities.[14] Even the Society's founder, George Fox, instructed slaves on at least one occasion "to love their masters and mistresses, and to be faithful and diligent in their masters' service and business."[15]

It was not until the 1750s that opposition to the institution intensified within the Quaker community. Some Friends were increasingly unable to reconcile slavery with their belief that all people possessed an inner light and, as such, should be treated as equals. Like Husband, a number of Quakers bemoaned the negative impact that slavery had on whites, fearing that it made them lazy and wasteful.[16] Additionally, for many Friends, slaves had become "symbols of conspicuous consumption," a sign that Quaker slaveholders "were more concerned with worldly than spiritual affairs."[17] Quaker minister Samuel Fothergill echoed such a sentiment when he visited fellow Friends in eastern North Carolina in 1754, complaining that "worldly-mindedness and lukewarmness" had corrupted many slaveholding members.[18]

The budding Quaker campaign against slavery reflected part of a broader reform movement intended to purify the church.[19] By the mid-eighteenth century, many Friends increasingly lamented what they believed to be a decline of morality within the entire Quaker community. In addition to the corrupting influence of economic affluence and political office, which they believed caused their members to fall victim to worldly temptations, Quaker reformers were most worried by the perceived lack of virtue among the younger generation. In particular, reformers pointed to a growing number of young Quakers who had begun to marry non-Friends and abandoned the practice of dressing simple, opting to wear gaudy and fine apparel, both signs that they were straying from the faith.[20]

In response to these disorders, Quaker leaders increased church discipline and oversight, which Husband initially welcomed. In 1750, he condemned members, young and old, who acted contrary to Quaker teachings, declaring that these Friends had "trampled [the Holy Spirit] under Foot, setting up Forms to shelter under, and loving the Pleasures of Life under the Form of Holiness, whose God is their Bellies, their Sweet Hearts, their costly and grave Apparel, the Esteem of Man, and their fellow Mortals."[21]

Although new to the Quaker faith, Husband quickly emerged as a prominent member in the Bush River Preparative Meeting in Baltimore County during the early 1750s, serving as its representative to both the East Nottingham Monthly Meeting and the Baltimore Yearly Meeting. He seems to have accepted the power of church authorities to regulate members' behavior, at least until he became the target of scrutiny in the 1760s. In 1752, he became the meeting's overseer, enabling him to enforce Quaker rules and regulations.[22] His duties included providing advice and help to Friends who committed sins, and then determining whether such disorderly walkers had reformed their ways. He reported those who had failed to do so to the monthly meeting, which would then investigate the matter and decide on the offender's punishment.[23]

The Quest for Economic Independence

By the early 1750s, Husband had become a promising merchant and well-respected member of the Quaker community.[24] Yet landownership continued to elude him, as it did other settlers in Maryland and Pennsylvania. Since 1725, both colonies had experienced rapid increases in population, making it more difficult for people to buy cheap, fertile land.[25] The situation along the Maryland-Pennsylvania border, where Husband resided, was particularly alarming. The price for an acre of land in Lancaster County, just north of Cecil County, rose threefold between 1740 and 1760.[26] The long history of extensive farming in Maryland and Pennsylvania further hampered economic prospects by causing soil erosion. While Husband initially pursued a mercantile career over farming, he, like most other eighteenth-century American colonists, believed that landownership was the key to achieving economic independence. Husband did purchase land for the first time in Cecil County in 1754, but only thirty acres, hardly enough to earn a living on as a farmer.[27] Unwilling to permanently forego his dream of becoming a planter, he would turn his sights on the North Carolina Piedmont, where affordable farmland was plentiful.

Since the early eighteenth century, travelers and boosters had touted the North Carolina backcountry as a newfound Eden, a region where explorer John Lawson claimed in 1708 that "you meet with the richest Soil, a sweet, thin Air, dry Roads, pleasant small murmuring Streams, and several beneficial Productions and Species."[28] Land there was not only fertile but also easy to obtain, at least in theory.[29] Beginning in the 1740s, the British Crown and John Carteret, 2nd Earl of Granville, who owned the northern half of North Carolina (known as the Granville District), attempted to increase white migration to the Piedmont, hoping to make money from quitrents, an annual tax that all landowners paid to either the royal governor or Granville. Both tried to encourage settlement by enacting land distribution policies that were fairly straightforward. To acquire a patent on a piece of land, a farmer needed to pay the required fees and file an entry, describing its location and size, with the Granville's office or royal land office, both in Edenton, North Carolina. If the land had not already been claimed, a government official would issue a warrant to survey the land, and upon the survey's completion, the prospective landowner received an official patent transferring the land.[30] At only five shillings per acre, the price of land in the North Carolina Piedmont was well below that of most other colonies.[31]

Like his grandfather and father before him, the promise of obtaining cheap and productive land appealed to the enterprising Husband, as did the prospect of making money as a land speculator. He had visited the Carver's Creek Quaker Meeting in Bladen County, located in the eastern part of North Carolina, shortly after returning from Barbados in 1751.[32] Recognizing the appeal of the cheap land and potential opportunities in the colony's backcountry, he formed a land company with ten other investors in 1754. The group agreed that Husband would serve as the advance man for the company, probably because he already had contacts in North Carolina. Venturing alone into the backcountry of Virginia and North Carolina, Husband's task was to buy ten thousand acres of the best available land and return to Maryland with a map and description of the region's cash crops and soils.[33]

In September 1754, just shy of his thirty-first birthday, Husband loaded up his wagon and headed to Virginia. He eventually reached the Great Wagon Road, a heavily traveled transportation artery that linked Pennsylvania with the southern backcountry, and followed it south, scouting out the best available acreage as he went. By this time, the possibility of buying productive and accessible land in the Valley of Virginia was bleak, with German, Scots-Irish, and other colonists already claiming most of the region's choice land. Husband continued on to North Carolina, finding what he was looking for in Orange County, situated in the Granville District.[34] "I gave it as my judgment that thy part of North Caralina exceeded any part of my travells," he wrote in 1755. It "was [distinguished by] a wholsome pleasant air, good water, fertile land, and beyond expectation according to its appearance, [having] a moderate and short winter and for 7 or 8 months in the year dureing my stay there free from all kind of troublesome insects."[35] By the fall of 1755, Husband, convinced that he had found "a second Pensylvania," had purchased for himself nearly two thousand acres of land near Sandy Creek, a tributary of the Haw River that flowed through the western part of Orange County. He also secured two lots in Hillsborough, the county seat founded the previous year, where he built a temporary home.[36]

Husband was one of thousands of settlers—mostly from the middle colonies—who began to pour into the North Carolina Piedmont in the early 1750s. "Great numbers of Families keep daily crowding into the Back Parts of this Country," North Carolina governor Gabriel Johnston reported in 1751. "They come in Waggons by Land from Pensylvania, a hardy and laborious Race of Men."[37] Like Husband, the settlers came seeking relief from population growth and rising land prices. Most were, according to Johnston's successor, Arthur Dobbs, in 1754, an industrious people who sought to "cultivate and improve [the land], as fast as they can."[38] Thousands more would move into the backcountry during the late 1750s and 1760s, raising livestock and cultivating wheat, the region's leading cash crop. By 1767, more than 42,000 souls, including 3,000 African Americans, lived in the region.[39]

Beneath the outward appearance of a thriving backcountry, Husband observed some troubling tendencies. He spoke out against corrupt officials, the growing presence of slavery, and religious persecution in the region, not necessarily motivated by moral outrage but more likely self-preservation. He believed that his own best chance for economic success would only come if the North Carolina Piedmont continued to be a prime destination of white settlement, and this was threatened by corruption, lack of opportunity, and oppression.

In 1755, Husband decided to investigate complaints about Rowan County land agent James Carter. Husband traveled to Granville's land office in Edenton with "upwards of 20 reciets from the people of this Carters for money paid towards their lands from two to 4 years ago," and found in the office's records proof that Carter had committed fraud. Husband wrote to Lord Granville, explaining that most backcountry migrants were unable to make the long trip to Edenton and relied on local agents like Carter, who worked for the royal governor or Granville, to deliver their fees to the land office. But unscrupulous agents often pocketed the money and/or secured the land for themselves and their friends. "There appeared in the office as near as I could learn about 170 odd returns made by this James Carter, and by what I could gether from the people there should been near if not quite a thousand," an angry Husband informed Granville. "But here and there the most leading men in a neighbourhood and particular favourites [of Carter] who voted him an assembly man could get their deeds." Such corruption resulted in hardship for many farmers, who, believing that they had obtained titles, continued to make improvements to the land, only to have it eventually taken away. Without "a shure foundation and title," Husband feared that migration to the backcountry would cease, which threatened his own livelihood. "The people like Israll of old," he warned Granville, "begin to wish themselves back to Pensylvania . . . and had rather rent land there from year to year than live under a goverment where they thought themselves not fairly used."[40]

The proliferation of slavery in the backcountry troubled Husband as well. Although few Orange County residents owned slaves in 1755, he believed that a growing number of settlers in the region had begun to purchase slaves, much to the detriment of laboring white men, who would find it difficult to acquire land or employment.[41] "For each of those Negroes the public is deprived of a white person, a white person deprived of a livelihood, the king of a subject, a soldiar, etc.," he informed Granville. "All this might be foreseen by a studious person but tis here spoke from knowledge taught by wofull expieriance." Further, Husband believed that the continued expansion of slavery would increase the threat of slave rebellion throughout the American colonies. "The Negroes are imported in [such] greater numbers . . . [that] unless the white people take to beat out their brains as they do the piggs when over stocked . . . [slaves] must unavoidably (according to the natural course of things) wholy over run in a [series] of time the whole provinces," he warned. "By the time they come to such a pitch on the continant . . . it will be morrally impossible to govern them, as alass how many thousands daily obscond from their masters in [the West Indies], which never could be got again had they such wide wildernesses to run to as there is on the continant."[42] In order for the backcountry to grow and prosper, Husband concluded, it had to remain a white man's land.[43]

Husband also advocated for religious tolerance in the region. He was especially critical of the 1754 Vestry Act, enacted to strengthen the Anglican Church, which had long struggled to gain converts throughout the colony. The law required that in each parish, freeholders owning fifty acres of land or more had to elect twelve men to serve on the vestry, which established the parish tax rates, distributed aid to the poor, and paid the local Anglican minister. All residents had to pay the vestry tax, capped at five shillings per year, or face a fine.[44] The act also created fifteen additional parishes and provided rectors with an annual salary of £80.[45] In 1755, Husband expressed his displeasure to Governor Arthur Dobbs, a staunch supporter of the Anglican Church. Writing that he had departed Maryland to escape "the yoke of bondage that our ancestors have brought us under," specifically "the authority there given to the [Anglican] clergy," Husband contended that the Vestry Act threatened to not only enhance the Church's power but also allow corrupt men to "crowd into those established benifices as tis too notoriously known to be the case."[46] Moreover, he argued, it placed a financial burden on backcountry settlers, many of whom already found it difficult to pay other taxes. "Thy Tennants Here are Much Disturb'd our Taxes this Year Being Double to what they us'd to Be," Husband complained to Granville in 1756. It is the "Opinion of Maney that one Half the People cannot Pay But Must Have their Goods Distrained (and truly few of them they Have)."[47] Such conditions, he warned, had already begun to discourage people from moving to the Piedmont, placing the well-being of North Carolina in danger.[48]

Husband was not alone in his deep distrust of both the Anglican Church and the 1754 Vestry Act. Most settlers in the backcountry belonged to dissenting sects and had, in fact, moved there to escape religious persecution. New Side Presbyterians, Separate Baptists, German Pietists, and Quakers, among others, poured into the region at midcentury, much to the dismay of Anglicans.[49] Influenced by the Great Awakening, these enthusiasts carried with them the notion that all humans possessed an inner light that allowed them to directly communicate with God and achieve salvation. This conviction threatened to disrupt the status quo, encouraging men and women to follow their own consciences, even if it brought them at odds with religious and political authorities.[50] In 1758, for instance, around seven hundred backcountry settlers gathered to voice their opposition to the Vestry Act, demanding reforms such as the elimination of vestries and denominations' right to pay their own ministers.[51] Although King George II annulled the

Vestry Act two years later, temporarily reducing tensions between officials and Piedmont evangelicals, local Anglicans continued to resent the presence of the dissenters. One itinerant, Charles Woodmason, complained in 1765: "The ... New Lights or the Gifted Brethern (for they pretend to Inspiration) now infest the whole Back Country.... [My] strongest Endeavours, must, and will be, to disperse these Wretches."[52]

Husband had high hopes for the North Carolina backcountry. He envisioned it as a "new government of liberty," a refuge for small, white farmers and religious dissenters, and it was also where he intended to make his fortune. Husband admitted to capitalizing on the widespread fraud that discouraged settlers from moving to the region. "The [land agents'] abuses had no other weight with me then as they turned to my advantage," he informed Granville in 1755, "as in the mean while I could make a cheaper purchase of land, as I cleerly saw those abuses, how great and gauling soever to the inhabitants, was eaisily to be removed and on their removeall land would likely rise."[53] Now, Husband believed, was the time to speculate in land.

In the spring of 1755, Husband returned to Maryland to secure additional funding from his land company's co-investors. But his visions for the backcountry fell on deaf ears. Fearing that the Vestry Act would discourage future settlement, his partners backed out of the business venture. Husband, who had purchased his land before the law was passed, remained undeterred, writing that he was "not willing to quit my schemes that I there projected."[54]

Determined to make a return on his investment, Husband returned to North Carolina and sought out potential clients, including Shubal Stearns, the leader of a group of Separate Baptists residing in Hampshire County, Virginia.[55] In 1755, Stearns and his followers, numbering between fifty and one hundred, left Tolland, Connecticut, for the Virginia wilderness, believing that God wanted them to perform "great work in the west." They eventually settled in Hampshire County's Cacapon River Valley but quickly grew dissatisfied with the region's harsh terrain and isolation. Husband contacted Stearns in the spring of 1755, encouraging him to relocate to Orange County. Husband must have been persuasive. That summer, Stearns and other members journeyed to Husband's temporary residence on Nutbush Creek in Granville County and then accompanied him to the Sandy Creek area, where they established a settlement.[56] Over the next decade, Husband worked closely with these Separate Baptists, witnessing the deed to their church, selling and renting lands to them, and encouraging them to protest against local corruption.[57]

Throughout the late 1750s, Husband continued to increase his property holdings. He acquired around ten thousand acres in Rowan and Orange Counties, which made him one of the region's largest landowners.[58] He also joined the Cane Creek Monthly Meeting of Friends, founded in 1749, and began to court a fellow Quaker, Mary Pugh.[59] In 1759, he abruptly moved back to Maryland, where he was part-owner of the Fountain Company, a copper mining outfit located in present-day Montgomery County.[60] Husband likely feared that the company, which would close in 1764, was on the verge of bankruptcy and decided to use his mining expertise to help resuscitate it. For the next three years, he managed the company's two copper works, hiring and supervising miners, negotiating disputes with the investors, and enumerating supplies needed to maintain the mines' operations.[61] In 1762, however, he resigned—perhaps convinced that he could not save the business venture—and made his way back to Orange County, where he married Mary Pugh that June.[62]

The Rachel Wright Affair

When Husband arrived home in North Carolina, he found the Cane Creek members bitterly divided. The conflict had begun in January 1761, when the men's monthly meeting appointed two Friends to investigate charges brought against Jehu Stuart "for spreading scandalous reports on several young women."[63] One of the women with whom Stuart was reported to have had sex was Charity Wright, the fifteen-year-old daughter of prominent Cane Creek members John and Rachel Wright. In 1749, the Wright family had migrated from Frederick, Maryland, to Orange County, where they helped found the Cane Creek Monthly Meeting. Rachel, in particular, became a leader in the congregation. Thanks to the Quakers' relative acceptance of female participation in church matters, she became a recorded minister and often conducted missionary trips to Virginia and eastern North Carolina.[64] The accusations against Charity threatened to destroy the family's reputation.

Despite Charity's assertion that Stuart had raped her, the women's monthly meeting disowned her in April 1761.[65] Infuriated, Rachel began to publicly denounce the decision, insisting that her daughter had done nothing wrong.[66] That August, Charity appealed her case to the Western Quarterly Meeting, a supervisory body of the Friends, which determined that Stuart had "overcome and defiled" the young girl but chastised Charity for not resisting "to the Utmost of Her power his wicked and lustfull design." Ultimately, the quarterly meeting found her guilty of having unseasonable relations with Stuart and ruled that she would have to sign a document admitting her guilt in order to be reinstated into the fellowship.[67] Charity refused, and Rachel once again openly condemned the handling of her daughter's case.[68] In response, the Cane Creek Monthly Meeting ordered Rachel to publicly apologize for her outbursts, which she did in a letter.[69] Perhaps due to this upsetting series of events, the Wrights moved to Camden, South Carolina, in early 1762. Rachel wrote to the Cane Creek Meeting to ask that it grant her a certificate of good standing, required for any Quaker who wished to join a new meeting.[70] Debate within the Cane Creek congregation ensued, sparking the so-called Rachel Wright affair.[71]

Upon his return to Orange County, Husband aligned himself with the group that opposed Rachel's request on the grounds that her earlier apology had been insincere. There was apparently no love lost between Rachel Wright and Herman Husband. According to Husband, two brethren had approached him shortly before moving back to Maryland in 1759, reporting that they had had sex with Rachel. Husband wrote a letter to Cane Creek leaders detailing the accusations, but church elders told him to drop the matter, which he reluctantly did. After his move to Maryland, he discovered that the Cane Creek Meeting had initially refused to grant him a certificate of good standing and had formed a committee to investigate accusations that he was a liar. Although he eventually received a certificate, Husband believed that Wright was among the Cane Creek members who had launched the campaign against him.[72] For Husband, the Rachel Wright affair offered an opportunity to repay her slights against him.

With the support of Husband, the anti-Wright faction successfully blocked the Cane Creek Monthly Meeting from making a ruling on Wright's certificate of good standing. She appealed to the quarterly meeting in November 1762, charging that some Cane Creek members continued to unjustly detain her certificate. In May 1763, the Western Quarterly Meeting granted Wright her certificate, pointing out that the Cane Creek Meeting's delay on granting such a certificate was not due to her behavior but due to a division within the congregation, one that had grown all the deeper since Husband's reappearance the previous spring.[73]

The anti-Wright faction remained defiant, however. The quarterly meeting complained in November 1763 that many of Wright's opponents continued to maintain "practices, Contrary to the wholesome Rules of Discipline Established in the Wisdom of truth among us."[74] This rebuke infuriated Husband, who once again publicly denounced the quarterly meeting as acting irresponsibly.[75] Wanting to end the affair once and for all, the Cane Creek Monthly Meeting decided to take action against Husband, whom they believed was the ringleader of the dissent. In January 1764, they officially ruled that "Herman Husband being complained of for being guilty of Making remarks on the actions and transactions of this meeting as well as Elsewhere as [is] his mind, and publickly advertising the Same, and after due labour with him in order to shew him the Evil of so doing, this meeting agrees to disown him, as also to publish the Testimony."[76] While the Cane Creek Friends likely thought that disownment would silence Husband and restore unity to the congregation, this proved to be wishful thinking.

Husband and his supporters again refused to concede defeat. Several members of the anti-Wright faction signed a dissenting minute protesting Husband's excommunication. In response, the quarterly meeting expelled those people, including Husband, as it "would be of dangerous Consequences to allow them the priviledge of active members, or to be made Use of as such in any of our meeting of business."[77] In November 1764, the faction appealed to the Yearly Meeting of North Carolina, the highest supervisory body, maintaining that the Western Quarterly Meeting had acted irresponsibly in both granting Rachel Wright a certificate of good standing and expelling those who had signed the dissenting minute. The yearly meeting sought to reach a peaceful resolution and reversed Wright's victory, arguing that the quarterly meeting "did not act Safe in the Case of granting [her] a certificate." It further requested that the Cane Creek Meeting—in order to resolve the conflict—reinstate those who had been disowned with one notable exception: Herman Husband.[78]

This experience would have a dramatic influence on Husband's religious and political views. Four years later, Husband would write *The Second Part of the Naked Truth*, a pamphlet that condemned the Society of Friends for expelling him, in which he portrayed the Rachel Wright affair as a conflict between church authority and individual conscience.[79] He explained that Quaker doctrine declared that all members, not just church officials, possessed the divine ability to "define what is Sin and Immorality." As such, Husband insisted, he had every right to denounce the quarterly meeting's decision to grant Wright a certificate, having been guided by the spirit within to believe that her apology was insincere. However, Husband argued that church leaders had increasingly abandoned the "Principles of the first Quakers" since he joined the brethren in 1743. "Pride and high Conceit, and a vehement Thirst for Power" had caused these elders to begin to control "the Thoughts and Consciences of Men" by imposing "Rules, Precepts, and carnal Ordinances, the Seeds of Bondage and false Power," on them.[80] This perversion of Quaker writings repulsed Husband, who used the Rachel Wright affair as a rallying cry against spiritual tyranny.

While Husband cast himself as a David-like character fighting Goliath, a man who dared to follow his own conscience and challenge church authority, other, less altruistic motives may have played a role in his actions. He conveniently overlooked the fact that Wright could have been following her own conscience when defending her daughter's honor, even if it brought her at odds with church members. Husband's attack on Rachel Wright, then, contradicted his own belief that the spirit within trumped the authority of the church, suggesting that other factors encouraged him to join the anti-Wright faction. Perhaps he hoped to use the affair to enhance his stature within the Cane Creek congregation and beyond. The removal of the Wright family, a fixture in the community since its founding in 1749, clearly eliminated a religious and potential economic competitor (Rachel's husband, John, was a land speculator) in the region, opening the door for Husband's continued ascent up the socioeconomic ladder. Or maybe Husband, unable to rise above his time and place, viewed Wright's leadership position as a threat to the gender status quo.[81] Whatever the motives, he attempted to garner support during the dispute by employing the evangelical rhetoric of spiritual independence and growing antiauthoritarian convictions, a strategy that would prove effective for him in the years to come.

Husband's disownment ultimately failed to restore unity among the Cane Creek congregation. In fact, it likely made matters worse, boosting Husband's popularity among the evangelical community and enabling him to build a broad base of support. Much to the dismay of church elders, the former Quaker continued to proselytize to supporters and encourage them not to compromise their spirit within. In February 1765, a Quaker minister visiting Cane Creek complained that a "considerable number here have unwarily got into a ranting spirit, that much opposes our discipline in the several of its branches, being led away by one Herman Husband; and there have been sorrowful scenes of division and discord among Friends in these parts."[82]

This ranting spirit caused further conflict later that year during the celebration of Husband's marriage to a young Cane Creek Quaker named Emey Allen shortly after his second wife's death.[83] Eleven Friends, several of whom would join Husband a few years later in the Regulator movement, attended the disorderly ceremony, a clear challenge to Cane Creek leaders, who promptly disowned the offenders, including Emey.[84] Even as a former member, Husband remained a thorn in the congregation's side.

Political Awakenings

In the midst of the Cane Creek controversy, Husband's future adversary William Tryon was on board a ship bound for North Carolina. Born in Surrey, England, in 1729, Tryon was the fourth son of Charles and Mary Shirley, both members of the British aristocracy. Raised on the family's grand estate, Norbury Park, Tryon entered the military in 1751, having received a commission as a lieutenant in the prestigious First Regiment of Foot Guards, no doubt bestowed on him due to his parents' wealth and political influence. Six years later, he married the heiress Margaret Wake and was shortly thereafter called up for active duty in the Seven Years' War. Tryon served with distinction

FIGURE 4. As governor of North Carolina, William Tryon struggled to quell the Regulators and would view Husband as a leader of the protest movement. (State Archives of North Carolina, N.53.16.1438)

during the conflict, participating in the Raid on St. Malo in northwestern France, where he was shot twice. Following the war, Tryon secured the position of lieutenant governor of North Carolina through his wife's political connections and set sail for the colony in 1764. He served in that post until March 1765, when the colony's ailing governor, Arthur Dobbs, died. Tryon became interim governor, and in June 1765 King George III appointed him governor of the colony, an office he would hold for the next six years.[85]

Even before officially taking the position, Tryon confronted a crisis that shook the foundations of North Carolina's social order. In March 1765, the British Parliament enacted the Stamp Act with the hope of raising revenue for colonial defense. The law required American colonists to pay a duty, collectible only in specie (gold and silver coin), on stamps or stamped paper used for legal documents, newspapers, playing cards, and other items. News of the impending direct tax sparked a wave of civil disobedience throughout British North America, including North Carolina. Opposition to the Stamp Act was most prevalent in North Carolina in the lower Cape Fear region, where residents in Brunswick, New Bern, and Wilmington formed Sons of Liberty organizations and staged several rallies calling for the duty's immediate repeal. Adhering to radical Whig ideology, these protestors claimed that Parliament had overstepped its authority by imposing a tax without the consent of the people, which broke the social contract between the citizens and government by threatening to take away the inalienable rights of life, liberty, and property. As such, opponents believed, the people had a duty to protest and, if necessary, rebel against the government. Tryon tried to diffuse the

"*A New Government of Liberty*"

situation that May by suspending the General Assembly to prevent it from passing resolves against the law and meeting with anti–Stamp Act leaders to find a peaceful resolution.[86]

While order would temporarily be returned in March 1766 with the reversal of the Stamp Act, the crisis gave Herman Husband a new ideology to embrace. For most of his adult life, he had placed his faith in the power of organized religion to help reform mankind and usher in the millennium. For more than twenty years, he had maintained that the Quakers, being the "best reformed society," would lead the way.[87] But the Cane Creek conflict had left the now-disowned Husband disillusioned, and he was convinced that all denominations rejected the spirit within. What he found to fill his spiritual void was, in fact, not a religion at all but civil government. This required Husband to completely reframe his worldview. In years past, he had linked politics with the secular world; by extension, he "Looked Upon Civill Government Separate from [the] Relegeous one as the business and Province of Kings, Nobles, Learned Men, [and] Lawyers . . . who in Generall were deists and nonbelievers." However, this attitude changed with the Stamp Act crisis. Embracing the radical Whig ideology of the protestors, Husband took up the banner of civil government as the agent of reform. "Convinced that the Authors who Wrote in favor of Liberty was Generally Inspired by the Same Spirit that we Relegeous Professors Called Christ," he argued that all men had to engage in political activism. Only then could they break free from the shackles of tyranny and create a just and moral government, one that, Husband insisted, would bring about the millennium. "Outward Civill Government was as much the object and design of God and the authors who wrote the History of the Scriptures," he explained, reasoning that Christians should no longer shun the political realm because "the Right Government of the Passions by the Grace of God in Man's heart is . . . the beginning of [the] kingdom of God."[88] Husband's conversion to political advocacy and protest of the Stamp Act did not immediately lead him to oppose the British Crown. Instead, it encouraged him to support a local crusade attempting, for the most part, to protect the economic interests of small and middling farmers in the North Carolina Piedmont.

Down and Out in the North Carolina Backcountry

By the mid-1760s, a growing number of backcountry settlers found themselves in a precarious situation. For one, many of them remained unable to secure land titles, due in part to the widespread corruption of land agents Husband had witnessed—and profited from—a decade earlier. The death of Lord Granville in 1763 and the subsequent closing of his land office exacerbated matters by preventing recent arrivals from obtaining titles to the farms they had purchased.[89] Elsewhere, large absentee landowners intensified efforts to identify squatters on their property and force them to purchase their farms or pay rents. These owners often used their wealth, social status, and political influence to ensure the support of local officials. One such was Henry McCulloh, a wealthy London merchant, who in 1761 sent his son, Henry Eustace, to the North Carolina backcountry to survey, subdivide, and sell his 1.2 million acre estate, which included land in parts of Orange, Mecklenburg, Rowan, and Anson Counties. The younger McCulloh quickly made enemies with local farmers, many of whom had unwittingly settled on his father's property, charging them £8 to £12 sterling per one hundred acres, "which far exceeded the cost at which the land could have been patented."[90] Unable or unwilling to pay such inflated prices, some squatters resisted McCulloh, and in March 1765, a group of farmers living near Sugar Creek in Mecklenburg County assaulted the young landlord and his men as they attempted to survey the area.[91] Most of the tenants, however, opted to either purchase their farms at the inflated price or leave the region altogether, knowing that McCulloh had the support of local elites.[92]

Among McCulloh's closest—and least popular—acquaintances was Edmund Fanning.[93] Born in New York in 1739, Fanning earned a degree from Yale College before moving to eastern North Carolina in the late 1750s, where he studied law. Ambitious, charismatic, and sociable, he soon integrated himself into the social circle of the colony's elite. After securing a commission as a colonel in the Orange County militia in 1759, Fanning moved to the booming town of Hillsborough in that county and established a law practice. There, he used his political connections to swiftly rise up the socioeconomic ladder, obtaining lucrative government posts including justice of the peace, public register, and town commissioner. In the 1760s, he joined forces with the McCullohs, who helped Fanning procure a judgeship on the Salisbury superior court, ensuring that the landlords would have the law on their side in their fight against squatters. Although his alliance with the McCullohs and later Governor Tryon enabled Fanning to amass a fortune, it also made him the most reviled man in the Piedmont, as he was often the author of writs of ejectment against unlawful residents on the landlords' property.[94] Backcountry farmers saw him as arrogant and corrupt and immortalized his unscrupulous path to riches in a popular song:

> When Fanning first to Orange came
> He looked both pale and wan,
> An old patched coat upon his back
> An old mare he rode on

"A New Government of Liberty"

> Both man and horse wa'nt worth five pounds
> As I've been often told
> But by his civil robberies
> He's laced his coat with gold.[95]

Fanning represented a new kind of elite emerging in the North Carolina backcountry during the 1760s, as lawyers, merchants, and other professionals replaced the planters who had dominated positions of power in the previous decades.[96] The most coveted and influential post was that of justice of the peace. Appointed by the governor, justices controlled the legislative, judicial, and administrative functions of each county and possessed, among other powers, the authority to impose fines, set local tax rates, supervise the collection of taxes, and order the sale of debtors' properties. They also handpicked officers of the county court, including sheriffs, who enforced tax laws, oversaw elections, and selected juries. Not surprisingly, justices of the peace nominated either themselves or other local professionals to fill these positions, ensuring that membership in the developing rings of courthouse officials remained small.[97] But this concentration of political power in the hands of a few inevitably led to continued corruption and economic exploitation, at least according to backcountry farmers struggling to hold on to their land and get out of debt.

Most settlers in the North Carolina Piedmont were subsistence farmers. Still, they also needed money to buy land, pay taxes, and purchase goods they were unable to manufacture at home.[98] As such, they often devoted a portion

FIGURE 5. A friend of Governor William Tryon and land speculators Henry and Henry Eustace McCulloh, Edmund Fanning became the most despised man in the North Carolina backcountry and a nemesis of Husband. (State Archives of North Carolina, N.96.4.3)

of their crop—frequently wheat, which fetched a better price than tobacco in the 1760s—to sell on the market. Husband, for instance, tended "about fifty Acres of as fine wheat as perhaps ever grew" on his Sandy Creek plantation, where he also operated a gristmill.[99] Other backcountry residents distilled their excess yields of corn and fruit into alcohol; raised livestock to produce commercial items such as beef, milk, cheese, and leather; and hunted and trapped wildlife.[100]

Despite these varied commercial enterprises, most farmers found themselves low on actual cash. Merchants, who were already filling the increased demand for store-bought goods, often served as impromptu bankers, extending credit and outright loans to farmers.[101] This became all the more necessary with growing currency shortages in the mid-1760s. In 1764, the British Parliament prohibited the American colonies from emitting new paper money, which caused the quantity of currency to plummet. By 1768 in North Carolina, only £60,106 in paper money circulated among a citizenry of more than 160,000.[102] Living in the colony's most populous region, backcountry residents were hit the hardest by this currency squeeze.

Rising taxes—which had to be paid in specie or paper currency—put even more pressure on these cash-poor farmers. For example, the poll tax ("levied on any white men over the age of sixteen and all people of color, or their spouses, over the age of twelve") increased from one shilling eight pence in 1754 to six shillings in 1765.[103] To add insult to injury (especially for backcountry evangelicals), the General Assembly, once again hoping to strengthen the Anglican Church, passed the 1764 Vestry Act and the Orthodox Clergy Act of 1765. The former act reinstated the vestry tax, now capped at ten shillings per year, while the latter imposed a tax to pay for the salaries of Anglican ministers in each parish.[104]

Largely due to these tax increases, indebtedness quickly became an unfortunate part of life for many settlers who had moved to North Carolina to achieve economic independence. Farmers relied on advances from merchants to obtain much-needed goods, improve their farms, and buy land and slaves. According to one estimate, the "average debt of farming families lay somewhere between £5 and £9," an amount higher than many yearly incomes at the time.[105] These loans proved difficult to repay. Farmers were always a bad harvest or two away from defaulting, and in the mid-1760s, droughts and unusually high temperatures caused widespread crop failures and economic devastation throughout the region.[106]

Indeed, backcountry courts became increasingly clogged with debt cases during the 1760s, as creditors scrambled to protect their investments. Between 1764 and 1767, merchants in Orange and Granville Counties prosecuted 591 suits for debt recovery.[107] Because most court officials were creditors and landowners themselves, they often ruled against debtors. Not only did defendants frequently lack enough money on hand to fulfill their financial obligations, but they also could not pay fees charged by clerks, sheriffs, and lawyers. Sometimes farmers could reach an agreement with all parties to work off their debt. Granville County resident William Cathon, for instance, reimbursed his creditor by building him a stable and performing "two or three little Jobs besides." Others were not as fortunate and were either taken to debtors' prison or had their property seized by the sheriff and sold at public auction. Local elites used these auctions to expand their landholdings by buying improved land well below the market value of "£10 to £20 North Carolina money per 100 acres." For example, when Orange County resident John Hern's two-hundred-acre farm was auctioned off on October 5, 1765, Edmund Fanning purchased it for £5 North Carolina currency. Later that day, Fanning also bought another local debtor's farm, which totaled a hundred acres, for £3.[108]

Among the reformers who called for an end to the abuses of small farmers was Granville County schoolmaster George Sims. In 1765, Sims publicly accused merchants, lawyers, and court officials of working in collusion with one another to exploit the common people. Embracing radical Whig ideology, Sims reminded Granville County farmers that they had an obligation to resist despotism and tyranny. "I look upon it as my indispensible duty," he proclaimed, "to exert myself in vindication of those rights and privileges which our Constitution has endowed us with, when either persons or things endeavour to destroy them. . . . I think it is high time we should all exert ourselves, in our defence against the common evil." While Sims's public address was ultimately a call for political action, he was not a revolutionary. He encouraged disgruntled inhabitants to remain loyal British subjects, insisting that they were not quarreling with King George III but "with the malpractices of the Officers of the County, and the abuses which we suffer by those empowered to manage our public affairs." Nor did he advocate violence as a solution. "Let us deliver them [officials] a remonstrance," Sims advised, "setting forth the necessity there is for a suspension of court business, till we have a return from the Governor, in answer to the petition, which we shall send to his Excellency on the occasion." In the meantime, he asked protestors to remain patient, keep the law, and behave themselves "with circumspection to the Worshipful Court." Only then, Sims believed, could they "appear what we really are, To wit, free subjects by birth, endeavouring to recover our native rights according to law."[109] But Sims's attempt to mobilize Granville County residents against local officials came to naught. Shortly after giving his so-called Nutbush Address, Sims was sued for libel and support for his cause evaporated.[110]

Herman Husband followed the events unfolding throughout the North Carolina backcountry from the vantage point of his farm along the Sandy Creek in Orange County. While years earlier he had predicted that the region would become "a new government of liberty," a land where industrious white farmers could achieve economic and religious autonomy, he now feared that lawyers, clerks, and merchants had begun to conspire against these men.[111] "The People of Orange," Husband recalled in 1771, were "insulted by the Sheriff . . . neglected and contemned by their Representatives . . . obliged to pay Fees regulated only by the Avarice of the Officer . . . and from all these Evils they saw no way to escape; for the Men in Power . . . were the Men whose interest it was to oppress, and make gain of the Labourer."[112] Such animosity toward the local elite stemmed in part from Husband's belief that the yeomanry formed the backbone of a just and moral government. Although he was one of the wealthiest men in the region, he claimed to sympathize with struggling farmers, describing them as men of honesty and virtue.[113] However, Husband's social critiques also reflected his anxiety over his own position in society. Power brokers like Edmund Fanning constituted a new kind of ruling class—merchants, lawyers, and public officials whose authority was not derived solely from landownership. Well-versed in the law, allied with wealthy merchant firms in England, and politically connected to the colony's eastern elite, they monopolized public office and ascended to the top of the socioeconomic ladder, often on the backs of backcountry planters like Husband.[114]

The Budding Political Activist

In August 1766, Herman Husband joined other like-minded farmers in forming the Sandy Creek Association, an organization addressing the plight of small and middling farmers in the North Carolina backcountry. Most of the members were Quakers who had sided with Husband during the Rachel Wright affair.[115] Like Husband, these men embraced radical Protestantism and believed they had to follow their own consciences, even if it brought them into conflict with Fanning and other local officials. They elected Husband to pen the group's manifesto, later known as "Regulator Advertisement, No. 1." Group member John Marshall carried the petition to Hillsborough, some twenty miles east of his farm along the Sandy Creek in Orange County, where he entered the courthouse, politely introduced himself to the audience, and read it aloud.[116]

"Regulator Advertisement, No. 1" reflected the Sandy Creek Association's desire to peacefully mobilize Orange County residents against corruption and oppression. It requested that each neighborhood in the county elect delegates to meet with local authorities at a mill owned by Joseph Maddock, a Quaker and friend of Husband, located along the Eno River near Hillsborough. The petition demanded the farmers be given a chance to "judiciously" enquire "whether the free men of this Country labor under any abuses of power or not." Espousing the ideology of radical Whigs, the petition continued, "This method will certainly cause the wicked Men in Power to tremble and there is no Damage [that] can attend such a Meeting nor nothing hinder it but a cowardly, dastardly Spirit . . . while Liberty prevails, we must mutter and grumble under any Abuses of Power until such a noble spirit prevails in our posterity."[117] Court officials approved the proposed conference. Thomas Lloyd, a justice of the peace and assemblyman from Orange County, "fixed the day of meeting, to the tenth of October" and promised that "nothing but death or sickness [would] prevent him" from attending it.[118]

Over the next several weeks, the association held public meetings for people to share their grievances and appoint representatives. In the neighborhood of Deep River, where Husband lived, residents elected Quakers William Cox and William Moffitt to attend the meeting. On October 10, Cox and Moffitt, along with ten other delegates, arrived at Maddock's mill, eager to call on local officials "to give an account of their Stewardship."[119] But their enthusiasm turned to disappointment when, as Husband later recorded, "none of the Officers appeared though they had frequently gave out Word beforehand that they would be there." The twelve men were on the verge of adjourning the meeting just as James Watson, clerk of the Orange County court, appeared carrying a message from Edmund Fanning. The nervous messenger explained that Fanning (and other authorities) had decided not to meet with them after observing the word "judiciously" in the petition, which implied to him that the representatives "intended to usurp the power of the county court."[120] Fanning also found the location of the meeting offensive, as he "could not brook the meanness of being summoned to a Mill, the Court House appearing to him, a more suitable place."[121]

The delegates instructed Watson to stay put while Husband drafted their response to Fanning's objections. The public meeting, the group argued, was solely a way to acquaint citizens with elected officials, not an attempt to override the court's authority. Given the fact that "no one Man in [Orange County] . . . was known by above $1/_{10}$ man of the Inhabitants," such an assembly was "absolutely necessary in order to reap the profit designed us in that part of our Constitution of choosing Representatives and knowing of what uses our money is called for." A public conference, they reasoned, would also allow authorities to consult with their constituents, thereby avoiding any future misunderstandings. Satisfied that they had made a strong case, the delegates concluded the petition by asking Fanning to reschedule the meeting at a place of his choosing.[122] They entrusted the paper to Watson, who, "on his Approbation of it, promised to present each of our Representatives with proper Transcripts."[123]

Their appeal proved ineffective. The petition not only failed to change Orange County officials' position on the matter but made them more determined to silence their critics. According to Husband, Fanning read a letter at the county court and militia muster that condemned the proposed meeting as an insurrection and claimed that the Sandy Creek Association members were deranged fools who had "a mischievous Design against the Government."[124] Disgruntled residents recalled later that local authorities began "to assume airs, threatening us behind our backs, which Menaces working on the imbecility of some, the Pusilanimity of others.... The Sheriffs now grew very arbitrary, insulting the Populace and making such Distresses."[125] The Sandy Creek Association responded by collecting £50 to sue Fanning and other officers but could not find a lawyer willing to represent them. This, along with the threats made by local officials against the organization, Husband remembered, "so discouraged the People, that the Affair dropped."[126]

For the time being, all was quiet in Orange County. But the forty-three-year-old Husband had found a new calling in life: political activism. Stubborn, outspoken, and intelligent, he had always challenged authority. As a youth, he had rebelled against the secularized Anglican world of his father, embracing evangelicalism and joining the Society of Friends. His faith in the spirit within inspired him to stand up to prominent coreligionists and ultimately led him to reject organized religion altogether. Combining radical Protestantism with radical Whig ideology, Husband would denounce local corruption and become politically active, insisting that common farmers, endowed by God with reason and understanding, had a civic and religious duty to combat all forms of tyranny. Only then could they create "a new government of liberty" and usher in the millennium.[127] But Husband was by no means a revolutionary. Like most other backcountry farmers, he supported the British Crown and only sought to curb local corruption. Along with the Sandy Creek Association, he also advocated for moderation, encouraging protestors to seek peaceful redress within the system. In the immediate years to come, Husband would continue his quest to establish a just and moral government. In the process, he would emerge as a leader of the largest agrarian uprising in colonial American history.

THREE

"Shew Yourselves to Be Freemen"
Husband and the North Carolina Regulation

> Oh Liberty! Thou dearest Name! and Property! thou best of blessings! Whither are ye flown from the inhospitable land of Tryon and Fanning! blasted by the perjurous breath of Villains, who sell their Conscience for an unworthy Price, the smile of an injurious Man, ye are forced from the Courts, (miscall'd) of justice.
> —Herman Husband, *A Fan for Fanning*

The Rise of the Regulators

In the early morning of May 2, 1768, Herman Husband awoke to a loud bang on his back door, followed by the sound of footsteps charging into his bedroom. "You are the King's prisoner," Thomas Hart, an Orange County official, declared to a startled Husband, "on Suspicion of having a Hand in the Mob."[1] The mob in question had formed three weeks earlier, on April 8, when approximately seventy men armed "with Clubs, Staves &c and cloven Musquets" marched into Hillsborough to rescue a mare that a local sheriff had confiscated from a farmer refusing to pay his taxes. The men also seized and tied the sheriff, parading him through the streets, a shaming ritual known as skimmington, long practiced by English protestors.[2] The procession ended at Edmund Fanning's house, where someone "fired a few Guns at the Roof" before the crowd dispersed and left town. Although Fanning had been out of town during the disturbance, he called for the arrest of Husband, believing that the former Quaker had organized and led the riot.[3]

The Hillsborough ruckus was the result of increased tensions between Orange County officials and disgruntled residents, which had only grown worse since Fanning's crackdown on the Sandy Creek Association in 1766. Husband and others accused authorities of continuing to intimidate and profit from the common people through the collection of illegal fees, excessive taxes, and unlawful confiscation of debtors' property. "These Things [repossessed property] were all sold in [Hillsborough] at under Rates, and became a constant trade," Husband complained. "Roguish People began to depend on these Sales to raise them Fortunes."[4] Relations further deteriorated in early 1768 when Orange County sheriff Tyree Harris announced that he would no longer collect taxes at people's homes. Instead, all citizens had to pay their taxes at one of five collection points in the county or pay a fee for Harris's visit.[5] This new mandate enraged residents, including Husband. "Every one could see this was quite insulting," he bemoaned, "for no one but had Sense enough to know this new Law was calculated for the Sheriff's Ease."[6]

The timing of Harris's decree could not have been worse. In 1766, the General Assembly had authorized £5,000 to begin construction of a new residence and government headquarters for Governor William Tryon in New Bern, but by December 1767, building costs had exceeded the original appropriation. In early 1768, Tryon asked assemblymen to allocate an additional £10,000 to finance the project, which they did.[7] The additional appropriation for the governor's residence—which became known as Tryon's Palace—was raised via a poll tax of one shilling six pence, payable only in North Carolina proclamation money.[8] This infuriated many backcountry settlers, who charged that the tax was regressive in nature and hurt poorer residents the most, especially those in the Piedmont, where currency was already in short supply.[9] "A man that is worth £10,000 pays no more than a poor back settler that has nothing but the labour of his hands to depend upon for his daily support," a Mecklenburg County farmer complained. A man "must be still more grievously oppressed if he has a large family, which 'tis ten to one but he has, as the women in these parts are remarkably prolific."[10] Even more insulting, the tax collectors were local sheriffs, who many people believed pocketed much of the money given to them.

In the spring of 1768, a group of farmers along the Haw River in southwestern Orange County took action against these perceived injustices. On March 22, they formed a new organization and wrote a public advertisement more defiant than those issued by the Sandy Creek Association. Arguing that taxes in Orange County were higher than elsewhere in the colony, they accused Fanning and other officials of denying them their rights as Englishmen to investigate and remedy this irregularity. They pledged to withhold their taxes "until we have a full settlement for what is past and have a true regulation with our Officers" and warned that they would not accept defeat. "The Inhabitants of this Province have not as a good a right to enquire into

FIGURE 6. The North Carolina assembly's allocation of £10,000 in 1768 to finance the completion of Tryon's Palace sparked a wave of protest across the backcountry and helped to mobilize support for the Regulators. (State Archives of North Carolina, N.53.15.1951)

the nature of our Constitution and Disbursements of our funds as those of our Mother Country," they declared. "We think that it is by arbitrary proceedings that we are debarred of that right, therefore . . . it is our intent to have a full settlement of you in every particular point that is matter of doubt with us."[11]

The advertisement struck a chord among resentful Orange County residents, and the new organization "spread every Way like Fire till it reached Sandy Creek," where Husband lived. While Husband remained hesitant to embrace the group, believing that its combative language and refusal to pay taxes was "too hot and rash," he was also careful "not to kill that Zeal for Justice and true Liberty" and agreed to meet with the group on April 4.[12] Hoping "to shew them the Danger of their Proceedings," Husband convinced members to begin calling themselves Regulators, a name that emphasized the organization's primary—and less militant—goal of "regulating publick Grievances & abuses of Power." He also persuaded them to draw up a new, more moderate petition that continued to endorse the nonpayment of taxes but did not make personal attacks on local officials and assured that the Regulators would seek peaceful redress of their grievances. This document maintained that the protestors simply wanted to preserve and enjoy the liberties and privileges the English constitution granted them. Fanning could not oppose this sentiment without alienating himself from the populace, and again asked Orange County officials to meet with the group to discuss charges of corruption in local government.[13]

Not all Regulators embraced Husband's moderate strategy. A group of radical activists called for more drastic action and organized the April 8 Hillsborough riot. The event alarmed moderates, who quickly distanced the Regulator organization from the militant wing, agreeing to return the seized mare to authorities and requesting a meeting with local officials.[14] Husband—fearful that the riot discredited the legitimacy of the Regulators and provided Fanning with an excuse to use military force—reached out to Hillsborough lawyer and merchant Ralph McNair for legal advice. He informed Husband that the April disturbance was "diametrically opposite to the law of nature and nations." "Their method of redress," McNair continued, "is wrong according to the opinion of all preceding Ages I need only put you in mind of the ancient Fable ascribed to Esop of the hands and Feet running in mutiny against the Head." But he advised that it was not too late for the Regulators to make amends with Fanning to avoid harsh punishment. "I can assure [you] with the utmost confidence that this affair if it stops here will never be represented by Colo Fanning any otherwise than as a Mob" and would thus be "treated generally with Lenity," he wrote, asking that Husband and other protestors visit Fanning to reach a peaceful resolution.[15]

This meeting would never take place. Fanning viewed the April 8 riot as an act of treason and was in no mood to negotiate with the Regulators. "Such an instance of a traitorous and rebellious conduct and behaviour such a lawless opposition to Government such an open defiance of Law and contempt of authority I could never believe or suspect the Inhabitants of my Darling my favourite County guilty of," he complained to an Orange County militia officer on April 13. Their "behavior is a disgrace to our Country and something more than a dishonor to our King." Determined to suppress the "spirit of riotousness," Fanning ordered officials to call up the militia, but their attempts to muster volunteers were unsuccessful, to say the least.[16] Only 120 men appeared when called for duty on April 16, and most of them, officers reported, opted to remain neutral, indicating local support for the Regulator cause.[17]

Such disaffection was not confined to Orange County. On April 21 in nearby Anson County, approximately forty armed Regulators entered the courthouse, protesting "the Payment of the Taxes now due from them." Although officials managed to convince the group to leave, the next week around a hundred men returned, making "a great deal of noise & uproar, behav[ing] very saucy and arrogant & threaten[ing] to come in and take the Magistrates off the Bench." Samuel Spencer, a court clerk and Anson County assemblyman, met the protestors at the door and demanded they disperse. But this time the group meant business. They forcibly removed the justices from the bench before debating whether to tear down the courthouse. They decided to let the building stand but passed a series of resolves, including a pledge to no longer pay unlawful taxes.[18]

Both Fanning and Spencer wrote to Governor Tryon, expressing their fears that the situation was getting out of control. "The People," Fanning explained, "are now in every part and Corner of the County, meeting, conspiring, and confederating by solemn oath and open violence to refuse to pay Taxes and to prevent the execution of Law, threatening death and immediate destruction to myself and others." Even more alarming, he warned, a rumored 1,500 Regulators planned to surround Hillsborough and burn it to the ground.[19] A distressed Spencer wrote to Tryon after the Anson County riot, uncertain how to proceed. While Fanning had wanted to raise a militia, Spencer cautioned that doing so would only "give the Disaffected an opportunity of being more mischievous and dangerous."[20]

The disturbances in Orange and Anson Counties took Tryon by surprise. The governor had toured the North Carolina backcountry the previous summer and was greeted with open arms. "It was with a very sensible satisfaction," he bragged in July 1767, "[that] I found on those hilly or back settlements a race of people, slightly, active, and laborious, and loyal subjects to his Majesty."[21] After this experience, Tryon had been certain that most settlers were not sympathetic to the Regulators. "Is it possible that the same men, who I received with so much pride and happiness last year . . . should now be loaded with opprobrious Titles of Insurgents and Violators of the Public Peace, that common right of Mankind in Society," he wrote incredulously to Fanning. "This surely can only be an infatuation, instigated by a few Persons, whose characters are as desperate as their fortunes."[22] On April 27, Tryon issued a proclamation demanding that all rioters disperse and instructed backcountry authorities to apprehend the organization's leaders.[23]

Fanning was more than happy to carry out the governor's orders. On May 1, he secured arrest warrants for William Butler, a farmer who had participated in the April 8 riot, and Herman Husband.[24] Fanning immediately set out to Sandy Creek with a posse of approximately thirty men. They apprehended Butler first, and twelve men in the group headed to arrest Husband, leaving Fanning and the others behind. When the posse returned with Husband in hand, the prisoner recalled that Fanning asked him "flutteringly, and with visible Confusion, Why I did not come to see him in so long a time—I told him I new no call I had—He said, Well, you'll come along now.—I said, I suppose I must." The prisoners were escorted to Hillsborough and placed in jail.[25]

The next morning, justice of the peace Thomas Lloyd summoned Husband to court, charging that the former Quaker "had a Hand in the mob." When Husband denied this, Lloyd called Fanning to the witness stand.

Fanning asserted that he had received a Regulator advertisement that was in Husband's handwriting, clear evidence that the prisoner at least worked on behalf of the organization. Another witness also testified that Husband had attended several Regulator meetings. Husband was returned to the jail, where he and Butler stayed the rest of the day. Around midnight, several guards collected the two prisoners, tied their hands and feet, and prepared them for transport to New Bern for trial. Alarmed, Husband requested to see Fanning, who decided to give the prisoners an audience. Pleading for his and Butler's release, Husband promised Fanning that he would "not concern myself any more whether you take too large Fees or not." Fanning contemplated the offer and agreed to release them if they promised "never to give your Opinion of the Laws,—nor frequent assembling yourself among People . . . and do every Thing in your Power to moderate and pacify them [the Regulators]." Although Husband accepted these terms, Butler remained defiant. "I have but one Life," he proclaimed, "and I freely can give that up for this Cause; for, God above knows, our Cause is just." Butler eventually consented to his release, but only after Fanning pledged "to clear him at the Court, without Cost." Promising to appear at the Hillsborough superior court that September to stand trial, Husband and Butler were then released on bond.[26]

Fanning's willingness to release the prisoners stemmed more from fear than leniency. News of the men's arrest had "alarmed the whole County, Regulators [and] Anteregulators," and by the morning of May 3, approximately seven hundred protestors had encamped near Hillsborough on the opposite side of the Eno River.[27] This spirit of enthusiasm—as Husband described it—troubled Fanning, and he made sure to release the prisoners before addressing the crowd.[28] Carrying a bottle of wine and rum as a peace offering, Fanning walked down to the river, calling to Regulator leader Ninian Bell Hamilton to send over a horse so he could cross without getting wet. "Yer none too gude to wade, and wade ye shall, if ye come over," Hamilton replied. When a dripping wet Fanning arrived at the camp, he did not find a receptive audience, and "no one would partake of his refreshments, or listen to his statements."[29] With Husband and Butler released and Fanning humiliated, the Regulators were elated. Rednap Howell, a local schoolteacher from New Jersey, commemorated that day's events in a popular song:

> From Hillsborough Town the first day of May
> March'd those murdering traitors.
> They went to oppose the honest men
> That were called the Regulators.
>
> [missing verses]

> Old Hamilton surrounded the Town,
> He guarded every quarter;
> The Regulators still marching on,
> Full fifteen hundred after.
>
> At length their head men they sent out
> To save their town from fire.
> To see Ned Fanning wade Eno,
> Brave boys, you'll all admire.
>
> With hat in hand, at our command,
> To salute us every one, Sir;
> And after that, kept of his hat
> To salute old Hamilton, Sir.
>
> But old Hamilton, like an angry man
> He still craved satisfaction
> For taking of Husbands away to the town
> It was a most villainous action.[30]

Order eventually prevailed when Tryon's private secretary Isaac Edwards intervened on Fanning's behalf. He assured the people that if they dispersed and wrote a petition to Tryon, the governor would "Protect and Redress them against any unlawful Extortions, or Oppressions of any Officer of Officers in the County," which seemed to appease the crowd. "No sooner was the Word spoke, but the whole Multitude, as with one Voice, cried out, Agreed," Husband recalled. "That is all we want; Liberty to Make our grievances known." Edwards passed out several bottles of wine to seal the deal.[31]

The promise that Tryon would accept a petition directly from protestors deeply troubled Fanning, who up to that point had controlled what information the governor received concerning conditions in the colony's backcountry. Determined to maintain his influence over Tryon, Fanning demanded that he would write the petition, and he attempted to coerce several Regulators to assist him or face charges of treason.[32] Despite this threat of execution, the Regulators refused to comply. On May 21, Regulators and other disgruntled farmers assembled at George Adam Sally's farm on Rocky River in Orange County, where they appointed an eight-man committee to draw up a petition without Fanning's input.[33] Signed by 480 residents, including Husband, the petition and attached narrative of events blamed the recent disturbances on local officials, "nefarious and designing men who being put into Posts of Profit" had used "every artifice [and practiced] every fraud ... to squeeze and extort from the wretched Poor."[34] The petitioners—careful not to present themselves as rebels—pledged loyalty to King George III, acknowledged the government's right to tax, and asked the governor for clemency.[35]

Tryon responded to the petition the next month, assuring protestors that the colonial government would prosecute every official who had extorted money from them. But he also chastised his unruly subjects. "The Grievances Complained of by no Means warrant the Extraordinary Steps you have taken," he observed. "If [this vigilantism had been] carried but a little farther [it would] have been treated as High Treason." Tryon ordered protestors to pay their taxes, stop threatening officials, and cease using "the borrowed Title of Regulators, assuming themselves Powers and Authorities (unknown to the Constitution)." He promised to pay a visit to Hillsborough soon, but in the meantime, he wrote, "I rest in full Confidence I shall again be made happy by seeing Industry prevailing over Faction, and Peace and Harmony triumphing over Jealousies and Murmering."[36]

As promised, Tryon traveled to Hillsborough in early July, where he issued a proclamation forbidding officials from collecting excessive fees. That August, however, several hundred Regulators met again at Sally's farm and penned a letter to Tryon, claiming that Fanning and other local authorities were continuing to charge double the amount of fees allowed by the law. Such blatant lawlessness, they warned, had caused many people to lose faith in obtaining justice. "Your Excellency is pleased to observe that you Hope again to be made happy on seeing a spirit of industry prevailing among us over faction and discontent," they explained. But "since the iron hand of tyranny [continues to display] its baneful influences over us with impunity how has dejection, indifference and melancholy . . . spread themselves far and wide among us."[37] Regulators also had a heated exchange at the meeting with Sheriff Tyree Harris. Although Tryon had ordered Harris to attend the event, the constable's presence infuriated Regulators, who reminded him that they would kill anyone who attempted to collect taxes from them. Harris heeded their warning, excusing himself from the meeting and riding back to Hillsborough.[38]

Relations between Tryon and the Regulators steadily deteriorated over the next couple of weeks. Regulators were now convinced that the governor was in league with corrupt local officials, a situation exacerbated by rumors that he wanted to raise a militia and recruit Native Americans to attack insurgent farmers. By August 11, more than a thousand Regulators had assembled at Simon Dixon's mill near Cane Creek, twenty miles from Hillsborough. In response, Tryon called up Fanning's Orange County militia regiment. With the threat of violence looming, Regulator leaders appointed eight men to negotiate with Tryon in Hillsborough on August 12. The governor was eager to diffuse the situation. In addition to denying that he conspired to use

Native Americans or the militia to quell the Regulators, Tryon promised not only that sheriffs would delay collecting taxes but also that Fanning would stand trial for extortion at the Hillsborough superior court in September and that local officials would meet with protestors at Sally's farm on August 17. The Regulator delegates endorsed Tryon's proposals and returned to Dixon's mill, where their compatriots agreed to disband.[39]

Tryon failed to uphold his end of the bargain. When the Regulators convened again at Sally's farm, only Sheriff John Lea appeared with a letter from Tryon. The governor, fearful that the Regulators would disrupt the upcoming trials of Husband and Butler at the Hillsborough superior court, had decided to take a harder stance against them. He chastised the protestors' refusal to pay taxes, accused them of being "bent [more] upon destroying the Peace of the Government . . . than a wish or Intention to wait for any Legal Process against those [they] imagine have Abused their Publick Trusts," and ordered them to send twelve of their leaders to Salisbury to post a bond for £1,000 "as a Security that no Rescue shall be made of William Butler and Harmon Husbands."[40]

Tryon also mustered around 1,100 troops from Rowan and Mecklenburg Counties to protect the upcoming court session in Hillsborough. For many Regulators, the governor's actions left them "at Liberty to Defend themselves."[41] Nonetheless, "We bear no ill-will to any but our cruel Oppressors from which number we exclude your Excellency," they wrote to Tryon. "But [if threatened] we are determined at all events to fall like men, and sell our lives at the very dearest rate."[42] Tryon's militia arrived in Hillsborough on September 19; shortly thereafter, approximately 3,700 Regulators assembled near the town. Military confrontation again appeared imminent.[43]

Meanwhile, Herman Husband considered fleeing the colony. Since his release from jail, he had maintained a relatively low profile. He did not attend Regulator meetings throughout the summer, and in fact denied that he was a Regulator at all.[44] Given his misgivings about militants within the organization, this may well have been true. But Tryon was unconvinced, pointing out that Husband had worked closely with Regulator leaders to formulate strategy and insisting that the "factious temper[ed]" man had orchestrated the April 8 riot.[45] With rumors circulating that the governor wanted to execute Husband, the former Quaker "took to the Woods." His close friend and Cross Creek merchant John Wilcox caught up with Husband about fifteen miles from his home, and accompanied him to the farm of John Pyle, a Cane Creek Quaker.[46] "I called to Hermon, and asked him what his Horse was shod all around for," Pyle later recalled. "To take the Mountains, or upper Roads, said he, so as to leave the Province.— I told him that would shew Guilt, forfeit his Estate, and bring his Family to

Want.—He said, better so than to be killed and then my Family be equally brought to Poverty."[47]

Wilcox and Pyle convinced Husband to remain at the house and went to Hillsborough to seek help from John Ashe, a militia officer, prominent Whig politician, and former Stamp Act protestor from New Hanover County in eastern North Carolina. Ashe promised to protect Husband if the would-be fugitive agreed to stand trial. Following their meeting, Wilcox and Pyle ran into Fanning, who was none too happy to see the pair. Fanning ordered them to leave Hillsborough immediately, and a heated argument ensued. Pyle told Fanning that the "Authority which drives me out of your Town [is] arbitrary." According to Pyle, Fanning "resumed his Countenance and stept towards me, and ordered me to be gone." Husband's friends—scared for their safety—determined it would be best to comply with Fanning's wish.[48]

Wilcox again asked Husband to stay put while he traveled to Cross Creek to speak on Husband's behalf to the colony's attorney general, Thomas McGuire. On September 20, Wilcox returned with promising news. McGuire had assured him that Husband would receive a fair trial and instructed the former Quaker to meet him at the Regulator camp in order to be safely escorted to Hillsborough. Husband did go meet McGuire but had misgivings about surrendering. Husband's friend William McPherson had warned him that a few days earlier in Hillsborough, Fanning had said that Husband would be executed, "as sure as [you] is born of a Woman."[49] Further, Regulator leaders refused to allow him to leave with McGuire "unless every Body had Liberty to go, as usual in all courts."[50] Husband ultimately abandoned the idea of surrendering and set out for Pyle's farm with Wilcox and McPherson. Along the way, Wilcox eventually convinced Husband to stand trial.[51]

On September 22, Husband and Wilcox rode into Hillsborough to secure the service of Abner Nash, a lawyer and future governor of the state of North Carolina who knew Wilcox. Nash and another attorney, James Milner, agreed to sue for damage for Husband's arrest and imprisonment before the superior court. Although Husband intended to prove to the court that he was not a Regulator himself, he later claimed that he had asked Nash to "Plead the whole Cause of the Regulation all over the Province."[52] Satisfied with the arrangement, Husband gave "all the Money [he] had, and Bonds and Notes for £150 more" to the two attorneys and secured lodging in Hillsborough for the night.[53]

The next morning, Fanning again ordered Wilcox to depart from Hillsborough, leaving Husband without any allies in the town. Husband decided that he, too, would return to the safety of his own community, where he could also recruit neighbors to testify on his behalf. However, before he could make it out of Hillsborough, several militiamen approached him with bayonets raised. After pushing him off his horse and dragging him into a tavern, Husband claimed, the soldiers placed him on a table and jeered him, even firing a gun over his head.[54] Fortunately, John Ashe, who had promised to protect Husband several days earlier, shoved the men away from the former Quaker and warned them to not "carry the joke too far." A relieved Husband took his leave and hurried back to Sandy Creek.[55]

While Husband sought redress for his grievances, Tryon was trying to restore law and order. On September 23, the governor extended a peace settlement to Regulators encamped on the outskirts of Hillsborough, requesting that nine of their leaders surrender to authorities and stand trial. All other Regulators would receive a pardon if they gave up their arms and pledged to pay taxes.[56] Unwilling to fight or hand over their guns, the Regulators opted to return to their homes and "leave the Governor to fight the Air."[57] While the conflict remained unresolved, violence had once again been averted.

Three days later, Husband returned to the Hillsborough courthouse, where Fanning greeted him with disdain.[58] He "accused me of Crimes committed since I had entered into the Recognizances," Husband remembered, "and signified they were of so high a Nature as concerned my Life." The court indicted Husband on four counts of inciting a riot and placed him in jail. He shared his cell with nine other prisoners, one of whom welcomed the new arrival by "pointing to a Gallows, erected between two Joyces of the Prison, right over the middle of the Floor."[59] Eager to post bail, he met with Nash and Milner that night. The attorneys agreed to loan their client the money, but only after he signed a promissory note. A desperate Husband agreed to the terms, a decision that would come back to haunt him.[60]

Over the next week, Husband and several other Regulators stood trial at the Hillsborough superior court before Chief Justice Martin Howard and Associate Judge Richard Henderson, a Granville County lawyer and planter.[61] Given recent events, Howard and Henderson thought it best to show leniency to the defendants. Some of them received small fines and short prison sentences, but Husband was found not guilty.[62] In an attempt to placate the Regulators, Fanning stood trial for extorting fees while serving as Orange County's register of deeds. He was found guilty, although the judges fined him only a penny for each offense.[63]

The court's leniency on Regulator defendants and Fanning's trial temporarily alleviated tensions in the backcountry. The Regulators announced that they would comply with the law, and that October, Tryon discharged the militia and pardoned "all persons concerned in the late insurrection," with the exception of Husband and twelve other Regulator leaders.[64] "The insurgents finding their ardor opposed and checked and that they were not the masters of government . . . [have changed their] disposition," Tryon wrote to his superior, Wills Hill, 1st Earl of Hillsborough, in December. "Those in Orange County have declared they will pay their taxes as soon as they can get the money."[65]

Disheartened but Not Defeated

When the General Assembly convened in November 1768, Regulators and other disgruntled farmers were cautiously optimistic. For weeks, they had bombarded their representatives with petitions calling for lower taxes, the removal of corrupt officials, and the creation of a small-claims court to limit court costs, confident that the recent events in Hillsborough signaled elected officials' willingness to now work on their behalf.[66] However, this would not be the case. Although legislators lowered the poll tax, they failed to repeal funding for Tryon's Palace nor did they crack down on local corruption or establish a small-claims court.[67] Indifferent to the protestors' grievances, assemblymen focused their attention on the British Parliament's controversial Townshend Acts of 1767, which placed import taxes on such items as paper, lead, and tea. In early 1768, Massachusetts legislators issued a circular letter inviting other assemblies to unite in opposition to the new levies. That December, the North Carolina lower house responded, introducing to the floor a petition to King George III protesting the duties.[68] An angry Tryon promptly suspended the assembly before it could do anymore damage.[69]

Although disappointed in the lack of results, most Regulators refused to engage in further civil disobedience, instead suing corrupt officials in court, a tactic endorsed by Husband and other moderates within the organization.[70] In March 1769, disgruntled Orange County farmers filed into the Hillsborough superior court to secure indictments against Fanning and other local officials.[71] In neighboring Rowan County, protestors followed suit, attempting to indict John Frohock—a wealthy land speculator and multiple officeholder—in the Salisbury superior court for extorting money from a widow.[72] However, according to Husband, Deputy Attorney William Hooper, a future signer of the Declaration of Independence, made it as difficult as possible for farmers to sue officials in the Hillsborough court. Those few officials who did stand trial, Husband argued, were shown leniency by juries composed of anti-Regulators.[73] Fanning, claiming ignorance of the law, received a verdict of not guilty, while the grand jury in the Salisbury superior court voted against indicting Frohock for extortion.[74] "We can get no redress in what is called Courts of Justice," a group of Regulators complained to Husband following Frohock's exoneration. "Our Crafty & cruel Oppressors . . . take the power of the Court in their own hands, & try it themselves, or at least deprive us of the Benefit of bringing our matter to any Issue."[75]

Despite these setbacks, the Regulators continued to seize opportunities to agitate for reform. In May 1769, Tryon dissolved the assembly for the first time in nearly three years and called for new elections to take place that summer.[76] Reinvigorated, Regulators scrambled to elect legislators sympathetic to their cause. In Orange County, they reached out to Husband, who had become a folk hero throughout the backcountry. A popular Regulator song championed Husband as a "hum-drum old fox" who had the courage to stand up against corrupt officials, and rumors that he was related to and corresponded with the famous Benjamin Franklin further enhanced the former Quaker's reputation as "a firebrand amongst the people."[77] With his popularity at an all-time high, the Sandy Creek farmer agreed to run in the upcoming election against his nemesis, Edmund Fanning.

Husband capitalized on pro-farmer sentiment and radical Whig ideology to mobilize support for his campaign. In his only extant speech, he argued that lawyers, clerks, and other officials had sacrificed the "Interest of their Country" for "the Promotion of their [own] Wealth." While controlling the General Assembly, he reminded voters, these men had designed laws to benefit themselves at the expense of hardworking farmers whose rights and properties wavered in the balance. Still, Husband insisted that the common people possessed the ability to act responsibly and elect honest men— preferably farmers like himself—who were "independent in their Fortunes" and thus enjoyed "no Places of Benefit under the Government." "Should we now through Fear or Favour act as we have done, contrary to Duty and Interest; so far as we do this, we contribute to all the Mischief consequent upon it," he proclaimed. "Shew yourselves to be Freemen, and for once assert your Liberty and maintain your Rights."[78]

Husband's words struck a chord with Orange County farmers. He, along with Regulator John Pryor, soundly defeated Fanning in the election, receiving collectively more than 75 percent of the vote.[79] Regulators elsewhere in the backcountry were also successful. In Rowan County, Christopher Nation prevailed against John Frohock, while Granville County residents elected Regulator sympathizer Thomas Person over Samuel Benton, an assemblyman whom George Sims had targeted in his Nutbush Address several years earlier. Anson County's Samuel Spencer, whom angry protestors had accosted at court that previous April, also lost his seat to a Regulator supporter, Matthew Railand.[80] The results of the elections left the colony's elite in disbelief. "The madness of the people must be great indeed," Henry Eustace McCulloh bemoaned, "to trust such wretches as Herman Husbands and Christopher Nation as their representatives."[81]

In October, Husband set out for New Bern to take his seat in the North Carolina lower house, carrying with him a petition signed by Orange County residents. Weeks earlier, the Regulators, emboldened by their success in the election, had organized meetings throughout the backcountry, allowing disgruntled farmers an opportunity to again voice their grievances and demand reform.[82] The resulting petitions, including the one packed in Husband's saddlebag, called for the creation of a government that worked on behalf of the common people and proposed sweeping reforms to the colony's political process, tax laws, land policy, and court system.

Central to their demands was political reform. Up to that point, each freeholder stood before the candidates and gave his vote.[83] The disgruntled farmers complained that this enabled corrupt officials to intimidate voters on election day, and they asked the General Assembly to implement secret balloting.[84] Orange and Rowan petitioners further demanded that clerks and lawyers be prohibited from serving in the assembly, declaring that they passed laws to solely enrich themselves "at the expense of the poor Industrious peasant." The complainants also called for accountability in government by requesting that "the votes of assemblymen" be recorded in "the House journals and distributed, along with copies of all new laws, to every justice of the people in the province."[85]

Petitioners likewise proposed extensive revisions to the colony's financial structure. They denounced the poll tax for placing a disproportionate burden on struggling backcountry farmers and instead called for a more equitable levy, in which "each person pay in proportion of the profits arising from his Estate." The protestors further demanded that they be allowed to pay their taxes in produce due to the shortage of paper currency, and that warehouses be erected for them to store their crops and receive notes that could be used as legal tender.[86] Additionally, they argued that sheriffs should not have the authority to collect these duties, recommending that legislators divide counties into districts and appoint officials in each to collect the taxes.[87]

The colony's chaotic land system, petitioners claimed, continued to be corrupted by officials who extorted money and conspired with large speculators to monopolize the backcountry's most fertile lands. They charged that these men often granted their friends headrights that exceeded 640 acres, a blatant violation of the law, and failed to comply with North Carolina's cultivation clause, which required all owners to improve a portion of their land annually. All the while, "great numbers of poor people" toiled "in the cultivation of bad Lands whereon they hardly can subsist."[88] To protect farmers who had labored several years to improve their land from losing it to absentee speculators, the petitioners further requested that the Granville District land office, which had closed in 1763, be reopened and required to give squatters preemptive rights "to at least 300 acres of their own improvements."[89]

Regarding the court system, disgruntled citizens suggested that in order to prevent lawyers, clerks, and other officials from charging exorbitant fees and extorting money, chief justices and clerks should be granted an annual salary and lawyers be restrained from demanding any fee that was greater than the law allowed. They argued that the assembly could further combat corruption by replacing current clerks with "Gentlemen of probity and Integrity" and by prohibiting judges, sheriffs, and lawyers from receiving payment until all court cases had reached a conclusion.[90] Finally, petitioners again called for the creation of a small-claims court, which they believed would help cut court costs and guarantee speedier trials.[91]

However, hopes for reform were quickly dashed when the General Assembly convened in New Bern that October 1769. Most legislators refused to consider the petitions, and Tryon, more concerned with growing colonial dissatisfaction with the British Parliament, focused on convincing assemblymen not to adopt the nonimportation resolves that Virginia's House of Burgesses had recently passed in protest of the Townshend duties. Moreover, many assemblymen remained reluctant to conciliate with the Regulators, agreeing with Speaker John Harvey that members of the organization were "a set of men . . . forgetful of their duty they owed their Sovereign, insensible of the Happiness" that Tryon's administration had brought to North Carolina, "and in Defiance of the Laws under which they Lived."[92]

Despite these setbacks, Husband attempted to deliver on his promises to backcountry voters. On October 27, he introduced the Orange County petition to the assembly, but no vote was taken on it.[93] Days later, his motion requiring land speculators to compensate evicted squatters "the Value of his Labour, and Damages of moving to another Place" failed to pass.[94] The only highlight of Husband's first term in the assembly was his appointment to a committee charged with investigating allegations of corruption regarding the colony's sinking fund.[95] The newly elected lawman no doubt cherished this opportunity, as Regulators had long accused officials of embezzling tax money designated for that fund.[96] Before the committee could make any headway, however, Tryon again suspended the assembly, fearing that a nonimportation agreement in remonstration of the Townshend Acts was imminent.[97] "All Things are left in Confusion and Disorder," Husband complained. "Our Assembly was dissolved before they could do any Business of Consequence."[98]

Disheartened but not defeated, Husband returned to his Sandy Creek farm that winter and penned the first of two pamphlets encouraging backcountry inhabitants to continue their fight for reform. Published in early 1770, *An Impartial Relation* chronicles the history of the Regulation up to 1769, emphasizing Husband's attempts to minimize violence. But more than just a narrative of the Regulator movement or a defense of Husband's actions, this tract also sought to further politicize farmers by merging radical Protestantism with radical Whig ideology.

At the end of *An Impartial Relation*, Husband included two sermons, both of which he plagiarized heavily from James Murray's *Sermons to Asses*, published two years earlier. Murray, a Nonconformist minister from Scotland, warned that Europe had fallen victim to civil and religious oppression and urged all Christians, having been endowed by God with reason and understanding, to assert their rights and peacefully resist "any yoke of bondage."[99] Expanding on Murray's argument, Husband insisted that North Carolinians were also not free. Politicians and clergymen, he explained, had thus far succeeded in depriving the people of their civil and religious liberties. But the people had only themselves to blame. "The reason of all civil and religious impositions hath been the slothfulness of the people.... As soon as we have elected civil or religious governors, we fall asleep in pleasure, indolence and inattention," he complained. "We loose our liberty by not asserting it properly.—It serves no purpose to cry out against government and officers if we don't properly bestir ourselves." Like Murray, Husband proclaimed that Christians had a duty to protect their God-given religious and civil rights by following their own consciences and participating in the political sphere. Only then could they establish a just and moral government. "Christians is the light of the world—this is a most certain truth, and when the state is deprived of the light of so many Christians as is among dissenters, her light become almost quite darkness," he elaborated. "If it is necessary to choose Christians to sit in synods, presbyteries, associations or yearly meetings, so it is necessary to have such in assemblies."[100]

In his second pamphlet, *A Continuation of the Impartial Relation*, also published in 1770, Husband went further by linking the Regulator movement with postmillennialism. He claimed that American colonists currently lived in a degenerate time in which corrupt politicians and clergymen used the law to oppress the common people. But Husband believed that the Regulators—like the ancient Israelites—possessed "God's Spirit to redeem their Country" and bring about a reformation. Husband's millennialism did not translate into a desire for American independence, however. He remained loyal to the British Crown, insisting that he and other protestors only sought to combat local corruption and urging disgruntled farmers to work within the political system to enact change. Shunning the use of violence, he concluded, "Methinks when a Reformation can be brought about in our Constitution by a legal and constitutional Manner, then will commence that Thousand Years Reign with Christ, and utter down of Mystery Babylon, who has truly made the Nations of the Earth drunk, poysoned their Understandings, and bereaved them of Sense as much as strong Drink will so."[101] Husband's call for nonviolence would ultimately fall on deaf ears.

The Fall of the Regulators

By 1770, many backcountry farmers had become convinced that their attempts to achieve reform through legal means had failed and resumed withholding their taxes and boycotting civil courts. Husband and other moderates feared that such actions would evoke the wrath of colonial authorities and sought to contain the damage. That February, Regulators William Butler and James Hunter agreed to serve as tax collectors in Orange County, hoping that their appointments would discourage residents from breaking the law.[102] This proved to be wishful thinking. "The Sheriffs of the several Counties in this District complain heavily of the opposition made to them, in the Execution of their Office, by the People who call themselves Regulators," a superior court justice in Salisbury complained in early March. "I am told there is no such thing as collecting the public tax, or levying a private Debt among 'em."[103]

In March, farmers sued several officials, including Fanning, for extortion at the Hillsborough superior court. However, most of the defendants won their cases. Fanning not only was found innocent but he successfully countersued two of his accusers for slander.[104] Livid Orange County Regulators promptly issued a warning to the judge of the court, Richard Henderson, that they would soon be driven to extremities if the situation did not change.[105] Violence again seemed imminent.

Even moderates like Husband had begun to lose faith in the legal system. That March, he too was denied justice at the Hillsborough superior court. Husband's legal woes dated back to 1769, when his former lawyers, Abner Nash and John Milner, sued him for debt. While jailed in Hillsborough in September 1768, Husband had borrowed money from them to secure bail and legal representation, but he later refused to repay the loan, claiming that he had signed the promissory notes under duress and that Nash had reneged on his promise "to Plead the whole Cause of the Regulation all over the Province." Nash and Milner each responded by filing a civil suit against Husband at the September 1769 court session. Each of the cases was continued until March 1770.[106]

While on trial, Husband pled duress and asked the court to permit witnesses to testify on his behalf. But the judges, on a technicality that Husband claimed not to understand, denied his request. Undeterred, he proceeded to read a prepared statement, but the court ordered him to stop and promptly instructed the jury to reach a verdict, "as the Defendant had no Evidence that could be admitted." The jury decided against Husband, awarding Milner and Nash £375.[107] An angry Husband now concluded that it was impossible for him and other Regulators to receive a fair trial or successfully sue corrupt officials in court, conceding that the organization's strategy of moderation had failed. "Our chance at the Law is entirely at this Time out of the Question," he wrote, "and that particular Horn of the Beast which reigns in our District [is] not to be brought down now by a legal and constitutional manner."[108]

As Husband predicted, violence against the "Horn of the Beast" soon erupted. On the morning of September 24, around 150 Regulators—led by Husband and other leaders—carrying whips, sticks, and clubs marched into Hillsborough and proceeded to the courthouse, where the superior court was about to go into session.[109] Perhaps Husband hoped that his presence there would limit the violence, but he also likely wanted to save face. In recent months, his popularity had declined throughout the region, a casualty of protestors' increasing disapproval of moderation.[110] Whatever the reasons for Husband's appearance, the passions of his compatriots could not be contained that day.

Around eleven o'clock, the mob stormed into the packed courthouse. Jeremiah Fields, a farmer and Regulator, approached Richard Henderson, the presiding judge, and announced that "he had something to say before [the court] proceeded to Business." Speaking on behalf of his fellow Regulators, Fields told the judge that they "had come down to see Justice done, and Justice They would have." He then began to describe the injustices that the March superior court had committed against ordinary citizens and demanded that Henderson remedy the situation. "He spoke that they [Regulators] understood that I would not try their cases . . . and if I would proceed to try those Cases, it might prevent much Mischief," Henderson remembered. "They also . . . objected to the Jurors appointed by the Inferior Court and said they would have them altered and others appointed in their room." After a heated thirty-minute talk with the Regulators, Henderson managed to convince them to leave and opened the court.[111]

The protestors did not disperse but remained gathered just outside the courthouse. When John Williams, a deputy attorney who had signed Husband's arrest order in April 1768, attempted to enter the courthouse, several men grabbed him and hit him "with Clubs and sticks of enormous Size."[112] The agitated crowd then reentered the courthouse, seeking out their nemesis, Fanning, who was hiding behind the judge's bench. The Williamsburg *Virginia Gazette* reported the event: "They seized [Fanning] by the neck, dragged him down the steps, his head striking violently on every step, carried him to the door, and forcing him out, dragged him on the ground over stones and brickbats, struck him with their whips and clubs, kicked him, spit and spurned at him, and treated him with every possible mark of contempt and cruelty."[113] Fanning escaped to a nearby store, and the mob turned on other unpopular officials.[114] By late afternoon, the Regulators' anger had subsided. They allowed Fanning to return safely to his home on the condition that he would stand trial the next day and permitted Henderson to adjourn the court before accompanying him to his lodgings. That evening, Henderson snuck out of town, leaving "poor Col. Fanning and the little Borough in a wretched Situation."[115]

At daybreak, news of Henderson's disappearance sent the mob back into a frenzy. Several Regulators went to Fanning's house, seizing the frightened man and debating putting him to death. While they spared Fanning's life "on no other Condition than that of his taking the Road and continuing to run until He should get out of their sight," the mob was not so generous with his home.[116] "The lawless & desperate men," one newspaper reported, "destroyed every piece of furniture in [the house], ript open the beds & threw all china & glass into the street, scattered all his papers and books in the winds, seized all his plate and cash . . . took his wearing cloaths, stuck them on a pole, paraded them thro' the streets, and to close the scene, pulled down & laid his house in ruins." Having taken their revenge on Fanning, the Regulators returned to the courthouse to hold a mock trial. They reportedly "took from his chains a Negro that had been executed some time, and placed him at the lawyer's bar [in the courthouse] and filled the Judge's seat with human excrement."[117] By the end of the next day, the protestors, having expended their energy, dispersed.

Outraged, Tryon was convinced that the September 1770 riot in Hillsborough was an act of treason and subject to capital punishment. In early October, the colony's attorney general, Thomas McGuire, however, informed Tryon that under current laws, the culprits could only be charged with riot, a crime not punishable by death, and could not be tried in New Bern, as Tryon desired, but "in the District where the offence was committed." McGuire suggested that the governor instead convene the assembly and let it enact laws that could effectually punish the Regulators.[118] Tryon did just this, calling for the assembly to meet at New Bern on November 30 and ordering the muster of several county militias to see how many men would serve if summoned to restore law and order.[119]

Meanwhile, conditions in the backcountry continued to deteriorate. On November 12, several Regulators burned down Judge Richard Henderson's house in Granville County, prompting Tryon to issue a £100 reward for the perpetrators' capture.[120] Even more disconcerting to Tryon were the rumors that the Regulators planned to march on New Bern to prevent Edmund

Fanning from taking his seat in the assembly.[121] That July, Tryon had agreed to incorporate Hillsborough, thereby granting the town a representative in the lower house.[122] The Regulators had protested the governor's action, arguing that it was a deliberate attempt to curb their heavily won influence in the assembly. Fanning's subsequent election exacerbated the Regulators' anger.[123] Now, alarmed that the Regulators intended to disrupt the upcoming assembly, Tryon fortified New Bern by securing six cannon from nearby Fort Johnston and enlisting the services of Pitt County militiamen to protect the town.[124] The Regulators' rumored attack on New Bern never materialized, and on December 3, the assembly opened, meeting for the first time in Tryon's Palace.

In his opening address, the governor urged assemblymen to take action against the Regulators, arguing that the recent events at Hillsborough were the result of a mob that had "torn down Justice from Her Tribunal, and renounced all Legislative Authority." "These Insurgents," he warned, had to be stopped before they "spread their Contagion through the Continent," and he asked the assembly to endorse and fund a military expedition against them.[125]

Although the assemblymen did not approve an armed response, they attempted to placate Tryon by expelling Herman Husband, who was serving a second term as an Orange County representative.[126] In mid-December, the legislature formed a committee, headed by anti-Regulator John Campbell, to investigate Husband's role in the Hillsborough riot. The committee ruled that Husband was not only a Regulator but had "been a principal Mover and promoter of the late Riots and Seditions in the County of Orange." It also charged Husband with libel for penning an anonymous letter in the *North Carolina Gazette* accusing superior court judge Maurice Moore of "having obstructed justice in 1768 when several charges were made against Fanning for assessing illegal fees."[127] The committee concluded that the "conduct of the said Hermon Husbands both as a Member of this House in particular and of Community in General has justly incurred the Contempt of this House and rendered Him unworthy of a seat in this Assembly." It removed him from office on December 20.[128]

To prevent Husband from "returning into the back settlements to inflame anew the insurgents by his seditious practices," Tryon immediately secured an arrest warrant for the Regulator on the charge of writing the libelous letter about Moore.[129] Husband, who denied any wrongdoing, was apprehended and held without bail. Regulators responded angrily to their compatriot's imprisonment, which perhaps was Tryon's plan all along. Rumors that the Regulators intended to march on New Bern to free Husband sent the colony's leaders into a panic.[130] New Bern inhabitants were also on edge, fearing the Regulators intended to murder everyone who opposed them. One opponent recalled that he found it difficult to sleep at night, not knowing if his "throat may be cut before the morning."[131] Tryon capitalized on these fears and built support for his call for military action, warning the public on December 31: "The Regulators are Assembling themselves in the Neighbourhood of Cross Creek, with a large quantity of Provisions, and a Number of Waggons, in Order to March down to this Town."[132]

It was in this tense atmosphere that the General Assembly passed the Johnston Riot Act. Ratified by Tryon on January 15, 1771, this law broadened the powers of government officials to preserve public peace. Under the new decree, any group of ten or more people deemed by a justice of the peace or sheriff to be acting unlawfully had to disperse within an hour if ordered to do so or be charged with a felony and tried within sixty days. Failure to appear for trial, which could be held at any county court regardless of where the offense occurred, resulted in an automatic guilty verdict, after which "it shall and may be lawful to and for any Person to kill and destroy such Offender or Offenders." The act was retroactive, making the Hillsborough rioters subject to the new law.[133]

While the act further empowered Tryon to mobilize the militia to maintain law and order, the threat of violence encouraged officials—including Tryon—to support legislation that addressed some of the Regulators' demands. The assembly established several small-claims courts, required that chief justices be paid a salary, and "set attorneys' fees on a definite and published scale."[134] It also created four new counties in the backcountry: Chatham, Guilford, Surry, and Wake. Husband and other Regulators had long championed such an action, complaining that the size of Piedmont counties made it time-consuming and often impossible for farmers to attend court.[135] Tryon endorsed these reforms in hopes that they would placate the protestors and make it easier for him "to suppress the Insurgents in the back Frontiers."[136]

However, the lawmakers' efforts did not appease the Regulators, who charged that the Johnston Riot Act violated English law and continued to protest Husband's imprisonment.[137] In early February, there were rumors that the Regulators intended to rescue Husband from the New Bern jail, and militia spies alerted Tryon that at least three hundred armed Regulators had assembled in Orange County. The protestors reportedly intended to march on New Bern on February 11 and burn it to the ground.[138] Tryon was further unnerved by the growing support for Husband and the Regulators: around four hundred Rowan County protestors reportedly planned to join their Orange County neighbors and break Husband out of jail, and the movement had begun to gain ground in eastern North Carolina.[139] After successfully recruiting a number of Halifax residents to the Regulator cause, Rednap Howell wrote, "If it once takes a Start here it will run into the neighboring County's of Edgecomb, Bute, and Northampton and . . . will undoubtedly facilitate Justice to poor Carolina."[140] Government authorities intercepted Howell's letter to Orange County Regulators. Alarmed by the message, Tryon ordered the construction of a 1,500-yard trench to protect New Bern, outlawed the sale of lead and powder throughout the colony, and alerted local militiamen to be ready to fight at short notice.[141]

On February 8, military confrontation was again averted when a grand jury failed to indict Husband for libel and ordered his immediate release from jail.[142] Husband, hoping to avoid violence, wrote to William Butler and James Hunter, both of whom headed Regulator forces now marching toward New Bern. "I lay at Mr. Joel Lanes last night [on] my way home from Newbern, having had my trial there and cleared by Proclamation [when] I heard that the Regulators were on their way to release me," he informed Butler and Hunter. "I thought it good to let you know I am gone along and expect to meet some of you who I am informed are to come by the Redfield Ford."[143] With Husband freed, the would-be rescuers agreed to disperse, though several Regulators returning home displayed a final act of solidarity and celebrated Husband's release by parading through Hillsborough.[144] Husband returned to Orange County without fanfare.

Despite Husband's court victory, Regulators continued to condemn the Johnston Riot Act and threaten local authorities with violence. "The Assembly have gone and made a Riotous Act, and the people are more inraged than ever," they informed Hillsborough attorney Waightstill Avery. "It was the best thing that could be for the Country for now We shall be forced to kill all the Clerks and Lawyers, and We will kill them and [we]'ll be damned if they are not put to Death."[145] Such threats led Rowan County officials to negotiate with the protestors. When several hundred Regulators converged on the outskirts of Salisbury on March 6 and demanded the opening of the superior court to redress their complaints, John Frohock and several other townspeople rode out to the Regulator encampment to reach a peace settlement. "We went to [the Regulators] found some of them Armed and others unarmed [and] desired to know their Designs and what they wanted," Frohock remembered. "They answered they came with no Intention to disturb the Court or to injure the Person or property of any one . . . and that their Arms were not for Offence, but to defend themselves if assaulted." Both parties agreed to form a joint committee to arbitrate disputes involving excessive fee collection and to discuss other Regulator grievances, and Husband was chosen to represent the protestors. Appeased, the Regulators rode into Salisbury, "gave three Cheers, and returned to their home without using Violence to any Person."[146]

News of the settlement infuriated Tryon, who chastised Frohock for compromising governmental authority. "The Mode . . . of your Agreement with the Insurgents," Tryon complained, "is unconstitutional, Dishonorable to Government, and introductive of a practice the most dangerous to the peace and Happiness of Society." Despite Frohock's concessions, the governor had already begun to raise a militia to quell the protest movement.[147] On March 15, the grand jury in New Bern indicted Husband and sixty other Regulators for rioting, and three days later, Tryon's council authorized the militia to arrest these men and "reduce [the Regulators] by force to an Obedience to the laws of their Country."[148] Tryon, who had recently been appointed governor of New York, hoped to subdue his unruly subjects before leaving the colony. By May, he had assembled a force of about a thousand troops and began to march his army to the backcountry.[149]

On May 11, Tryon's militia arrived in Hillsborough and continued west, crossing the Haw River and setting up camp. There, Tryon learned that General Hugh Waddell, along with four hundred troops in Rowan County, would not rendezvous with the governor's militia near Hillsborough as planned. Three days earlier, Regulator forces had compelled Waddell's troops to retreat back to Salisbury. Determined to reach this army, Tryon marched his militia toward Salisbury, eventually stopping at the Great Alamance Creek in Orange County on May 13, where Husband and several hundred Regulators had assembled to confront the militia. The governor ordered his men to arms.[150]

For the next two days, both sides refused to take action. On May 15, the Regulator camp, which now numbered more than two thousand men, sent a petition to Tryon, expressing their disappointment that the governor had failed to listen to their complaints but nonetheless hoping to avoid violence. The Regulators again asked Tryon to address their grievances, an act that would "promulgate such Harmony in poor pensive North Carolina," and requested a "speedy and Candid Answer."[151] Tryon promised that he would give them an answer by noon the following day.

On the morning of May 16, Presbyterian minister David Caldwell, along with Regulators Robert Thompson and Robert Matear, visited Tryon's camp to attempt last-minute peace talks.[152] But Tryon was unwilling to negotiate. He arrested Thompson and Matear and ordered Caldwell to inform the Regulators "that nothing could be done in the way of compromise."[153] In a formal reply to the Regulator petition, the governor notified his rebellious subjects that they had one hour to disperse before the militia opened fire.[154] Caldwell further warned the Regulators that Tryon would not back down and pleaded with them to disband. Husband was one of several Regulators who followed the preacher's advice. Perhaps Husband's Quaker principles compelled him to flee or maybe it was cowardice. Regardless, he now believed that the threat of violence had backfired against the Regulators and that military defeat was certain.[155]

Shortly before noon, Tryon signaled Colonel James Moore to fire cannon into the Regulator ranks, beginning the Battle of Alamance. Husband's fears were quickly confirmed. Lacking adequate military leadership, discipline, or ammunition, the Regulators proved no match for Tryon's forces, who soundly defeated them within two hours.[156] An estimated 20 Regulators and 9 militiamen died in the battle, with more than 150 men from both sides wounded.[157] A proud and relieved Tryon informed his superior, Lord Hillsborough, of the victory, writing, "This Success I hope will lead soon to a perfect Restoration of Peace in this Country."[158]

Over the next several weeks, Tryon consolidated his control over the North Carolina backcountry. Perhaps to intimidate residents, he ordered the execution of James Few, one of fifteen Regulators taken prisoner and a friend of Husband.[159] Tryon moved his army to the Sandy Creek settlement, where, on May 21, they burned James Hunter's home to the ground. Hunter, who Tryon called the General of the Rebels, escaped capture by taking refuge in the mountains.[160] The militia proceeded to Husband's six-hundred-acre plantation and set up camp.[161] Husband was already safe in Virginia, on his way to Maryland, but the soldiers left his estate "without a House or Fence" standing. Tryon's army continued west, destroying farms and crops in Deep River, Cane Creek, and other Regulator strongholds.[162]

By June, Tryon's military expedition had quelled the Regulators once and for all. Disheartened, nearly 6,500 Regulators accepted the governor's offer to pardon those who agreed to give up their arms, pledge allegiance to the government, and pay their taxes.[163] Tryon refused to provide such leniency to Husband, Hunter, William Butler, or Rednap Howell. Declaring them outlaws, the governor issued a reward of £100 and one thousand acres of land for their capture.[164] However, the rewards would go uncollected. Butler and Howell moved to Virginia and Maryland, respectively, and never set foot in North Carolina again. Hunter, after a ten-month absence, ventured back to the Piedmont, where neighbors, viewing the former Regulator as a hero, protected him from authorities.[165] Husband, too, would live to fight another day. Eventually settling in southwestern Pennsylvania, he soon became embroiled in a new rebellion: the American Revolution.

FOUR

"Perfecting a Free Government"
Husband and the American Revolution

> And to you an open Door is now set, which no Nation before you ever had. You may now hold the Crown, without the Use of a Sword, or a Gun, forever; and if Tyrants oppose you, they must throw off the Mask which they have ever wore to deceive you; they must openly fight against all the Principles of their own Societies, and all the Principles of our Constitutions, which they have solemnly swore to defend.
> —Herman Husband, *Proposals to Amend and Perfect the Policy of the Government of the United States of America*

Going Home

One afternoon in late May 1771, Samuel Gilpin, a prominent Cecil County, Maryland, planter and miller, spotted a traveler approaching his farmhouse.[1] The man, Gilpin observed, "was between fifty and sixty years of age, rather shabbily attired in Quaker costume . . . [and] rode a bay horse of middle size, strong, square built, but of ordinary appearance and gait." When the rider arrived at the front gate, he dismounted from his horse and "glanced across the landscape with an air of familiarity that plainly told that he had known these scenes in bygone days." Drawing closer, Gilpin was surprised to recognize the stranger to be his brother-in-law and childhood friend Herman Husband. The former Quaker and wanted rebel had, at last, reached the sanctuary of kinfolk in Maryland.[2]

It had been a long journey for Husband, one that remains shrouded in myth. According to family legend—as recorded by his grandson David in

1870—Husband had returned to Sandy Creek shortly after the Battle of Alamance on May 16, 1771. That afternoon, he received a message that Tryon had sent eleven soldiers to arrest him at his home. Husband quickly packed his belongings, bid his family goodbye, and "left his house only in time to save himself and get under cover of the forest into which he had plunged to avoid meeting his pursuers." He then made his way to a nearby friend's house, where he "disguised himself by throwing off his Quaker costume and assuming a travel-worn appearance," exchanged horses with his neighbor, and set out for Cecil County along a road leading to Virginia.[3]

All the while, Tryon's posse was in hot pursuit. The men eventually caught up with Husband, who remained calm and collected. "Old man," one of the soldiers called out, unaware that he was speaking to Husband, "did you see anything of a man flying on horseback, as you came along?" "I did not," Husband replied. Satisfied with the traveler's response, the patrol proceeded down the road. Shortly thereafter, the soldiers grew discouraged and turned their horses, riding back the way they had come. Husband, the story goes, "carelessly moved out of the way, freely giving them the road while he was unconcernedly eating a biscuit taken from the wallet that hung across his saddle." One of the soldiers asked the old man where he was traveling. Donning the character of an itinerant minister, Husband answered, "It matters little where I go; I'm about my master's business." The ruse worked. The posse informed him that "a man named Husband . . . has made his escape, and you will do the King good service by putting the good people on the alert to have him apprehended if he flees in this direction." Before riding away, one of the soldiers handed the preacher a letter and ordered him to deliver it to authorities in the next village, warning them that Husband remained on the run.[4]

This letter would prove a blessing for Husband. At the next farm, he learned that soldiers had blocked the river up ahead, instructing the ferryman to carry only government messengers across. Husband was alarmed at first, "but upon reflection was astonished to find how Providence was working out his delivery." With the letter in his possession, he was indeed "a messenger of the Government." He presented the letter to the ferryman, who took the fugitive to the other side. Husband continued to a nearby village and delivered the note to a constable. The sheriff gave him a legal permit to pass on, which he used to leave North Carolina without further incident.[5]

Husband's travels in Virginia are the source of another legend, recorded by historian Eli Caruthers in 1842. According to this account, Husband was nearly apprehended by a Regulator named Robert Messer, who had been captured at the Battle of Alamance and sentenced to hang. On the morning of Messer's execution, however, Tryon received a visit from the Regulator's wife and ten-year-old son. The weeping boy begged the governor "to hang him and let his father live." Taken aback, Tryon asked the boy who had instructed him to say such a thing. "No body," he replied. When the governor inquired why he would make such an offer, the boy answered, "Because if you hang my father, my mother will die, and the children will perish." According to Caruthers, Tryon was so moved by the boy's request that he pardoned Messer under one condition: that the Regulator apprehend Husband. Messer accepted the proposal and rode out of camp, leaving his wife and son in the custody of Tryon. Messer eventually caught up with Husband in Virginia but was unable to detain his former comrade for want of more force. A disheartened Messer returned to North Carolina, where "he was put in chains until the time of [his] execution" and his son "retained as a foot page to the governor."[6]

Although solidifying Husband's status as a folk hero, these uncorroborated stories are steeped in fiction. However, the limited evidence of the details of his journey does indicate that it was likely an eventful trip. Following the Battle of Alamance, Husband may have first fled to the Moravian community of Bethabara, located about fifty miles west of Sandy Creek. On May 19, locals reported that "an unknown man (possibly Herman Husband)" visited the town to find a doctor to tend to wounded Regulators. News of the fugitive's presence in the vicinity reached the nearby Moravian village of Bethania, where a man in the town's tavern boasted that he would capture Husband in order to collect the reward on the fugitive's head. According to Moravian Church records, the man set out in pursuit of Husband, meeting "five Regulators, and one of them shot at him (very likely it was Husband who did it)." The man did not capture Husband but escaped the melee relatively unharmed. The ball from one of the Regulator's guns had "passed through his waistcoat, which was open, barely scratching him."[7]

Following this encounter, there are no more first-person accounts of Husband's travels until he arrived at Gilpin's estate in Cecil County. While there, the fugitive spent the next several days visiting with family and contemplating his next move. Gilpin advised Husband to settle in Bedford County, located in southwestern Pennsylvania's Allegheny Mountains. This region offered a number of advantages. Husband's childhood friend and hunter Isaac Cox lived in a region known as the Glades and could help protect him.[8] Although it was remote, two major transportation arteries, Braddock's and Forbes's Roads, ran through the region, linking it to the eastern part of the colony and Maryland.[9] This would allow Husband to hide from authorities while continuing to correspond with family and friends. Most importantly, the Pennsylvania backcountry had cheap and plentiful land.

The New Frontier

Western Pennsylvania was hotly contested terrain in the early eighteenth century and had only recently become safe for Anglo-American settlement. In the 1720s, the Shawnee and Delaware Native Americans, attempting to escape white encroachment, had migrated from the eastern seaboard and established villages along the Allegheny and Ohio Rivers.[10] By the 1730s, Pennsylvania traders were beginning to operate in the backcountry, selling English manufactured goods to the Shawnee and Delaware in exchange for pelts.[11] With its abundant wildlife and arable lands, the region also caught the attention of speculators. A group of wealthy Virginians founded the Ohio Company, a joint stock venture that sought to promote trade and white settlement west of the Alleghenies. In the late 1740s, the company received 500,000 acres of land in that region from the colony of Virginia, which claimed jurisdiction over southwestern Pennsylvania. The Ohio Company instructed agents to survey the area and negotiate a trade alliance with local Native Americans at Logstown, located near the forks of the Ohio River.[12] Meanwhile, a steady stream of German, Scots-Irish, and English settlers, unable to obtain land elsewhere in Pennsylvania, moved west across the Susquehanna River, establishing farms and hunting camps in the Juniata Valley and beyond.[13]

Further complicating matters, France also coveted western Pennsylvania, hoping to secure trading alliances with the area's Native American population and prevent the British from gaining a foothold west of the Alleghenies. The growing interest of Pennsylvania traders, the Ohio Company, and migrant settlers posed a direct threat to French goals. In 1752, Ange de Menneville, the Marquis Duquesne, governor-general of Canada, attempted to assert France's claims to the territory by dispatching militia units to expel Pennsylvania traders and ordering the construction of several forts near Lake Erie. In response, Virginia governor and Ohio Company shareholder Robert Dinwiddie directed agents in early 1754 to build a fort along the forks of the Ohio. That April, however, French forces took possession of the uncompleted garrison and began construction on their own military outpost a few miles upstream, calling it Fort Duquesne.[14] Dinwiddie sent George Washington, a twenty-one-year-old militia colonel, to capture the French fort. Outgunned and outmanned, the young colonel surrendered on July 4. London authorities intervened, dispatching 1,400 British troops under General Edward Braddock to expel the French from the forks of the Ohio, but the French and their Native allies defeated the British troops just outside of Fort Duquesne.[15]

Following Braddock's defeat, tensions between Britain and France culminated in the Seven Years' War, a global conflict that would devastate the

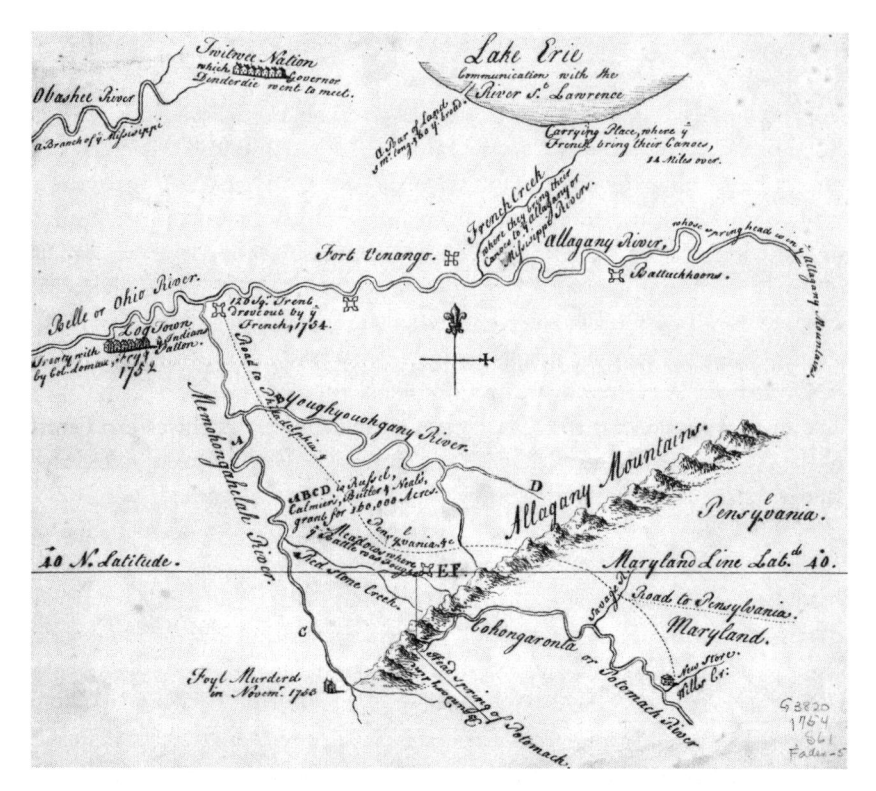

FIGURE 7. This 1754 map—drawn by a "Captain Snow"—shows the locations of several forts in southwestern Pennsylvania on the eve of the Seven Years' War, including Fort Duquesne, located at the confluence of the Ohio, Monongahela, and Allegheny Rivers. (Capt. Snow, *Captain Snow's sketch*, 1754; Library of Congress, Geography and Map Division)

Pennsylvania backcountry and bring a temporary halt to white migration. The Shawnee and Delaware, allies of the French, launched raids on civilian and military targets throughout the region. Many panic-stricken white settlers subsequently abandoned their farms and retreated to eastern Pennsylvania; others took refuge in hastily constructed forts that soon dotted the countryside and waged war against their Native American adversaries, killing innocent women and children in the process.[16] Britain's ultimate victory over the French in 1763 did not end the bloodshed. That year, the Shawnee, Delaware, and other Ohio Valley American Indians, hoping to forestall further white settlement on their lands, orchestrated a series of raids in the Pennsylvania backcountry and besieged several British military outposts, including Fort Duquesne, now called Fort Pitt. Known as Pontiac's War, this uprising lasted nearly two years before British forces and backcountry vigilantes compelled the western Native American tribes to sue for peace.[17]

By 1765, the Pennsylvania backcountry had again opened for Anglo-Americans. With the French gone and local Native Americans weakened by a decade of warfare, farmers, squatters, hunters, and speculators increasingly ventured into the territory. Some, including Husband, stopped in the Juniata Valley, where Bedford County would be established in 1771. Others moved farther west, setting up farms along the forks of the Ohio and in the Monongahela Valley.[18] Thousands of land-hungry colonists snatched up the cheap land, which could be purchased for only £5 per one hundred acres.[19] By 1771, an estimated ten thousand families had migrated to the area.[20]

It was in this context that Husband set his sights on southwestern Pennsylvania. The availability of cheap land made it an ideal place for him to thrive as a farmer and speculator, a goal he had been working toward for most of his adult life. He found the Glades, where his friend Isaac Cox resided, particularly appealing. Most whites had bypassed that region, opting to establish their farms farther west in the Monongahela Valley, which featured a warmer climate and longer growing season.[21] Those who settled in the Glades were mostly hunters, like Cox, who lacked the capital to accumulate large tracts of land, and the area remained wide open for land speculation.[22] After spending a week with Gilpin, Husband—having likely received money from his Maryland relatives—departed for Cox's camp to try his luck in the Pennsylvania backcountry.

A New Home

In early June, Husband set out on his horse, Old Tom, traveling west to Hagerstown, Maryland, where he purchased a surveyor's compass, clothing, food, and other provisions. He made his way to Fort Cumberland, Maryland, via Braddock's Road, and proceeded north into "the dark and pathless wilderness" of Pennsylvania's Allegheny Mountains. It took him several days to ascend the lofty range. "[I] tramp[ed] . . . through deep gorges, along rugged precipices; through tangled thickets and dark, doleful forests of towering pines and hemlocks, along the beds of streams, with towering bluffs in every contorted form," Husband wrote in his journal. "The sound of water murmuring among the rocky crags, occasionally relieved by the soft moan of the breeze in the tree tops, the distant croak of the raven or the shrill voice of the whippoorwill . . . served as an interlude to the monotony of the scene."[23]

On June 5, Husband crested the mountain and turned toward the valley below. There, he startled a group of playing children, who raced to a nearby cabin, where their father, a German farmer named Philip Wagerline, stopped his oxen and greeted the stranger in broken English. Husband, calling himself Tuscape, boarded with the Wagerlines for the next two days and surveyed the landscape for the first time. He was pleased with what he saw. "Nothing [can] exceed in beauty and luxuriance these plains when vegetation [is] at its full growth," Husband observed in his journal. "In many places for acres, grass [is] as high as a man, of a bluish green color with a feathery head of bluish purple."[24]

From the Wagerlines' homestead, Husband headed north in search of Isaac Cox's camp. Forced to zigzag around rocks and thickets, he moved at a snail's pace. When he finally reached the Glades just before nightfall, he came upon an unoccupied cabin. Tired and hungry, he entered the cabin and fell asleep without taking much note of his surroundings. When he woke the next morning, he was pleasantly surprised to discover "a half dozen venison hams suspended to the ridge poles of the roof." The cabin's owner, a hunter named William Sparks, appeared shortly thereafter, a bit taken aback by the stranger's presence in his home. Sparks, as it turned out, had just visited Cox, who was on a week-long hunting expedition, and invited Husband to stay with him until Cox returned. Husband spent the next several days exploring the immediate countryside and continued to be impressed. "This valley," he observed, "is what may be properly termed rolling in its general features, divided into hills, bottoms and glades.... The streams usually rise in hills and worm themselves sluggishly through the glades, then break through high banks and dark forests." Husband wrote in his journal that he could envision himself settling down in the region and "cultivating the soil as a business."[25] He had found his new Garden of Eden.

The next week, Sparks accompanied Husband to Cox's cabin, which was located a few miles northwest of the future community of Somerset in Bedford County. Cox at first did not recognize his old friend. "Cox looked at me for some moments, evidently with a vague recognition of my features, but time and circumstances seemed to bewilder his recollection," Husband recalled. "At length he said: 'Didn't we once go to school together? I think we did, as well as row together on the Chesapeake Bay. I know you now—Herman Husband,' and at the same time shaking me heartily by the hand, welcomed me to the privileges of his camp." Husband explained to the men why he had come to southwestern Pennsylvania and asked them to call him Toscape. Sparks believed that such a name was too formal for the backcountry culture and suggested they give Husband a "short characteristic name." Noticing that Husband did not have a gun, Cox suggested the name Quaker, a name that stuck with Husband until the American Revolution.[26]

Throughout the summer, Husband lived as a tenant on Cox's property. He constructed a cabin, built a shed for his horse, and cured meat. That August,

Husband accompanied Sparks to the town of Bedford, where he received a letter from Gilpin with news that his family was now safe in Maryland.[27] However, it also carried disturbing news about the fate of those Regulators captured at the Battle of Alamance. On June 15, six of them—including James Pugh, the brother of Husband's second wife—were convicted of treason and executed near Hillsborough four days later.[28] Pugh remained defiant to the end. With the noose around his neck, he used his final words to admonish his adversaries one last time. He charged that Tryon "had brought an army there to murder the people instead of taking sides with them against a set of dishonest officers," and that Fanning "was not fit for the office which he held." Moments before being "launched into eternity," Pugh reportedly told the onlookers that "his blood would be as good seed sown on good ground, which would soon produce a hundred fold."[29]

While in Bedford, Husband also likely read newspaper accounts about the Battle of Alamance and its aftermath. The town was situated along Forbes's Road, a busy transportation artery connecting western Pennsylvania to Philadelphia, Carlisle, and other eastern towns. Copies of the *Pennsylvania Journal* and other colonial newspapers were readily available there. Husband may have found some consolation in reports that Tryon's treatment of backcountry settlers following the battle led many colonial elites to sympathize with the Regulators, viewing them as victims of a tyrannical government. The *Massachusetts Spy*, for example, justified the Regulators' actions, explaining that Piedmont farmers had "suffered a series of the most cruel extortions and illegal plunderings that ever men under any shadow of civil government were subjected to."[30] A correspondent for the *Pennsylvania Journal* concurred, insisting that the Regulators were not rebels but brave men protecting their liberties. Lashing out at Tryon, the writer continued, "When those who are entrusted with the conduct of the affairs of the public, oppress the people, instead of protecting them, and do them wrong, instead of distributing impartial Justice among them, they, and not the people who resist them, are Rebels."[31] Although Husband still needed to keep his identity secret, he was likely heartened by the popular support of the North Carolina Regulation.

Husband also confirmed on his trip to Bedford that the region held promise for land speculation. Months earlier, Pennsylvania assemblymen had created Bedford County out of Cumberland County and made the town of Bedford its county seat, encouraging a wave of outside investors to enter the region and purchase land before its value increased. Ever the opportunist, Husband sought out several prominent speculators, including John Cisna, for whom he agreed to work as a surveyor. He returned to the Glades, eager to convince Cox and other hunters to sell their claims.[32]

Cox proved open to the idea. Like many hunters, he recognized that his days were numbered in Bedford County. Hundreds of Scots-Irish, English, and German farmers had already begun to settle in the region, driving away deer and beaver. The shrinking wildlife population did not concern Husband, as he was not interested in hunting for a living and in fact found it unnatural. "The killing of inoffensive animals merely for their pelts and furs appears unjust," he wrote in his journal, "but when required for the support of man, the objection vanishes and it appears right and legitimate, in accordance of the Creator, Gen. 1st, 20 and 30." He ultimately purchased the claims of several neighboring hunters, including Cox and Sparks, who remained in the Glades and became a farmer.[33] By 1772, Husband, using the alias Tuscape Death, had acquired six hundred acres of land.[34]

Throughout the summer, Husband continued to improve his farm, building a new cabin and raising wheat, rye, and potatoes.[35] He also made plans to reunite with his family. Emey had written that spring that she and his children were in Hagerstown, where they awaited his arrival to transport them to the Glades, and that she had recently given birth to a son.[36] Husband wrote back to assure her that he would return to Hagerstown that fall and asked her to name their son Isaac Tuscape (the first name in honor of Isaac Cox and the middle name "to preserve his own escape and history"). As promised, Husband arrived at Hagerstown in October and escorted his family to Bedford County. During the two-week journey, Husband's eldest sons, John and Herman Jr., each carried a gun for protection. They apparently did not share their father's Quaker proclivities.[37]

Over the next three years, Husband would prosper as a farmer and land speculator. With the help of his sons, he continued to expand his farm, clearing additional acres of land for cultivation; building a barn, which included a floor to thresh wheat; and erecting two stables that housed the family's livestock.[38] Husband also financed the construction of a gristmill in the Glades, though that project was cut short by the onset of the American Revolution.[39] Meanwhile, he accumulated more land, perhaps even acquiring some of it illegally. Pennsylvania had enacted a law prohibiting backcountry settlers from claiming more than three hundred acres of land, though speculators often evaded this decree by applying for land in a relative's or business associate's name.[40] Husband may have done the same in 1774, likely using the names of his sons and his younger brother John to claim 1,500 acres of land in western Bedford County's Turkeyfoot Township. Along with his birth name, he also used the aliases Toscape Death, Toscape Death Sr., and Toscape Death Jr. to claim an additional 1,150 acres of land by 1775.[41] In a region where the average farm size was 182 acres, Husband now towered above most of his neighbors in landed wealth.[42] At fifty years old, he had once again rebuilt his fortune.

The Woods Faction

Husband, of course, was not the only ambitious man in Bedford County. A handful of settlers similarly hoped to profit from land speculation, including George Woods, who would emerge as the leader of a courthouse ring that controlled the county's political machinery. Woods was a surveyor who had, as a young man, traveled throughout the Juniata Valley and worked with private speculators to find the region's most valuable lands. In 1759, he settled near Fort Bedford, a British garrison that doubled as a trading post in the heart of the Juniata Valley, making it a safe and lucrative location to establish himself.[43]

During the 1760s, Woods prospered as a surveyor and land speculator. His success was in part due to John Lukens, a member of Philadelphia's inner circle and surveyor-general of Pennsylvania.[44] The ambitious and charming Woods soon befriended Lukens, a relationship that would pay dividends for Woods. In 1766, when the Pennsylvania Board of Property directed Lukens "to lay out a town of two hundred lots at and around Fort Bedford," he selected Woods as one of the surveyors.[45] With his surveying business thriving, Woods also began to invest in real estate. By 1771—the year that Husband arrived in Pennsylvania as a fugitive—Woods had acquired six lots in the new town of Bedford and issued land warrants totaling 690 acres in Cumberland County, which at that time encompassed all of western Pennsylvania.[46]

The creation of Bedford County in 1771 further enhanced Woods's financial prospects. He continued to speculate on land but also became involved in an even more lucrative enterprise: public service.[47] With his wealth and influential political contacts, he quickly gained a great deal of control over the new county's legislative, judicial, and administrative offices. The governor named the surveyor to the much-desired position of justice of the peace, which he held for the next four years. He also supervised the construction of the county's first courthouse and prison, served as county treasurer, helped his brother Thomas secure the post of deputy sheriff, and was elected in 1773 to represent Bedford County in the General Assembly.[48] On the eve of the American Revolution, Woods had become the region's most powerful citizen.

Another ambitious man who would become part of Woods's political machine was Thomas Smith. Born and raised in Scotland, Smith migrated to Philadelphia in 1768 at the urging of his older brother William. In 1751, William left Scotland to work as a tutor in New York before moving to Philadelphia, where he became a successful professor and administrator at the Academy of Philadelphia (now the University of Pennsylvania). William's aspirations extended beyond academia, however, and he sent for Thomas to work as a surveyor and land speculator on his behalf. Upon arriving in

Philadelphia, the twenty-three-year-old Thomas quickly secured an apprenticeship with Surveyor-General John Lukens, no doubt arranged by his well-connected elder brother. In 1769, Lukens selected him to serve as a deputy surveyor in western Pennsylvania.[49]

Thomas eventually made his way to the new town of Bedford. There, he purchased a town lot and began to travel throughout the backcountry, conducting surveys and informing William of prime tracts of land not yet claimed or designated for auction.[50] Thomas did not share William's interest in land speculation but instead wanted to earn a living as an attorney. In 1771, he established a law office in Bedford and accumulated many affluent clients, including George Washington, who often hired the young man to evict squatters from his lands in western Pennsylvania.[51] The Smiths' powerful professional connections brought Thomas into Woods's inner circle and access to all the perks that came with it. By 1774, Thomas served as the county's prothonotary, deputy register of wills, clerk of the courts, recorder of deeds, and justice of the peace.[52]

Another confidant of Woods was Arthur St. Clair, a Scot who first arrived in North America in 1757 to fight in the Seven Years' War. Described as "a man of superior talents, of extensive information, and of great uprightness of purpose, as well as suavity of manners," St. Clair distinguished himself in battle and emerged as a favorite among his superiors. He married Massachusetts governor James Bowdoin's half-niece Phoebe Bayard, a union that made him a wealthy man. In 1762, St. Clair resigned his military commission and settled in Boston with his young bride.[53]

Through his political contacts, St. Clair soon befriended several prominent Pennsylvania speculators, including William Smith, whose glowing tales of the colony's backcountry piqued St. Clair's interest in that region. By 1764, he had joined the ranks of land speculators and headed to southwestern Pennsylvania. He initially settled at Fort Bedford, likely where he first met Woods, and then moved sixty miles west to Fort Ligonier, where he purchased a large tract of land and built a house and gristmill. St. Clair's wealth and political connections eventually landed him the lucrative position of surveyor for the District of Cumberland. Upon the creation of Bedford County, the governor appointed him the county's prothonotary, recorder of deeds, clerk of the court, and justice of the court. St. Clair received these same posts, along with justice of the peace, in Westmoreland County when it was established in 1773. He later became governor of the Northwest Territory and would remain friends with Woods throughout his political career.[54]

What Husband thought of the so-called Woods faction is unknown. The snippets of his journal that survive never mention Woods or his associates.[55]

Given his recent experiences in the North Carolina Piedmont, however, Husband likely viewed them with suspicion. In many ways, these men were cut from the same cloth as Edmund Fanning. They were ambitious, well-educated young men who had a taste for high living and fancied themselves the better sort. Allied with speculators, merchants, and lawyers, they belonged to an emerging backcountry elite that, at least in North Carolina, had failed to protect the interests of small and middling farmers. While Husband probably believed that these men, like Fanning, should be watched closely, he kept his views on the Woods faction to himself. Still a fugitive, he maintained a low profile and avoided politics altogether, at least until the onset of the American Revolution.

The Glorious Cause

In April 1775, a crowd of curious residents filed into the Bedford County courthouse to witness the arraignment of several persons—among them Herman Husband—charged with sedition and disturbing the peace. Months earlier, these men had staged a rally in the town of Bedford protesting against the British government.[56] Although the first of its kind in Bedford County, such demonstrations had become common throughout the colonies, especially after the British Parliament passed the Tea Act of 1773, which many Americans believed impinged on their rights as Englishmen.[57] While the Woods faction had up to that point remained reluctant to take a firm stance against Great Britain, it seems that Husband had grown impatient with the county's leadership and again felt compelled to join a rebellious cause. None of the rioters would serve jail time; instead, the presiding judges, Arthur St. Clair and Bernard Dougherty, elected to hit them where it hurt most: in the pocketbook. The defendants were released under bonds to keep peace. Knowing that Husband was a wealthy man, the judges set his bond at £2,500, a far greater amount than the others received.[58] The threat of financial ruin appears to have convinced Husband to at least temporarily abandon political activism. Over the next year, he abided by the law and attended each court session to pledge his good behavior.[59]

Meanwhile, two hundred miles to the east in Philadelphia, Pennsylvania's Quaker-dominated assembly was also scrambling to contain citizens there who had begun to unite in opposition to Britain, convinced that the Parliament's policies threatened to destroy colonial economic and political independence. Their conviction was not completely off base. Largely due to the Currency Act of 1764, the supply of paper money had steadily declined throughout the American colonies, making it difficult for farmers and merchants alike to pay off their debts. To make matters worse, British trade and tax laws—if imposed—would further deplete the supply of gold and silver and deepen an economic recession that had already adversely impacted all ranks of society. As Husband witnessed in the North Carolina backcountry, small and middling farmers were hardest hit by the recession. Strapped for cash, they defaulted on loans made to colonial merchants, who in turn found themselves in a precarious situation. They had purchased goods from British manufacturers on credit and, unable to procure cash or specie, also fell into debt. By the early 1770s, thousands of colonists had lost their farms and businesses. In Bedford County alone, between 1772 and 1775, judges there "issued enough writs to foreclose on 57 percent of the taxable population."[60]

Such economic hardship threatened the political liberties of white men, whose voting rights were secure only if they owned property. Well-versed in the ideals of republicanism, colonists viewed political and economic independence as inseparable from one another. If unable to acquire land, they feared, ordinary white men would lose their suffrage and fall victim to corrupt politicians. Many Americans further believed that British monetary, tax, and trade policies—if imposed—would weaken their financial prospects by concentrating wealth in the hands of the few, most notably English creditors who allegedly profited from the labor of industrious men. Across the colonies, farmers, artisans, and other ordinary folk increasingly envisioned the creation of a government that functioned to distribute wealth more equally among white men. Only then, they insisted, could political liberty become a reality. By the 1770s, these citizens would unite in support of progressive taxation and other reforms that benefited "the middling and poorer class[es]," demanding that the better sort support their cause.[61]

Tensions between the colonies and Great Britain escalated following the December 1773 Boston Tea Party. In the spring of 1774, the British Parliament enacted the Coercive Acts, which introduced such measures as closing the port of Boston and outlawing town meetings in Massachusetts.[62] These laws sparked a wave of protests throughout the colonies. In Bedford County, most citizens had thus far remained neutral in the growing colonial dispute with Great Britain. However, on July 12, a group of angry residents gathered to reconsider their position. Husband chose this moment to reenter the political arena and joined his neighbors at the assembly. The participants agreed to condemn the Coercive Acts in a resolution, later published in the *Pennsylvania Journal*. The "act of Parliament lately passed," they complained, "is repugnant to the fundamental principles of the constitution of Great Britain and her Colonies—subversive of that liberty and freedom which is the birth-right of every British subject—[and] contrary to natural justice and equity." The attendees also endorsed the creation of a Continental Congress and selected men to serve on the county's newly formed Committee of

Correspondence. The charismatic, outspoken, and intelligent Husband was chosen, along with George Woods and several of his cohort.[63]

Over the next two years, a growing number of Americans mobilized against British rule, organizing public meetings, creating county committees, staging protest rallies, and, after the Battles of Lexington and Concord in April 1775, forming militia units.[64] The publication of Thomas Paine's *Common Sense* in January 1776 added fuel to the fire, inspiring even more colonists to embrace independence.[65] In Pennsylvania, however, the Quaker-dominated assembly refused to break ties with the mother country. On May 10, the Continental Congress, reacting to Pennsylvania delegates' refusal to vote on independence, approved a resolution "essentially calling on Pennsylvanians to overthrow their government unless it joined with the other colonies."[66] Those who supported independence endorsed the resolve and selected delegates to serve in the provincial conference, which that June declared Pennsylvania's support for independence and called for a constitutional convention. On July 8, voters elected ninety-six men, mostly farmers, to write a new state constitution that would reflect what many ordinary folk had long wanted: a government that promoted political and economic equality, at least among white men.[67]

On July 15, members of the Pennsylvania constitutional convention assembled at the statehouse in Philadelphia, just across the hall from the Continental Congress, and proceeded to draft one of the most democratic governing documents in the Western world. Their first order of business was to open the political system by eliminating property requirements for voting. Voters were no longer required to own at least £50 of property or fifty acres of land. Now, all white men above the age of twenty-one who paid a local tax could vote as well as hold office, estimated to be "90 percent of the adult male population." To remove internal checks against the will of the people, the convention also instituted a unicameral house and created a plural executive branch without veto power. And to make politicians accountable to voters, the delegates "instituted annual elections for every representative," imposed term limits, and required that the assembly publish "a detailed record of votes and debates."[68] The more radical notion of economic equality proved more complicated to address. Although agreeing that the concentration of wealth "vested in a few individuals [was] dangerous to the rights and destructive of the common happiness of mankind," the delegates remained unsure exactly how to combat that problem.[69] Several members proposed that the new government place restrictions on the amount of land a citizen could own, but most viewed that measure as too extreme and voted it down. They ultimately decided to include a clause in the constitution that at least alluded to the state's responsibility to equalize wealth. "Government is, or ought to be, instituted for the common benefit, protection, and security of the people," the document pronounced, "and not for the particular emolument or advantage of any single man, family, or set of men who are only part of the community."[70] Finalized that September, the 1776 constitution quickly garnered a wide base of support throughout the state, especially among common farmers and urban artisans who found themselves empowered as never before.[71]

Husband embraced Pennsylvania's new constitution and welcomed American independence with open arms. He had long advocated for the formation of a government that protected the political and economic interests of common folk. The state constitution included several reforms that Husband championed as crucial to—as he put it—"perfecting a free government": annual elections and terms limits for every representative, freedom of speech and religion, and the expansion of white male suffrage. Husband wrote that such improvements had "been Preparing and forming in the Minds of the Workmen" since the English Civil War in the 1640s.[72] He also applauded these men for embarking on the creation of a new nation in order to secure "the Safety, Liberty and Happiness of every Individual in the Community," rather than "the Emolument of one Man or Class of Men."[73] Continuing to embrace postmillennialism, Husband viewed the American Revolution as divinely inspired. Even if the authors of the state constitutions considered themselves deists, he argued, they were nonetheless carrying out God's plan to rid the world of arbitrary power and tyranny.[74] For Husband, the American Revolution would ultimately usher in the millennium by inspiring other nations to rebel against despotism and allow God's grace to "cover the Earth as the waters Cover the Sea."[75]

Husband's proclamations were not unique. Countless other Americans believed that their new nation would become "the principal Seat of that glorious Kingdom, which Christ shall erect upon Earth in the latter Days."[76] Many were convinced that Britain had allied with the Antichrist, especially after the Quebec Act of 1774, which legalized Catholicism west of the Appalachians. According to Christopher Marshall, a prominent Philadelphia patriot and acquaintance of Husband, England sought "to destroy the liberties and freedom of this new world" and subject it to "papal power." However, Marshall declared, Americans would defeat "the prince of the power of darkness" and create a new heaven on earth.[77] Thomas Paine echoed those sentiments in *Common Sense:* "We have it in our power to begin the world over again. A situation, similar to the present, hath not happened since the days of Noah until now. The birthday of a new world is at hand."[78]

Such civic millennialism convinced many Americans that theirs was a glorious cause against popery, arbitrary power, barbarity, and vice. God had chosen them to "display His glory to all the nations of the earth, and improve social happiness and rights to a higher degree of perfection that hath yet taken place in the world."[79] Their fledgling nation had been anointed as the New Israel and was destined to usher in the millennium.[80]

But support for the American Revolution was far from universal. Throughout the colonies, perhaps one-third of the white population remained loyal to Great Britain.[81] Others attempted to stay neutral. In Pennsylvania, for instance, many Quakers were unwilling to compromise their religious beliefs, refusing to bear arms or take the controversial test oath, a clause included in the state constitution that required voters to denounce the king and pledge allegiance to the state.[82] Several hundred miles to the south, in the North Carolina Piedmont, former Regulators were also divided over the issue of independence. Much to Husband's dismay, many of his old friends supported the British Crown, unable to reconcile themselves with the eastern Whigs who had previously ignored their calls for reform and now championed independence.[83] According to one source, Husband visited Staunton, Virginia, during the Revolution and met several of his former compatriots imprisoned for fighting against patriot forces. He pleaded with the men to embrace the colonial cause, insisting that "the revolutionary struggle was what he intended at the time of the Regulation."[84]

Those who endorsed independence disagreed on how far the American Revolution should transform society. In Pennsylvania, there were two main political factions. Constitutionalists, like Husband, were more radical and embraced the commonwealth's attempts to expand white male suffrage and equalize wealth. They envisioned a government that—to use Husband's words—empowered "the labouring people" at the expense of "wicked Men" of "unworking Callings."[85] The Woods faction aligned with Republicans, also known as conservatives, who condemned Pennsylvania's constitution as "being too loose and Democratic."[86] Like other Republicans, Woods and his cohort were outraged by several clauses in the new document. They found the test oath particularly offensive because it forced them to support the constitution or face disenfranchisement.[87] The Woods faction likewise criticized the constitution for allowing new ranks of men to hold office. "Our principle seems to be . . . that any man, even the most illiterate, is as capable of any office as a person who has had the benefit of education," Thomas Smith complained to Arthur St. Clair in 1776. "Every person who is to be chosen into any office that was formerly supposed to require some degree of human knowledge and experience to enable the person to execute it with justice—every such person, I say—is to be turned out."[88] According to Smith and other conservatives, such a leveling principle had encouraged most delegates to "go to the devil for popularity" and draft a constitution granting suffrage to those they believed least capable of governing responsibly: the lower sort.[89]

Throughout 1777, Republicans protested, refusing to take the test oath and demanding that their representatives boycott the new government.[90] In February, Woods, Smith, and four other Bedford County Republicans elected to the state assembly walked out of a legislative session in opposition to the constitution.[91] "Those members who now sit, and assume to themselves the powers of an Assembly, are not the representatives of the People," Woods wrote, defending the delegates' withdrawal from the government. "They were elected by a small number. The majority in most of the counties were excluded from their right of voting by arbitrary oath."[92] That March, Bedford County Republicans Richard Brown and Abraham Cable refused to serve as officers in the militia after assemblymen appointed John Piper, a prominent Constitutionalist, as the county lieutenant.[93] Months later, the Woods faction pleaded with state officials to remove Piper, claiming that he had committed "fraudulent practices ... with regard to the election for Field Officers." That election, they complained, had placed unworthy people in power.[94]

Constitutionalists fought back. That spring, the Constitutionalist-led Supreme Executive Council removed Thomas Smith as Bedford County's prothonotary and replaced him with Robert Galbraith, an ardent radical. Smith refused to hand over the records to his successor until the assembly agreed to hold a new constitutional convention, so the council issued an arrest warrant for him.[95] Patriots in eastern Bedford County also lashed out at local Republicans, criticizing the Woods faction's withdrawal from the assembly in a public letter: "We think ... you have not been ingenuous with us, in that you allowed yourselves to be elected, when, as it appears unto us, you have no design to act. Your conduct, Sirs, has disgraced the whole county [and] wronged us entirely out of our share in legislation for one whole year." The men denounced a petition that Woods and Smith had sent to the legislature calling for a convention to annul the state constitution. Opponents of the Woods faction in eastern Bedford County feared that such a measure would "blow up discord, contention, and confusion." "We choose to give the New Government, being well satisfied with it, a fair trial," they concluded. "We have not time ... to contend about Forms of Government. Our attention is wholly engaged about the defence of our country, against a most cruel enemy."[96] Shortly thereafter, local Constitutionalists asked that the assembly hold a new election of representatives for the county.[97]

In October, Republicans across Pennsylvania made one last desperate attempt to discredit the new government by boycotting upcoming assembly elections. This largely symbolic move proved catastrophic. Constitutionalists, running virtually unopposed for office, swept the elections and solidified their control over the state legislature.[98] In Bedford County, voters elected six Constitutionalists to the assembly, including Husband, who in September

1776 had been appointed by the provincial government to the county's Board of Assessors, perhaps as a reward for his outspoken opposition to conservatives.[99] For the next year, the former Quaker would work with other legislators, most of whom had never served in office, to fulfill the promise of the American Revolution.[100] He would find that experience both gratifying and frustrating.

The Politician

When Husband assumed his seat in the assembly in December 1777, Pennsylvania was in turmoil.[101] Three months earlier, British forces had captured Philadelphia, forcing the provincial government and the Continental Congress to flee to Lancaster. The Pennsylvania legislators quickly "turned their attention to internal security" and hoped that by cracking down on political dissenters, they could prevent the British from seizing control of the entire state.[102] That summer, assemblymen had already targeted several disaffected groups, including Quakers, who continued to refuse to pledge allegiance to the new government or serve in the militia on religious grounds. In June, they passed the Test Act, which required all men over eighteen (not just those who voted) to swear loyalty to Pennsylvania or risk imprisonment. Now, with the British occupation of Philadelphia, legislators intensified their efforts to quell political dissent. Days before Husband arrived in Lancaster, they enacted a law that suspended the writ of habeas corpus for suspected traitors and deported several Quakers to Virginia.[103]

While in the assembly, Husband took advantage of this political climate to get back at his old nemesis, the Society of Friends. In February 1778, six representatives from the Western Quarterly Meeting petitioned the legislature to address their complaints.[104] Among them was Husband's younger brother Joseph, who—like his sibling—had converted to Quakerism as a young man. But while Herman eventually abandoned his faith in organized religion, Joseph remained dedicated to the Society and its doctrine of peace.[105] Joseph and his fellow brethren now stood before the assembly to defend their pacifist convictions and demand an end to the prosecutions committed against them.[106] They explained that, despite rumors to the contrary, the Society did not oppose the new government. "We do believe the present assembly to be the representatives of a body of the people of Pennsylvania, chosen for the purpose of legislation," they informed the legislators. When questioned about their stance on the test oath, the Quakers replied, "We believe it to be our duty to obey the principle of grace and truth in our hearts . . . yet it hath ever been our principle and practice . . . to submit to whatever power in the course of providence we may live under." Legislators were unmoved.

They denounced the brethren's answers as evasive and opened the floor for discussion.[107]

If the Quaker delegates thought that Joseph's presence would encourage Herman to support their cause, they were mistaken. Instead, the older brother seized the opening to lash out at the Society of Friends. He insisted that the group's obstinate rules had forced its members to betray their conscience and the new nation. The Quakers, he explained, belonged to "a Lesser Wheel" that made up "the Great Machine of Government." But their adherence to false laws had caused them to huddle together in their "small Sphere" and reject the "Larger Wheel Above": civil government, which Herman believed was "conducted by the Spirit [of Christ]" and thus destined to bring about the millennium. The Quakers' stubbornness now placed them in a precarious situation. "That [same] . . . Spirit of laws that thrust me out among you," Herman took pleasure in saying, "is leading you to Rebellion and Resistance and takeing Part in this Great Contest against us." The Society had to submit to the laws of the new government or risk losing everything. "I . . . am Pleading with you to Conform or you will throw your Selves out of our Protection," he warned. "Your discourses and writings . . . [have] become Quite unintelegable to any but your Selves [and will lead] to your . . . destruction."[108]

Although condemning the Quakers, Husband sympathized with other religious groups that remained neutral during the war and worked on their behalf as a legislator. Twice he rejected bills imposing harsher penalties on conscientious objectors. On December 26, he voted against a measure that levied a double tax on "the estates, real and personal, of every person not subject to nor performing military duty by the Militia Law of this State."[109] Months later, he withdrew from a committee charged with drafting a bill obliging all white men to pledge allegiance to the state. His opposition to the committee's recommendations denying pacifists their civil rights and prohibiting them from entering into certain professions was unpopular with his fellow Constitutionalist assemblymen, most of whom viewed neutrality as an act of treason.[110]

One reason Husband felt compelled to side with Republicans on this particular issue was Bedford County's large German Dunker population, which opposed the government's test oath on religious grounds. He was well acquainted with these men and women, as Brothersvalley, a thriving Dunker community, lay just a few miles from his estate in the Glades. Its inhabitants consisted mostly of hardworking yeoman farmers, the exact demographic that Husband had long championed as the backbone of a successful republic.[111] Politically, he probably thought it best not to further antagonize this constituency by backing legislation that punished religious dissenters. He also likely respected them and sought to preserve their civil rights, even if it brought him at odds with Constitutionalists.

Despite his sympathy for religious neutrals, Husband remained popular among Constitutionalist assemblymen. In March, legislators appointed him to investigate government officials suspected of defaulting in their payments of public monies, something for which his experience in the North Carolina Piedmont had prepared him.[112] He also united with Constitutionalists to combat the state's most pressing problem: inflation.

By 1778, Pennsylvania's economy teetered on the brink of collapse. Attempting to fund the war effort, legislators had the previous year issued £200,000 in paper currency, an amount far too great for the economy to bear. The value of the new notes quickly depreciated, resulting in runaway inflation.[113] Husband and other Constitutionalists blamed the state's financial woes on merchants, who, they argued, had monopolized the marketplace and artificially raised prices on essential goods. "Instigated by the lust of avarice and devoid of every principle of public virtue and humanity," they complained, "[merchants] are assiduously endeavoring, by every means of oppression, sharping and extortion, to accumulate enormous gain to themselves." Husband and his Constitutionalist colleagues subsequently instituted price-control regulations to lower inflation and relieve "the great distress of private families in general, and especially of the poorer and more dependent part of the community."[114]

Husband's solution to the state's financial problems went beyond enacting price controls. He recommended that the government completely overhaul its monetary system, presenting several Constitutionalist assemblymen with a plan to do just that.[115] He proposed that the government no longer use gold and silver to back its paper currency. Specie, he argued, had long been "rated above its true Value in England and America," which inevitably caused paper money to fluctuate unpredictably and increased the likelihood of runaway inflation. As such, Husband suggested replacing current notes with new bills not supported by metal. Each paper bill, he explained, would depreciate in value annually at a set rate until it became worthless after $33\frac{1}{3}$ years. Husband believed that his plan would not only regulate the rates of currency depreciation and price inflation but also end the commonwealth's (and nation's) dependence on other countries for specie.[116]

Above all, Husband was convinced that this monetary scheme would discourage merchants, speculators, and other wealthy men from hoarding cash and force them to finally pay their fair share in taxes. To help finance the sinking fund, he urged his fellow assemblymen to endorse progressive taxes on land, which would ensure that the burden of bankrolling the government no longer fell disproportionately on common farmers and artisans. "It will be found that every Man in the Community (from him who is richest, or holds the most moveable Property, to the poorest)," he proclaimed, "[should] pay the most equitable Proportion of Taxes, according to the Property they possess." Such a tax would also enable the government "to regulate the Quantities engrossed by Office Titles," thereby thwarting the concentration of land in the hands of a few.[117] However, even more radical legislators balked at Husband's plan and told him to lay it aside.[118]

During Husband's time in the assembly, relations between Republicans and Constitutionalists improved; conservatives, having failed to shut down the new government, now opted to work within the system to enact change.[119] In Bedford County, Thomas Smith surrendered his records in February 1778, nearly a year after being removed from his office as prothonotary, and took the test oath.[120] Woods and other Republicans followed suit, giving local Constitutionalists "their sincere intentions of burying all past disputes in oblivion and their hearty . . . endeavours to assist government and its Laws."[121] Robert Galbraith, Smith's replacement, who had earlier condemned Woods and his cohorts for inducing "maney of the inhabitants to deny the authority of our Present Legislators," was convinced these men now wanted friendship and reinstated Smith to the county bar.[122] By summer, one Bedford conservative declared that the powers of those "best acquainted with public Business & capable of managing the affairs of the County" had been restored.[123] In October 1778, reassured voters elected Woods and Smith to the assembly, while Husband appears to have not run for reelection.[124] Perhaps the former Quaker had become disenchanted by Constitutionalist legislators' lack of zeal for his brand of justice and equality. Whatever the reasons, Husband retreated back to his farm in the Glades, though, as usual, he would not remain silent for long.

Cautious Optimism

When Husband returned home, he was confronted with another brutal war being waged between white frontiersmen and Native Americans throughout western Pennsylvania. In 1777, the Delaware, Shawnee, and other Ohio Valley Indians—unwilling to tolerate white encroachment on their dwindling lands—allied with the British and began conducting raids on backcountry farmers. White settlers responded in kind, and both sides committed atrocities, torturing and killing combatants and civilians alike.[125] The western part of Bedford County, where Husband lived, was particularly ravaged by violence. "The Savages have . . . murder[ed] and destroy[ed] the property of the inhabitants upon the frontiers of this State," residents there complained to legislators shortly before Husband returned to the Glades in May 1778.

"Those who have escaped their barbarities, fearing least they may also fall a prey into their hands, are flying to the more secure parts of the Country."[126] Making matters worse, Tories (those who remained loyal to the British Crown) also took refuge in the western counties, where they united with the local Native American tribes.[127] Despite the danger, Husband opted to remain on his estate for the time being.

By 1780, white frontiersmen in Pennsylvania were on the verge of defeat. "Our Militia Companys are Intirely Broke up and whole Townships Layd waste," one authority informed state officials that year, begging for military support.[128] Unable to harvest their crops, many farmers struggled to feed their families. "Our County Seems to be pointed for Distruction," Woods lamented. "Our poor, Starving Contery, when they have Got Something on the Ground for Gethering, Dare not Go out to Save it."[129] In July 1782, news that a large band of Seneca warriors had decimated the white settlement of Hannastown in neighboring Westmoreland County convinced most Bedford inhabitants to abandon the region.[130] Husband and his family were among those who left, seeking refuge to the south at Fort Cumberland, Maryland. By April 1783, confident that the frontier war had been resolved, they returned to the Glades, where five months later they learned that Great Britain had officially signed a peace treaty with the United States.[131]

During this period, Husband increasingly became alarmed at the dwindling support for the Constitutionalist-controlled assembly, which was unable to curtail inflation or reduce the state's deficit. In 1780, Republicans regained control over the legislature and blamed Constitutionalists for the current fiscal crisis, claiming that in an attempt to placate the masses, they had passed legislation that victimized creditors, who were crucial to economic recovery.[132] Republicans argued that legal tender laws had caused currency to depreciate, which, in turn, discouraged "the mercantile Part of Society" from further investing in the market by driving down the value of and interest paid on loans to borrowers.[133] Conservatives also criticized statutes allowing citizens to pay taxes in paper money, insisting that relief measures actually prevented the government from getting out of debt.[134] Championing unrestricted free enterprise and sound money as a panacea for the state's financial woes, the newly elected Republican assemblymen quickly chipped away at Constitutionalist legislation.[135] In June 1780, they passed a bill repealing all tender laws that required traders and vendors to accept state-issued and Continental currency, forcing debtors to settle their loans in specie.[136] The following year, conservative legislators enacted new taxes payable only in gold and silver, which they believed would help fill the state's coffer with hard money, reduce depreciation, and balance the budget.[137]

Husband viewed the Republicans' crackdown on debtors and taxpayers with disdain. He believed their austere monetary policies would create a government that no longer worked for the common good of society, instead benefiting the community's most unproductive members: merchants and other so-called wealthy idlers.[138] In a 1782 pamphlet called *Proposals to Amend and Perfect the Policy of the Government of the United States of America*, Husband warned that Republican policies would soon deplete what little specie remained in the countryside, making it impossible for farmers, whom he considered the lifeblood of any successful republic, to pay their taxes or debts, causing them to lose their land and other possessions. Again, the crux of Husband's opposition to Republicans was that their fiscal measures victimized common folk by transferring the fruits of their labor to men of "unworking Callings." Those men, he believed, would squander that produce on luxury and superfluity, thus jeopardizing the future of the new nation. While "we lay the Burden on, and distress the Labourer," he cautioned, "we . . . lessen our Stock of Property, and destroy that Fountain out of which it rises, and make good the Proverb, of killing the Hen that laid a golden Egg every Day." Husband continued to champion the creation of a new currency divorced from specie as well as a progressive tax on land, insisting that these measures would allow the government to control the rate of currency depreciation and prevent working people from being unequally taxed.[139]

Husband also criticized the Continental Congress for its 1780 enactment of the so-called forty-for-one funding measure, an attempt to increase the value of national currency—by then virtually worthless—and restore public credit. The resolution called for the creation of a new currency based directly on the value of gold and silver. Congress required the states to remove $15 million of old Continental bills a month at a rate of forty to one: for every forty Continental bills turned in, one new bill, valued at one dollar in specie, would be reissued. To encourage the transition, the new bills would earn 5 percent interest, and to prevent depreciation, Congress capped emissions of the new certificates at $10 million. By 1781, most states had voted to accept the new currency as legal tender, acceding to Republicans' assurances that it would curb inflation and restore investors' faith in the economy.[140]

Husband was far from convinced. He lashed out at the congressional monetary scheme, not only for its continued reliance on the gold and silver standard but for encouraging speculation by increasing the value of the old bills and exacerbating the shortage of currency. Husband correctly argued that speculators would buy up the old currency at low rates, knowing they could earn a profit by exchanging it with the new, interest-bearing certificates. Further, he complained, the forty-for-one funding measure actually reduced the amount of currency available in the countryside, leaving farmers at the mercy of merchants and other speculators. "All our latter Regulations to raise the Value of Paper Money ... [has] cause[d] Money to become scarce [forcing] the Publick ... to buy it at full Value, from a few, who had engrossed it for little or nothing," he explained. "This Kind of Robbery has been always secretly practiced by a few."[141]

For Husband, the root of the problem was that state governments had failed to democratize enough. He believed that the most unfit men—merchants, lawyers, and other greedy individuals—continued to obtain political office and use their power to enact policies benefiting the wealthy at the expense of the common people. Pointing to Pennsylvania as an example, Husband argued that such men found it easier to gain office there because election districts were too large, which made it difficult for voters to make informed decisions. Knowing little of the candidates, they often supported the few men who were generally known in their district but who were—according to Husband—"generally the most unsuitable, they being chiefly Tavern-keepers, Merchants, &c. in the County Towns, with the Officers, Lawyers, &c." He insisted that large election districts prevented constituents from directly communicating with their representatives and holding them accountable.[142]

As an alternative, Husband advocated for the creation of county legislatures composed of representatives from every township in the county, who would then choose members of the state assembly, "the Board of Commissioners, and all other [county] Officers which we used annually to choose heretofore." Husband believed that these elected bodies would naturally be dominated by farmers and artisans, as such men were well acquainted with voters in their communities and could easily win office. Despite their inexperience in politics, these ordinary citizens, Husband believed, could govern responsibly and effectively. "A Man who will make a good Mechanick, or good Farmer, who can rule his own Family well," he wrote, "is also capable, with a few Years Practice ... to make a good Assembly-man to rule the State." The county legislature, then, would not only allow common people greater political control; it would give them the confidence and experience to run for other offices against those who sought to trample on their rights.[143]

Husband claimed that his vision for the creation of county legislatures was inspired by the story of the prophet Ezekiel, who was instructed by God to build the holy city of New Jerusalem based on the principle of gradation.[144] "As the city ... seen [in Ezekiel] was to be measured according to the measures of a man," he explained, "government [should also] be laid out by measure uniform, and to have all the same parts in due proportions to each other, as in a man's body."[145] Husband equated the lack of county legislators to a human hand missing joints in the fingers. "Our Want of the proper Use of those lesser Joints in the Body-politick," Husband bemoaned, "is as though we wanted our Finger-joints in our Bodies natural; without which we could not carry on the finer Parts of mechanick Work." By allowing the joints (common people) to maintain control over the hands (state assemblies), limbs (Congress), and head ("Commander of our Forces") of the body politic, county legislatures ultimately served as the lynchpin of any truly representative government. When "every Man in any Township [has] an Opportunity to converse with the Representative of his own Township, and those will stand more on a Level to converse with the State Representative, and they with the Congress . . . and so on to the general Commander of our Forces," he concluded, "a sweet Harmony will be diffused through every Limb and least Joint of our Body-politick, as the Blood is in our Bodies natural."[146]

Despite his distrust of established politicians and the gains made by Republicans, Husband remained devoted to the ideals of the Revolution and believed that the new nation was destined for greatness. Beginning in 1780, he penned a series of patriotic entries in William Goddard's *Pennsylvania, Delaware, Maryland, and Virginia Almanack* and David Rittenhouse's *The Continental Almanac*. These types of yearly almanacs enjoyed a wide readership throughout the eighteenth century. They were initially utilitarian texts that contained weather forecasts, agricultural advice, astrological predictions, mileage tables, and other useful information for the upcoming year, but with the onset of the American Revolution, their purpose and content changed. Popular among all ranks of society, almanacs became a vital weapon wielded by patriots to build support for their cause and forge a new national identity. For example, editors removed important British holidays from almanac calendars and added "new 'American' dates that commemorated battles for liberty fought throughout the new states."[147] They also invited talented writers like Husband to compose jingoistic essays, anecdotes, and songs.[148]

Under the pseudonyms Allegany Philosopher and Hutrim Hutrim, Husband portrayed himself as a wilderness prophet with a long, white beard who lived alone in a mountain cave. He described the Allegany Philosopher as "remarkably tall, his visage thin, and his eyes piercing." "He spends his time among the mountains, in searching into the nature of herbs and other wonders of the creation," he wrote in 1780. "The Dreams of this great man are said to be so remarkable, that many are induced to think he is capable of foretelling future events."[149] In reality, however, Husband was far from an impoverished hermit. He lived with his wife, Emey, and children in a comfortable home on more than four thousand acres in western Bedford County, where he remained one of the largest landowners.[150] But like the Allegany Philosopher, the farmer did care little about his personal appearance, as visitors often

FIGURE 8. Almanacs such as David Rittenhouse's *The Continental Almanac*, to which Husband contributed several entries during the 1780s, helped to mobilize support for the patriot cause. (Library of Congress, Prints and Photographs Division)

commented on his unkempt hair and ragged clothing, and he thought that dreams and visions enabled people to predict the future.[151]

As the Allegany Philosopher, Husband reassured readers that American victory was at hand, predicting in 1780 that the British economy would soon collapse because of the country's wartime deficit.[152] That following year, he urged patriots to not lose hope, foreseeing the defeat of British forces in the southern states. He also predicted that several European countries

"Perfecting a Free Government"

would rise up against the English and ally with the United States.[153] In 1782, the Allegany Philosopher celebrated the British surrender at Yorktown in October 1781. With American independence now virtually assured, he was ecstatic, proclaiming that the United States would "rise, among the Nations, to Victory, Liberty, and Glory." He praised the state constitutions, which he believed would "firmly secure our persons and property, and give us such a share of Liberty, as will be equal, if not superiour, to any other people under Heaven."[154] His optimism for the new nation continued in 1783. "Where ... is there a greater degree of political liberty enjoyed," he asked readers jovially. "'Tis true, that liberty is the natural birthright of mankind; but if we examine the several governments on the face of the globe, we shall plainly discover that a small proportion of our fellow-men enjoy that liberty, which we have so effectually secured to ourselves in America."[155]

Like his alter ego the Allegany Philosopher, Herman Husband had high hopes for the future and envisioned the nascent nation as the leader of a new era in world history. Already, American patriots—chosen by God to break the curse of arbitrary power and usher in the millennium—had begun the process of "perfecting a free government" that promoted political and economic equality.[156] "You, the Body of good People in America ... have an open Door" to "unite in [the] greater Wheel of the State" and "govern the Whole in true Justice and Righteousness," he proclaimed in 1782. "Through the growing Arts of Government, [we] will effect the End and Design aimed at, to wit, universal Peace and Order."[157] Husband's optimism for the new republic, however, would soon turn to despair.

FIVE

"The New Jerusalem"
Husband and the Early Republic

> I have been under an engagement of mind from my youth to understand the scriptures, concerning the promises therein made to our fathers... where God said, "I will put enmity between thy seed, and the seed of the serpent; (that was between the seed of tyranny and oppression, and the seed of freedom and liberty) he shall bruise thy head, and thou (tyranny) shalt bruise his heel." That is, freedom and liberty shall prevail in the end, to bruise the whole head and power of tyranny; and with this agree all the promises from this first to the end of the revelations.
> —Herman Husband, *XIV Sermons on the Characters of Jacob's Fourteen Sons*

The Vision

In September 1783, German botanist Johann Schoepf found himself lost in the wilderness of the Pennsylvania Glades. He had accidentally veered off of the main road and wandered aimlessly for hours, finally reconciling himself to the fate of sleeping outside as darkness approached. He later recalled his relief when he came upon two friendly boys who welcomed the tired and hungry stranger to spend the night at their house. There, he met the boys' father, a strange man, dressed in dirty clothes and barefoot, named Herman Husband. Schoepf described his host as courteous but terse, "with no waste of words and with no impertinent questions—almost the American habit."[1]

After supper, the two men sat by the fireplace and talked about one of Husband's favorite topics: geology. His years as a mine owner left the farmer fascinated with the subterranean science, and he had several geological works stacked on his bookshelf. His conversation with Schoepf centered around Thomas Burnet's *Sacred Theory of the Earth* and John Woodward's *An Essay toward a Natural History of the Earth and Terrestrial Bodies*. Husband criticized the scientists' theories and bombarded Schoepf with his ideas on the subject, including his belief that volcanoes were not "Coal Pitts of Sulphur Set on fire Accidently"—as Burnet argued—but instead burning mountains whose warmth kept the earth alive.[2] As the evening progressed, Schoepf found his host's words more and more astonishing. When the conversation "fell on the mountains, their valleys, inhabitants, soil and the like," Husband claimed that he had "travelled more than 400 miles along the Alleghany southwards," and was planning another journey in order to finish a map of the mountains. Schoepf was amazed at Husband's knowledge of the region's geography, remarking that during his yearlong tour of the young nation, he "had met no one, not even among those citizens of the United States better housed and clad, who appeared to have given so much attention to the mountains." The botanist recalled:

> Husband was over-interested in the regularity and straight line of the Alleghany which he compared to a solid wall, reckoning off-hand that the foot-hills of the mountains signified neither more nor less than the little inequalities made by the protruding stones of a wall. He estimated the width of the Alleghany [in southwestern Pennsylvania] . . . some 80 miles in breadth. Then taking the one, two, and three-mile jutties as so many eightieth parts of the whole, he compared them to the projecting stone-points of a wall, say four feet in thickness, and found that the apparently formless off-shoots from the chief mountain wall are merely to be regarded in relation as so many jutting stone-points, of half an inch or more, in a wall of thickness mentioned, and therefore are quite insignificant. I could at that moment make nothing of this vindicatory estimate.

Husband promised to show his surprised guest the unfinished map of the region the next day.[3]

What Schoepf saw the following morning left him baffled. Husband had drawn a quadrangle on the map, beginning at a point in Hudson's Bay, running south to Georgia, west into Mexico, north to a point near the Pacific Ocean, and finally back east to Hudson's Bay. Confused, Schoepf asked Husband why he had arranged his northeastern mountains in a quadrangular course. Husband's answer was not observation but divine inspiration. "Not I but the Prophet Ezekiel so set down the walls of the New Jerusalem," he explained. The sides of the quadrangle on the map corresponded with mountain ranges that formed the walls of New Jerusalem, a city described by Ezekiel in the Old Testament that would usher in the millennium. "Step by step and mile by mile, [Husband] expound[ed] how the Prophet Ezekiel has delineated with the utmost exactness the geography of America and its future states.... His allusions of the day before to walls, masonry, and gates were no longer a mystery," Schoepf recalled. "So wholly was [Husband] absorbed in the glory of this future kingdom that it was quite impossible for him to admit a reasonable thought." Anxious to make his exit, Schoepf thanked his host for the hospitality and went on his way, thoroughly convinced that the "loneliness of his mountain sojourning-place" and Husband's "lively powers of imagination" had driven him to insanity.[4]

Husband claimed that his vision of the New Jerusalem first appeared to him in June 1779 while searching for a natural highway through the Alleghenies near Pittsburgh. It dawned on him that the mountains formed the eastern wall of a glorious city that would someday contain more than 100 million people.[5] He abandoned his task and returned home, seeking the source of his inspiration in the Old Testament. He found what he was searching for in the book of Ezekiel, where he learned about New Jerusalem, a city surrounded by four walls with three gates each.[6] Husband believed that the dimensions of Ezekiel's New Jerusalem matched his own measurements of the trans-Appalachian frontier or—what he called—the western country, and was convinced that the walls of the city were the region's mountains and the gates were the passes between them.[7] He found further support for his theory in the New Testament's book of Revelation, which describes the walls enveloping the New Jerusalem as containing twelve precious stones. Husband insisted that these stones were actually iron-ore and other mineral deposits found in the North American mountains.[8]

Initially, Husband believed God had chosen the United States as the location for the New Jerusalem because it promised to perfect a government that worked on behalf of farmers, artisans, and other common folk, allowing the "tree of life" to grow to maturity and "remove the Curse and Calamities of Mankind in this World."[9] By 1790, however, Husband would lose confidence in the new nation. Corrupted by waste and luxury, he bemoaned, its leaders had begun to "live in disobedience to the dictates of God's spirit in their own consciences" and exploited common people.[10] Although he would be disheartened, Husband did not lose faith in New Jerusalem entirely, increasingly looking further west for salvation. There, he believed, would be the glorious land of New Jerusalem, where ordinary people would possess

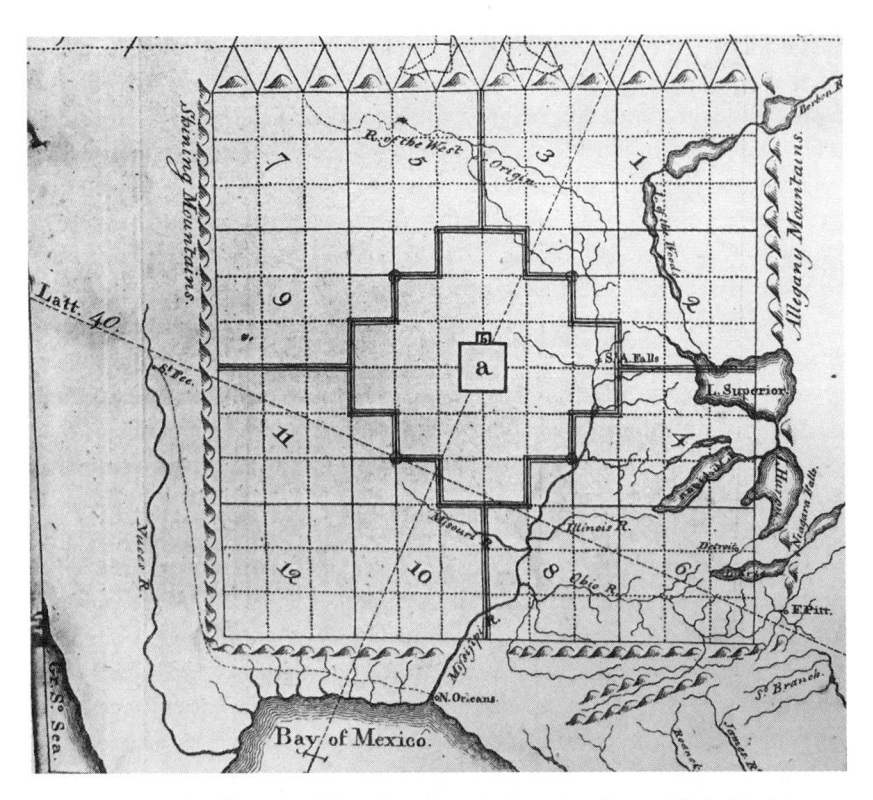

FIGURE 9. Husband's map of New Jerusalem in America, first published in his *XIV Sermons on the Characters of Jacob's Fourteen Sons* (Philadelphia: William Spotswood, 1789), facing page 17.

"all supreme power and authority" and "at last produce an everlasting Peace on Earth."[11]

Economic Recession and the Troubled Young Republic

Herman Husband was not the only American disappointed in the lack of change brought about by the Revolution and who sought new ideas in which to place their faith. In the fall of 1783, a group of Bedford County farmers— confronting high taxes, rising inflation, and the scarcity of money—waged a smear campaign against George Woods, who was running for reelection to the state assembly. Woods was an enemy of the people, the men charged in a letter displayed at several meeting places throughout the region, reminding voters that the candidate had initially opposed the call for independence, remained a harsh critic of Pennsylvania's 1776 constitution, and refused to compensate former militiamen. Even more damning, they claimed that Woods's endorsement of specie taxes and other recent monetary reforms had "almost ruined [our county] with ... lawsuits and extravagant fees." By siding with lawyers attempting to enact laws "made to suit themselves," Woods had betrayed his constituents. The letter encouraged voters to oust the corrupt politician from office. "Let us have a set of Farmers to serve us this year," it concluded, "and no doubt but we shall be honestly represented."[12]

These Bedford County farmers were part of a larger movement of ordinary Americans convinced that representatives like Woods had abandoned their responsibilities to the people in favor of pandering to the interests of so-called moneyed men, sparking an economic recession that threatened to undermine the new republic. The farmers argued that these politicians were no different from the British of the 1760s and 1770s, enacting legislation that raised taxes, imposed duties payable only in specie, and eliminated paper currency. For many common folk, such policies betrayed the Revolution by perpetuating economic inequality among white men. "No observation is better supported, than this that, a country cannot long preserve its liberty, where a great inequality of property takes place," Pennsylvania farmers explained in 1793. "Is it not therefore the most dangerous policy in this republic, to combine the wealthy in order to make them powerful?"[13]

Indeed, independence from Great Britain did not translate into economic prosperity for most Americans. Throughout the country, paper currency remained in short supply during the 1780s, making it difficult for ordinary citizens to pay their taxes or debts.[14] "The situation of this Country at present is very alarming for the want of Money," complained a Pittsburgh merchant in 1787. "Very few in this Town can procure Money to go to market. And as to pay ... a Debt it is out of the question."[15] Just as before the Revolution, farmers bore the brunt of the new nation's financial woes. Unable to obtain cash or procure loans, many of them were forced to sell their property well below market value, and tenancy subsequently increased throughout the countryside. As the young republic slid into an economic recession in the 1780s, it appeared that the opportunities for common folk to achieve economic independence were quickly fading away.[16]

Like elsewhere in the nation, ordinary Pennsylvanians lashed out at state leaders—Republican and Constitutionalist alike—whose reluctance to enact relief legislation, they believed, had caused the economic recession. Poor and middling citizens particularly bemoaned their representatives' endorsement of the Bank of North America, a private corporation chartered by the Continental Congress in 1781.[17] Critics charged that this bank threatened democracy by concentrating wealth in the hands of a few. In Pennsylvania, the Bank of North America issued loans mostly to merchants and other moneyed men, forcing ordinary people to borrow money from private lenders at exorbitant interest rates.[18] William Findley, a western politician and acquaintance of Herman Husband, warned in 1785: "This institution having no principle but that of avarice ... will [if continued] ... engross all the wealth, power, and influence of the state."[19]

Many struggling Pennsylvanians also resented state leaders for enacting specie taxes and reducing the amount of paper currency in circulation, which they viewed as a deliberate attempt to enrich creditors and bond speculators. These policies began during the American Revolution, when the Continental Congress issued millions of dollars in promissory notes to soldiers, farmers, and merchants as payment for services rendered. The IOUs quickly plummeted in worth, encouraging many original owners to sell their certificates at drastically reduced rates. Consequently, by the 1780s, these notes ended up mostly in the hands of speculators, who now demanded they be repaid in full with interest.[20] In response, Pennsylvania legislators, many of whom were certificate-holders themselves, scrambled to amass the funds to compensate speculators by cracking down on delinquent taxpayers and passing new levies payable only in specie. Moreover, in 1785, the Constitutionalist-controlled assembly earmarked a sizable portion of newly emitted paper money to pay the interest on the IOUs. Small and middling farmers were most affected by these actions, which reduced both the amount of specie and paper currency in circulation.[21] While common folk found it impossible to settle their debts, they claimed that unvirtuous bond speculators had become the wealthiest men in the state.[22] "The distress of the country people, from the weight of their taxes, is very great—and all this for what," an angry Pennsylvanian remarked in 1787: "To enrich a few men who have never done or suffered any thing for America ... to maintain in idleness a few speculators."[23]

As he had in the North Carolina backcountry, Herman Husband joined the chorus of opposition against stringent monetary policies, which he believed hampered economic growth and promoted wealth inequality. He argued that specie taxes and pro-creditor laws reduced agricultural output by forcing farmers to sell their means of production—tools and livestock—as well as their land to get out of debt. Even more alarming was the unfair transfer of wealth created by "the labouring Part of Mankind" to merchants, lawyers, bankers, and bond speculators, who squandered it on European goods and other superfluities.[24] The only talents of these vipers, as Husband called them, were the "robbing and living on the labour of others." This waste of men's labor on luxury, he claimed, had not only caused the economic recession by preventing the common people from enjoying the fruits of their labor but also threatened to incite the wrath of God. "To depend on the labour of other people for a living ... is the source of all other sins and the most provoking to God," Husband complained in 1789. It "ought to be treated with the greatest indignation by all, who would be accounted good men and Christians." He ultimately feared that legislators had begun to abandon the chief responsibility of any just government: to protect the property of those who had acquired it through their labor and industry.[25]

The vehement opposition to the assembly's fiscal policies was far from universal. Republicans and many Constitutionalists endorsed the Bank of North America, supported bond speculators, and called for monetary austerity, arguing that the commonwealth's (and nation's) economic challenges could be solved by distributing "Property into those Hands which could render it most productive": merchants, bondholders, and other moneyed men. According to Robert Morris, a prominent Philadelphia merchant, Republican, and founder of the Bank of North America, tax and debt relief legislation had prevented "the mercantile Part of Society" from acquiring what it most needed to promote economic growth: capital.[26] Like other fiscal conservatives, Morris insisted that only by cracking down on delinquent debtors, enforcing tax codes, reimbursing bond speculators, and privatizing finance could state leaders restore the faith of affluent Americans and foreign investors in the credit system and provide them with the funds to invest in the economy. For these men, economic development depended on the government's ability to channel wealth to the rich.[27]

Many ordinary Pennsylvanians took exception to this approach, continuing to champion tax abatements, debtor relief, and the emission of state-issued currency. Only through such equalizing measures, they maintained, would the promise of the Revolution be fulfilled and the new republic be saved. These men and women increasingly lost faith in the electoral process and relied instead on individual and collective resistance to enact change, staging protest rallies, ignoring tax laws, and sometimes accosting revenue agents.[28] They also frequently received the support of local officials, including Husband, who, as a constable and tax collector for Bedford County's Milford Township during the 1780s, refused to arrest delinquent debtors or collect taxes.[29]

This kind of protest occurred throughout the nation, as farmers, artisans, and other common people charged that austere fiscal policies had sparked the economic recession and undermined the "liberty and happiness of the middling and the poor."[30] When their petitions for reform went unheeded by state legislators, angry citizens took more radical direct action, halting sheriffs' auctions, closing courts, and assaulting tax collectors to protect their property.[31] In Massachusetts, opposition turned to outright rebellion, when some 1,500 farmers, calling themselves Regulators, attempted to seize the federal arsenal at Springfield in order to procure enough weapons to overthrow that state's government.[32]

These outbreaks of violence alarmed affluent Americans. Many blamed the disturbances as well as the economic recession on overly democratic state constitutions, which had allowed the people to not only engage in rebellion but also gain control over the government.[33] They claimed that legislators continued to cater to the masses or—as Robert Morris called them—"vulgar souls whose narrow Optics can see but the little Circle of Selfish Concerns," enacting currency emissions, tax abatements, and other relief measures that impeded economic growth by defrauding creditors and discouraging investment.[34] This "excess of democracy," the wealthy believed, threatened to undermine the young republic and needed to be contained in order to revive the nation's struggling economy.[35] Some proposed that the only way to avoid "democratical tyranny" was to establish a new, national government that restricted some of the powers that the states enjoyed under the Articles of Confederation, most notably the authority to tax and raise an army.[36] A stronger federal government promised to protect the wealthy from "domestic violence and the depredations which the democratic spirit is apt to make on property."[37]

These ideas heavily influenced the so-called Founding Fathers, who drafted a new federal Constitution in Philadelphia during the summer of 1787. The delegates of the constitutional convention sought to protect bondholders and creditors from unjust state laws.[38] In the proposed document, the federal government was granted the power to collect taxes and control war debt, ensuring that bondholders would be reimbursed in full.[39] The states were also barred from issuing paper currency or enacting any law that impaired the obligations of contracts, and debtors would now be required to pay creditors only in gold and silver.[40] The authors of the new Constitution further hoped to form a "stronger barrier against democracy" at the national level by creating an executive branch, which could veto congressional laws that threatened the interests of moneyed men, and a bicameral legislature, where the Senate could check legislation passed by the House, the only branch of the federal government elected directly by the people.[41] Finally, the delegates championed the creation of large congressional election districts, a measure that—as Husband had argued years before—would prevent ordinary folk from uniting in a common interest and make it easier for the elite to gain political office.[42]

Husband's Retort

Throughout the summer of 1787, Husband anxiously awaited news about the outcome of the Constitutional Convention. Like many other postmillennialists, he feared that the United States—mired in economic recession, internal strife, and moral decline—had fallen victim to the spirit of tyranny and was on the verge of collapse. It increasingly seemed possible that the young republic was not destined to usher in the millennium, after all.⁴³ But Husband, taking solace in the book of Revelation, remained confident that "the good and divine spirit of God" would ultimately triumph over Satan. This "patriotic spirit" had led Americans to break free from British oppression, and he continued to have faith that it would guide the framers to create a federal government that promoted "universal peace and [the] distribution of justice, judgment, and mercy throughout its extensive dominions."⁴⁴ He assured himself that biblical prophecies revealed that "the Perfection of our Protestant Constitution of Government" would occur in North America.⁴⁵

His optimism turned to despair, however, when he received a copy of the proposed federal Constitution. "I began to read [the Constitution] with full expectation to find something very agreeable.... But I [became] so far disappointed, that I got out of all patience, and condemned it before I read it near through," he remembered. "After a night's sleep, I read the whole over again very coolly, and was convinced that ... [the framers] were introducing tyranny, which has slain its millions." Husband was particularly concerned by the large congressional election districts, which he believed were designed to "rob the people of their liberty." He had long opposed this method of election, arguing that it allowed corrupt men unconcerned with common people to continue to acquire political office. These men "will never be able nor have an inclination to attend to the local circumstances of such distant inhabitants, to protect them and defend them from the violence and oppression of their rulers," he warned. "They will be deaf to any petitions or remonstrances of the people." Ultimately, Husband felt that the proposed Constitution failed to provide sufficient checks against the federal government at the state and local levels. "The congress, senate, and president, are created powers from one and the same jurisdictions, and sit in one place, and will join together to support their own authority, importance, emoluments, and interests, against all the United States," he predicted. "They will oppress; and, unless they can keep the people ignorant of their great strength, they (the people) will revolt [and] rebel."⁴⁶

Alarmed, Husband penned a series of pamphlets that condemned the Constitution and provided an alternative plan for "perfecting a free government."⁴⁷ He again drew his inspiration from the Old Testament, insisting that God's mandate to Ezekiel to build the temple of New Jerusalem on the principle of gradation revealed the true form of a just government.⁴⁸ The book of Ezekiel described that temple as having an enlargement at the base that tapered as it grew higher. Husband believed this was based on a natural law of design and that it could also be used as a blueprint for constructing a representative government.⁴⁹ Like the temple of New Jerusalem, such a government had to rest on a strong foundation. In others words, the lower parts of the body politic—township councils, county legislatures, and state

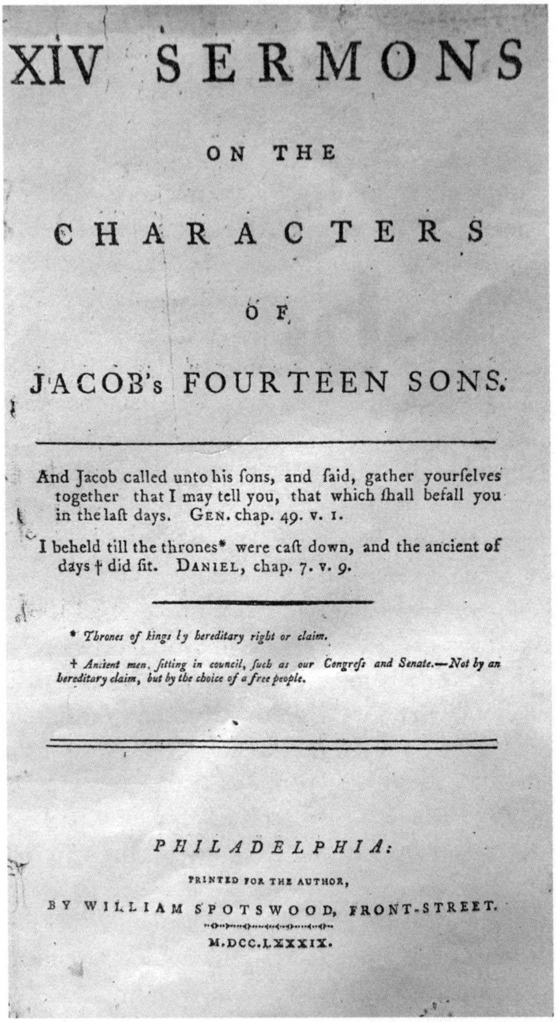

XIV SERMONS

ON THE

CHARACTERS

OF

JACOB's FOURTEEN SONS.

And Jacob called unto his sons, and said, gather yourselves together that I may tell you, that which shall befall you in the last days. GEN. chap. 49. v. 1.

I beheld till the thrones* were cast down, and the ancient of days † did sit. DANIEL, chap. 7. v. 9.

---

* *Thrones of kings by hereditary right or claim.*

† *Ancient men, sitting in council, such as our Congress and Senate.—Not by an hereditary claim, but by the choice of a free people.*

PHILADELPHIA:

PRINTED FOR THE AUTHOR,
BY WILLIAM SPOTSWOOD, FRONT-STREET.
M.DCC.LXXXIX.

FIGURE 10. Husband's most ambitious pamphlet, *XIV Sermons on the Characters of Jacob's Fourteen Sons,* not only laid out his plan for creating a just government but also encouraged farmers to protest peacefully against civil and religious oppression.

assemblies—had to be improved on before the upper parts—Congress and the executive branch—could be erected.[50] Husband believed that the Framers sought to raise the upper parts of government "a whole story without enlarging the foundation at bottom," and he warned that this top-heavy structure would allow the new federal government to consolidate power in the hands of a few and "reduce us again to tyranny."[51]

Husband's solution was to create a multilayered government that ascended gradually from the common people through the lower parts to the upper parts of the political hierarchy.[52] His plan allowed politicians to obtain state office only after first serving on a series of local, autonomous legislatures, the most important being the township assembly. Each state would be divided into ten-mile-square townships governed by a popularly elected council, with small election districts ensuring that all voters knew the candidates and could select virtuous men to manage township affairs. Councilmen who proved themselves the servants of the people could, in time, be appointed to the upper parts of local government—district assemblies and county legislatures—and then to a unicameral state assembly.[53] Husband believed his design assured that inept or corrupt politicians would quickly be voted out of office before they could use government to exploit their constituents. By "purging and expelling rotten Members downwards" and "giving the lower Classes of Power a free Examination," Husband concluded, his form of government would purify politicians and keep them beholden to the will of the people.[54]

Husband further called for the formation of a multitiered national government staffed by members of the state assemblies. Just as "a state is properly a confederation of townships," he explained, "so our federal government ought to be a confederation of states."[55] Under Husband's plan, the country would be divided into four empires: southern (Georgia, South Carolina, North Carolina, and Virginia), eastern (Maryland, Delaware, New Jersey, and Pennsylvania), northern (Connecticut, New York, Massachusetts, Rhode Island, and New Hampshire), and western (all territory "westerly and northerly . . . of the Allegany mountains").[56] These empires would serve as the limbs connecting the lower and upper parts of the body politic, thereby creating a government in which all branches remained united in a common interest and shared "the same care . . . for [one] another, as the different [parts] of the body natural have for each other."[57]

Each empire would be governed by a unicameral legislature, called a senate, composed of members chosen out of each state assembly and apportioned on the basis of population. To qualify as a senator, assemblymen had to have served at least three years in their respective state legislatures and be between the ages of thirty-five and sixty-five. Each senate would convene annually in a town in the center of the empire, where its members, serving only three-year terms, could establish legislation regulating trade and commerce, levy duties on imports, raise and collect taxes, and "divide the several states of their empires on the same principles as states now divide counties." The senates would also "have power to settle any difference between the states of their empires, and between citizens of one state against another state." Perhaps more importantly, they had the authority to veto any law passed by member states that violated the rights of citizens.[58]

The highest story in Husband's federal government would be a supreme council, composed of twenty-four men "chosen by the senates out of their own members," which would coordinate national affairs. To ensure that they were experienced leaders and fully devoted to their office, councilmen had to be between the ages of fifty and sixty when elected, take a vow of celibacy, and remain unmarried (if single). They would also be required to serve without financial compensation, a measure that would help prevent the supreme council from falling into the hands of the wealthy few. "If we annex no salaries to [this office], the ambitious mind, sweating with the desire of gain, will not seek after it," Husband explained, "and nature will work in those twenty-four elderly men . . . to become as careful, as industrious, and as frugal for the good of the body politic, as such aged fathers are for the good of their families." Serving a single ten-year term, councilmen would reside in a town central to the four empires and—like "the first saints of Jerusalem"—hold all their property in common.[59]

Under Husband's plan, the supreme council possessed an array of powers. Its members would appoint "supreme judges for all the United States," elderly men who could be trusted to deliver "impartial justice, according to the equity and laws of each state." The supreme council could also veto any law passed by the senates, resolve disputes among state assemblymen and senators, and divide overpopulated empires in order to "keep them as even as possible." Councilmen were responsible for selecting a commander in chief, who would be empowered to defend the nation against foreign aggressors and suppress domestic insurrections but who could not act independently. Only the senates (by a majority vote) could declare war, "make peace, enter into an alliance for assistance, and appoint and receive ambassadors." And the commander in chief could not use force to subdue domestic upheavals until the supreme council had the opportunity to review the petitions of protestors and address their grievances.[60]

For Husband, the supreme council's most important duty was to oversee the settlement of the trans-Appalachian frontier. He believed that the eastern states had been lost "to a despotic form of government," monopolized by speculators, stockholders, and other corrupt men who betrayed "the spirit and design of our state constitutions" and used government as a tool to engross their wealth and "live in luxury and waste on the labour of others."[61] But Husband had high hopes for the western territory. There, common people—if granted equal access to land—could escape tyranny, forge a truly representative government, and usher in the millennium, serving as an example for the rest of the nation. However, he feared that the framers of the federal Constitution would try to use the western region to further their own agenda by giving open land to large-scale speculators, thereby creating a nobility that would force most citizens to live in misery and slavery.[62]

To prevent the concentration of wealth and power in the hands of a few westerners, Husband's supreme council would limit the amount of land that settlers could own. Each family would be granted—at the price of £10 per one hundred acres—a maximum of two thousand acres ("three hundred acres for every man, two hundred acres for his wife, and one hundred for each child"). Absentee speculators would not be welcomed in the region. Only those settlers who showed "proof of improvements and residency" after three years would be permitted to retain possession of their land.[63] To further stop the monopolizing of lands, the supreme council would also impose inheritance laws that prohibited entailments of more than three hundred acres to any single heir. Once the region was settled and divided into small portions, councilmen would then require "the fathers estates to be equally divided among their own children."[64]

The supreme council would also be responsible for purchasing the "federal vacant territory" from Native American tribes and laying out the new western states.[65] Although Husband viewed American Indians as savage, he rejected the use of military force to confiscate their lands. He believed God had granted them first possession of the continent's uncultivated lands and, as such, should be fairly compensated for their loss.[66] After the supreme council purchased the western lands, it would open up the region to white settlement, creating a new state once two thousand families petitioned for admittance in a particular area. To ensure that the western states remained "as equal in Strength to one another as possible" and that election districts remained small, the supreme council would divide those states whose population had grown too large.[67] Ideally, Husband wanted each state to contain 144 townships.[68]

Husband's pamphlets not only provided a blueprint for creating a just government but also encouraged ordinary folk to engage in political activism.[69] He complained that the complacency of most freemen had resulted in a weakened and corrupt federal government. Content with a life of ease, regular individuals—like Issachar in the Old Testament—blindly accepted the authority of corrupt men determined to profit from their labor and enslave them, ultimately opting to remain neutral in the conflict between "the patriotic spirit and the spirit of tyranny."[70] However, the common people could still regain their voice, Husband argued, by using the vote and other legal measures to peacefully "throw off the yoke of their tyrants." Endowed by God with reason and understanding, they could elect virtuous men to office and, at last, create a government that was beholden to the will of the people.[71] But before that could become a reality, Husband believed "the labouring part of the community" had to reject the proposed federal Constitution, a vile document proceeding "from the spirit of the serpent."[72]

Ratification

Husband's voice was just one in a chorus of opposition to the federal Constitution. Generally called Antifederalists by their opponents, they were all critical of the proposed document because they feared it would create a tyrannical government beholden to the interests of the elite. "These lawyers, and men of learning, and moneyed men, talk so finely, and gloss over matters so smoothly, to make us poor illiterate people swallow down the pill, expect to get into congress themselves," one angry Massachusetts ratifying convention delegate declared in 1788. "They expect to be managers of this Constitution and get all the power and all the money into their own hands, and then they will swallow up all us little folks, like the great Leviathan."[73] Throughout the country, such discontent was most prevalent in rural areas like Bedford County, where voters elected two Antifederalists to serve in the state's ratification convention in late 1787.[74]

Countering this popular backlash were the Federalists, who lauded the proposed document as a panacea to the nation's economic woes and scrambled to get it approved by the states before opponents could effectively mobilize against them. Federalists in Pennsylvania had control over the assembly and scheduled the election of delegates to the state's ratification convention to take place on November 6, 1787, a mere eight weeks after the Constitution was read in public for the first time. The tactic worked, as Antifederalists in the state proved unable to organize their campaign against ratification quickly enough. The Federalists subsequently won a majority of seats in the Pennsylvania convention, which on December 12 approved the federal Constitution. Six months later, New Hampshire became the ninth state to ratify the Constitution, thereby making it the law of the land.[75]

Opponents like Husband were livid, insisting that Federalists had deliberately not given the people enough time to study and debate the proposed Constitution before its ratification. "The overhasty proceedings with which the new plan is hurried on," Husband complained in 1788, "shews that the authors are conscious it will not bear a strict examination of the body of the freemen of America."[76] Husband directed his anger at several prominent Federalists, most notably George Washington—who he now believed cared more about creditors and bondholders than "the people (who were all half ruined in their estates by the war)"—and Pennsylvania lawyer and signer of the Declaration of Independence James Wilson, who had publicly championed the new federal Constitution as the harbinger of liberty and insisted that its ratification reflected the voice of the people.[77] Wilson claimed that delegates had done due diligence and that the Constitution was only ratified after it had been "discussed and scrutinized in the fullest, freest, and severest manner . . . by its friends and by its enemies."[78] Husband dismissed Wilson's attestations, which he believed would one day "be a proof of the fraud by which the new constitution was obtained. . . . The result of their deliberations were laid before the people; true, and I might say, 'But there was no time allowed.'"[79]

Convinced that the framers of the federal Constitution were "lost to all truth, reason, and justice," Husband proselytized for his idea of the New Jerusalem.[80] He published more pamphlets and, dressed in homespun like a biblical prophet, preached to nonreaders, telling them that the western territory would soon become "the glorious land of New Jerusalem."[81] There, if his plan for creating a government was implemented, every farmer would own land, participate in the political process, and enjoy the fruits of his labor. Wage earners would also find economic salvation, no longer being exploited by large manufactory owners who kept their employees' wages as low as possible in order to live in luxury. Instead, these workers would partner with their employers and "receive a proportionate share of the profits, equivalent to his labor." In Husband's vision, "When every workman and laborer has such an interest in the whole, it will excite industry and care through the whole; and like the members of the natural body, each one will care for the rest." He ultimately believed that the trans-Appalachian backcountry would someday separate from the eastern states and pave the way for the Second Coming.[82]

Many contemporaries, especially the educated elite, scoffed at this vision. Hugh Brackenridge, a Pittsburgh attorney and Princeton alumnus, concluded in 1780 that Husband's "church [was] composed, like many others, of the ignorant and the dissembling."[83] German botanist Johann Schoepf remarked three years later: "Fortunate it is for the Congress and the entire thirteen United States that they know nothing as yet of Herrman's and Ezekiel's prophesies, and careless of the subjugation threatening them, live on tranquilly in the sweet, giddy pleasure of their new-won freedom."[84] Albert Gallatin, a Pennsylvania assemblyman and future founder of New York University, labeled Husband "the crazy man of Bedford," believing him "to be out of his senses as to politics."[85] Gallatin's friend John Badollet, who met Husband in 1793, agreed. "By too constantly reading & musing upon, the Scriptures, he is come to be compleately persuaded, that the prophecies of the old Prophets & unintelligible dream of St. John, find their application in these times & in this Country," Badollet scorned. "You must not laugh at the conceit, for he is in earnest & . . . has actually persuaded his family, amongst whom his wife, who appears a woman of good breading & of some degree of literature."[86] Testifying at Husband's sedition trial in 1795, Congressman Robert Smilie belittled the former Quaker for writing "some foolish things about the New Jerusalem."[87]

Despite being rejected by elite politicians, Husband maintained the respect of ordinary folk in Bedford County. He was described by one of his neighbors in 1795 as "a sober [and] industrious man."[88] Farmer James Wilson did not believe that Husband was crazy but that he simply "employed in writing upon prophets, & making riddles." This was an undertaking that Wilson and other evangelicals did not find odd, as they placed great faith in the power of one's inner light to decipher biblical passages and predict the future.[89] Even among those who "sometimes thought him a tolerably sensible man and sometimes not," Husband gave his beleaguered readers and listeners hope in a time of political and economic distress, reminding them that, "in the last days, the labouring, industrious people . . . shall prevail over the standing armies of kings and tyrants."[90] The people responded to his message, and his popularity soared in Bedford County in the 1780s. Voters elected him as a county commissioner, constable, tax collector, overseer of poor, and supervisor of highways. In 1789, they selected him to serve in the state assembly, which would be his final stint in public office.[91]

An Assemblyman Again

When the newly elected assemblyman arrived in Philadelphia in November 1789 to take his seat, relations between Antifederalists and Federalists remained tenuous throughout the country.[92] In September, the First Congress had responded to Antifederalists' call for a Bill of Rights by sending the states twelve articles of amendment to the federal Constitution for ratification. The most controversial of these articles, at least in Pennsylvania, was the first one, which sought to maintain actual representation in the House of Representatives. During and after Pennsylvania's ratification convention in 1787, Antifederalists had advocated for an amendment to the Constitution guaranteeing that the House would be reapportioned as the population rose, arguing that such a measure would keep election districts small and make representatives accountable to their constituents. The proposed amendment on representation was a concession to these Antifederalists, fixing the "maximum number of constituents for each representative" at fifty thousand.[93]

Most Antifederalist assemblymen were appeased and endorsed the amendment, believing it was enough to hold elected representatives accountable to the will of the people. "The legislature of a free country should . . . have a competent knowledge of its constituents, and enjoy their confidence," insisted an editorial in the *Pennsylvania Packet*. "To produce these essential requisites, the representation ought to be fair, equal, and sufficiently numerous, to possess the same interests, feelings, opinions, and views, which the people themselves would possess, were they all assembled."[94] However, Federalists generally opposed the idea of compromise and—as they controlled the General Assembly—eventually defeated the amendment's passage in the Keystone State. Proponents of virtual representation, they favored keeping election districts as large as possible to make representatives less dependent on their constituents and thus able to act in the interests of the entire nation.[95] They also charged that the amendment would make the House too large and unwieldy.[96]

Despite his general alignment with Antifederalist ideology, Husband opposed the proposed article, agreeing with Federalists that it would make the House too numerous. Husband predicted that as larger states were subdivided due to increased population, the nation would eventually be composed of approximately ninety states. Such growth, he warned, would "increase the number of the members of Congress to one thousand members, on the lowest calculation," rendering the House unmanageable. More importantly, Husband rejected the amendment because he felt it was not radical enough to ensure that representatives would remain accountable to local voters. He wanted even smaller constituencies than the amendment proposed and encouraged assemblymen to consider his plan of government based on the prophecies of Ezekiel, which he believed adequately addressed this challenge.[97]

On February 23, 1790, Husband made his case to the state assembly. Legislator Jacob Hiltzheimer remembered that Husband referred often to biblical scripture, "in particular the Kings of David & Nebuchadnuzzar."[98] His appeal fell on deaf ears, although it provided Husband's opponents with an opportunity to castigate the so-called Pennsylvania madman. That March, Assembly speaker Richard Peters wrote a letter to James Madison to inform the "Father of the Constitution" about Husband's idea of the New Jerusalem. Husband "must be a prodigious Genius," Peters jeered, "having drawn the Principles of the federal Government from higher Sources than we ever thought." While Peters conceded that it was necessary to have members of the legislature who represented opposing viewpoints, he dismissed Husband's plan as balderdash. He did recommend that Madison relay Husband's plan to Thomas Jefferson, but only for the sake of a chuckle. Jefferson "has a Head for deep Speculations," Peters wrote, "perhaps our great political Investigator may afford him some Amusement."[99]

Husband was undeterred by his critics and continued to advocate for reforms that he considered crucial in creating a just government. Near the top of that list was overturning an ordinance passed by the Federalist-dominated General Assembly in 1788 specifying that members of the state's House of Representatives be elected at large. He believed that this law not only further separated officials from the people but also gave Republicans, who enjoyed widespread support in the more populous eastern part of the state, "an electoral advantage over western and interior Constitutionalist candidates."[100] In August 1790, Husband and several colleagues proposed an alternative bill that divided the state into congressional districts, but to no avail. Their measure was overwhelmingly rejected by the General Assembly.[101]

Although Husband was often on the losing side of politics, he did experience an occasional victory. While in Philadelphia, he allied with Antifederalists to defeat the First Congress's second proposed amendment to the Constitution, which prohibited senators and representatives from receiving pay raises between elections.[102] The fact that congressmen would receive compensation in the first place, let alone have the authority to increase their salaries, alarmed Husband. "Our supreme councils" should "be above the influence of money, honor, or dress," he argued in 1790, warning that high salaries would encourage men to seek office only to accumulate wealth and act contrary to the will of the people. "Has it not been this object of getting money in the supreme rulers of every state and in every age, that has been the principal cause of all wars and desolation of kingdoms," he elaborated. "It engaged the Popes in wars as well as Kings—it is called filthy lucre and the stinking carcass, which our Lord alluded to when he said, 'Where the body is, there the eagles will be gathered together.'" Removing salaries from the equation promised to purify government by encouraging only "qualified men to run for office. These public servants would not be those "educated from their infancy in the courts of Kings, and in higher stations of life," whom Husband considered unfit to lead a nation. Instead, they would consist of successful farmers, artisans, and laborers, "whose merits and natural abilities [had] raised them to . . . higher stations in life from among the common people; as David was raised from being a keeper of sheep." Husband believed these self-made men, having acquired their wealth before entering into politics, would be able to serve the public in office without financial compensation, and thus "be wholly divested of all desire of gain" and govern responsibly.[103]

Husband enjoyed the support of most Antifederalists in opposing Treasury Secretary Alexander Hamilton's first "Report on Public Credit." By 1789, the country's financial standing had reached an all-time low, as the federal government continued to owe around $42 million to Americans who had purchased bonds or received IOUs during the American Revolution. Congress tasked Hamilton with preparing a plan for reviving the nation's

FIGURE 11. Acting on Alexander Hamilton's recommendations, the U.S. Congress passed the Funding Act of 1790, which Husband and other Americans believed benefited the elite at the expense of the common people. As secretary of the treasury, Hamilton became a staunch opponent of the Whiskey Rebellion and helped convince President George Washington to use force to quell the protest movement in 1794. (*Alexander Hamilton, -1804, half-length portrait, facing right*; Library of Congress, Prints and Photographs Division)

public credit, which he submitted in January 1790. In his report, Hamilton insisted that the federal government could only gain financial credibility by dealing fairly with its past creditors. To that end, he recommended that the domestic debt be "funded—but not repaid immediately—at face value," and that Congress allow investors to exchange their depreciated IOUs for new interest-bearing bonds.[104] Hamilton also urged the federal government to assume the debts accrued by the states, which would increase the domestic debt to $67 million, and permit holders of state certificates to exchange their securities for new national bonds. To fund the interest and principal payments on the national bonds, Hamilton advised Congress to impose excise taxes on domestically distilled whiskey and other luxuries.[105]

Along with other Antifederalists, Husband condemned Hamilton's "Report on Public Credit." He charged that the financial scheme was unjust because—like state fiscal policies in the 1780s—it defrauded original bondholders, most of whom had been forced to sell their certificates well below face value to an "unmerciful set of speculators." Husband instead favored the policy of discrimination, whereby speculators would be required to share a portion of their profits with the original bondholders.[106] He called Hamilton's plan "the curse of all curses," believing that it would prevent the federal government from fulfilling its "moral obligation to liquidate the [national] debt in a single generation."[107] Burdening future Americans with financial insolvency, he argued, "is as unjust as if we were by law to oblige insolvent debtors to black their children in their infancy and sell them slaves for life."[108] Husband recommended his 1778 paper money scheme as a solution, but Congress again disregarded his suggestions and passed the Funding Act of 1790.[109]

Husband likewise continued to fight political battles on the state level. In 1789, the Federalist-controlled Pennsylvania assembly had secured the creation of a convention to revise the state's 1776 constitution. The convention met in Philadelphia during Husband's tenure in the assembly, and the resulting document sought to contain democracy through a bicameral legislature, an executive branch with veto power, and "a top-down legal system with governor-appointed judges replacing the locally elected justices of the peace." The convention also targeted debtors, granting state-appointed judges the authority to enforce tax laws and punish local officials who neglected their duties. Further, it strengthened the influence of state officials over local affairs by permitting the governor to appoint county sheriffs. Although elections would still be held, the governor would choose "the winner from the top two vote getters."[110]

The convention adjourned on February 26, 1790, with members planning to reconvene on August 9. During the recess, Husband penned *A Dialogue between an Assembly-Man and a Convention-Man*, a pamphlet that lambasted the proposed state constitution and demanded that legislators reject it. While Husband conceded that the 1776 constitution was imperfect, particularly when it came to checking the authority of the assembly, he insisted that the creation of a bicameral legislature was not the solution. "That check," he argued, "ought to be possessed of more wisdom and more power—as well as [be] less interested in the law to be examined." Instead, Husband urged the constitutional convention to form a council made up of legislators in Pennsylvania, New Jersey, Delaware, and Maryland that could check laws passed by the assemblies in those states. Such a group would "have the wisdom and power of the four; and at the same time would be less interested and more impartial judges of the laws under their examination," he explained. "Besides this one council could serve these four states at the same expense that it would cost each of them on the other plan." Once Pennsylvania, New Jersey, Delaware, and Maryland set a precedent with this senate, Husband believed that other states would follow suit, dividing the new country into four empires. This would ultimately complete the creation of a "Federal Government and body politic, with every useful and necessary joint [in operation], similar to the body natural, as ... shown in a vision to the prophet Ezekiel."[111]

Husband's hopes that the constitutional convention would lead the way in "perfecting a free government" left him disappointed yet again.[112] On September 2, 1790, the delegates—without allowing a popular vote on the document—adopted the new state constitution.[113] Husband remained defiant to the end, insisting that the current unicameral General Assembly not be dissolved, despite the fact the new constitution vested legislative power in a Senate and House of Representatives. He argued that the assembly had been elected by the people and therefore continued to possess legal power to enact legislation. Moreover, he reasoned that the continuance of the assembly would allow the government to remain operational before the ensuing election. Husband rationalized that this would ensure a smooth transition. "I should think," he explained, "that common sense would dictate to every man, that in cutting the head off from any body, in order to put on a new head, that the said new head should be all in readiness before the old one is cut off—Gardeners always take this care in grafting a new head on an old stock."[114] Husband's pleas again fell on deaf ears, as fifty-six assemblymen, convinced that "the power vested in the late Convention was necessarily superior" to theirs, opted to retire from their positions, thereby ending the final state assembly formed under the 1776 constitution.[115]

Frustrated, Husband left Philadelphia and returned to his home in the Glades, much to the delight of Emey, who had been running the family farm in his absence. The adoption of the 1790 state constitution and Congress's embrace of Hamilton's fiscal plan had shaken his already fragile faith in the young republic. Although it appeared that his initial vision for the New Jerusalem would not come to pass, he remained optimistic about the future. The news of the French Revolution, especially, reassured him that the spirit of liberty had not been extinguished.[116] "In Europe, a great and enlightened people, the French nation, [are] throwing off the shackles of despotism, and establishing political and religious liberty," Husband proclaimed in 1790. "This progress of . . . free government bids fair to bring on that happy era, when nations shall no more learn war."[117] Still convinced that the "tree of Life" would reappear in the United States, he composed an essay analyzing the visions of Daniel in the Old Testament.[118] It would never be published and ended up being his final manuscript.

Husband had contemplated writing such a tract for nearly a decade. He had long believed that the book of Daniel predicted that the trans-Appalachian backcountry would usher in the millennium.[119] He was especially fascinated with chapters 7 through 12, in which Daniel describes the rise and fall of four kingdoms and the "ultimate triumph of God through the fifth kingdom."[120] According to Husband, the ancient civilization of Babylon was the first of those four kingdoms, followed by the Eastern Roman Empire, the Western Roman Empire, and the "Protestant Kingdoms of Europe." Husband argued that Daniel had foreseen the emergence of Great Britain as the head of that fourth kingdom and—by adopting a mixed constitution—had come the closest in the old world to ending arbitrary rule. However, the continued influence of the corrupt Anglican Church prevented this, causing "Men induced with the Spirit of Grace" to leave the country and settle in British North America.[121]

These religious dissenters, Husband concluded, were the ones Daniel had prophesized who would establish the fifth kingdom and pave the way for the Second Coming of Christ. Husband believed that the American Revolution had ultimately failed to create this final kingdom, in which the common people would have the power to choose their governors and see their will become "the Supreme Law of the Land." Despite gaining independence from Great Britain, Husband bemoaned that, as in "every Revolution where the People at Large are called on to assist Promised true Liberty," the nation's leaders, having "thrown off . . . the foreign oppressor," embraced idolatry and worshiped false Gods, leaving everyday Americans to continue to live in oppression and slavery. Meanwhile, he argued, the "tree of Life" had replanted itself in Europe, sparking the French Revolution and a war between France and England. Although disappointed in the American Revolution, Husband maintained that Daniel had predicted such a dark time would precede the true founding of the fifth kingdom. He remained confident that the laboring classes in America—inspired by "those who dethroned the French king and are now fighting to Save the French Nation and gain its Liberty"—would again resist their rulers and, like the "Israels Coming out of Egypt," forge a righteous government in the western country.[122] Husband's faith in biblical prophecy, however, would again prove misplaced.

The Whiskey Rebellion

On September 16, 1792, George Clymer, the federal supervisor of revenue for Pennsylvania, arrived in Pittsburgh to investigate a series of protest meetings that had recently taken place in the southwestern part of the state.[123] In September 1791 and August 1792, delegates from Westmoreland, Allegheny, Fayette, and Washington Counties had assembled at Pittsburgh to draft petitions to Congress denouncing Hamilton's financial program. Topping their list of complaints was the Revenue Act of 1791, which imposed a duty on distilled alcohol to help fund the national debt. The delegates charged that this so-called whiskey tax threatened to ruin western farmers who relied on liquor manufacturing to market their crops and obtain cash, which remained a scarce commodity in the region.[124] However, this new impost was not an isolated event but the offspring of the Funding Act, a piece of federal legislation that delegates found even more detestable.[125] The delegates bemoaned the act's "unreasonable interest of the public debt," rejection of discrimination, and endorsement of a national bank. In their eyes, Congress, acting on Hamilton's recommendations, had yet again betrayed the laboring many by supporting fiscal policies that further allowed "men to make fortunes by the fortuitous concurrence of circumstances, rather than by economic, virtuous, and useful employment."[126]

Hamilton viewed the Pittsburgh meetings as treasonous, and he instructed Clymer to provide a firsthand account on the true state of the western counties.[127] Afraid to venture outside Pittsburgh, however, Clymer relied heavily on information provided to him by John Neville, head of the state's fourth collection survey of Westmoreland, Fayette, Washington, Allegheny, and Bedford Counties.[128] One of the wealthiest residents in the region, Neville was also one of the most hated. Many of his neighbors considered him a traitor and threatened to assault him for becoming an excise tax collector.[129] Basing his reports on Neville's accounts, Clymer informed Hamilton that most westerners were in "a state of actual insurgency against the government of the union."[130]

To a certain extent, Clymer was correct. Western Pennsylvanians had increasingly become outspoken critics of the new nation.[131] Like Husband, these men and women saw the excise tax and Funding Act as the latest in a series of laws dating back to the 1780s that had "created a new monied interest" and made "politics favourable to aristocracy and monarchy in the states which were once the most republican in the Union."[132] But Clymer's supposition that most westerners wanted to overthrow the government was misguided. Instead, they only sought to regulate it. The point of contention was how to best proceed. Some backcountry residents favored the use of extralegal tactics—closing courts, blockading roads, and accosting tax officials—to initiate political reform. Others feared that such methods would provoke a military response from the Washington administration and encouraged their angry neighbors to enact change at the ballot box.[133] Only by working within the existing system, they insisted, could the people reestablish "a well regulated republican government."[134]

Regardless of tactics, Hamilton believed that all forms of opposition to his financial plan undermined federal authority. Even before Clymer arrived in Pittsburgh to take stock of the situation, the treasury secretary had asked President George Washington to send troops to the region, warning him that inaction would indicate the national government was "wanting in decision and vigour."[135] Several members of Washington's cabinet disagreed, urging the president to remain patient. Attorney General Edmund Randolph, for instance, countered that Hamilton did not have enough evidence to call for military intervention, arguing that the Pennsylvanians were exercising one of the rights most dear to the American Revolution. "To assemble to remonstrate, and to invite others to assemble and remonstrate to the Legislature, are among the rights of Citizens," Randolph reasoned, and cautioned that hasty action might cause the dissatisfaction to spread even to those who disapproved of the "spirit of the Pittsburgh meetings."[136] Washington followed the advice of his cabinet, and on September 15, 1792, he issued a proclamation denouncing resistance to the excise and ordering westerners to "refrain and desist from all unlawful combinations and proceedings."[137]

The president's mandate went unheeded. Disgruntled residents continued to oppose the excise law, including the mysterious Tom the Tinker, who posted articles in the *Pittsburgh Gazette* encouraging distillers not to pay the whiskey tax.[138] By 1794, displeased western Pennsylvanians—like those elsewhere in the nation—had also formed several Democratic-Republican societies in the hopes of mobilizing voters against the Washington administration.[139] That summer, events in western Pennsylvania turned violent. On July 17, about six hundred militiamen from Allegheny County surrounded the mansion of the reviled tax collector John Neville and demanded that he resign his post. An ensuing gunfight resulted in the death of James McFarlane, the militia's popular commander.[140] In response, approximately seven thousand angry men converged on Braddock's Field, located just south of Pittsburgh, on August 1 to consider creating their own independent government. For the time being, cooler heads prevailed; the men agreed to return home to debate the matter and elect delegates for a regional meeting, scheduled to take place on August 14 at Parkinson's Ferry.[141]

Up to this point, resistance to the whiskey tax in Bedford County, where Husband lived, had been minimal. Two years earlier, Clymer had reported that the influence of George Woods and his "friends of the town of Bedford" caused citizens there to remain "well attached to the federal government." But Clymer cautioned revenue officials not to aggressively enforce the law, fearing that would provoke farmers in the county to engage in violence.[142] This warning proved prophetic. By 1794, Bedford County residents had begun to accuse collector John Webster of "unlawfully seizing liquors on the road from poor people who were carrying it to [barter for] their necessities." That July, around 150 men from Bedford and Westmoreland Counties took matters into their own hands, seizing Webster from his home at Stony Creek, setting fire to his stables, and escorting him to Westmoreland County.[143] The group eventually released Webster unharmed, though only after he agreed to "mount a stump [and] hurrah three times for Tom the Tinker."[144]

Shortly after Webster's abduction, news of the demonstration at Braddock's Field reached western Bedford County, and residents organized a meeting at Berlin to elect delegates for the Parkinson's Ferry conference. Husband attended and—as he had attempted to do nearly three decades earlier during the North Carolina Regulation—endeavored to steer his neighbors down the path of moderation. He warned that the recent attacks

FIGURE 12. On August 1, 1794, more than seven thousand protestors from Allegheny, Fayette, Washington, and Westmoreland Counties met at Braddock's Field, located just south of Pittsburgh, near the banks of the Monongahela River, in opposition to the federal government's whiskey tax. (*Braddock's Battlefield*, ca. Nov. 23, 1908; Library of Congress, Prints and Photographs Division)

on Neville and Webster were a wrong step in attaining justice. "If [we] resist and overpower government then there [will] be no security at home, and [we will] be left without protection," he explained. "Whatever [is] the will of the people ought to be the law of the land. If a law [is] bad, the same power [can] repeal it; and the voice of the people by their representatives [is] the only way of getting redress."[145] The majority agreed, and the Berlin gathering resolved to ally with the protestors only if they favored peace. They selected Husband and Robert Philson, a Berlin storeowner and former patriot general, to represent them at the upcoming convention.[146]

On August 14, Husband and 225 other delegates converged on the high bluff overlooking the Monongahela River at Parkinson's Ferry, surrounded by 250 spectators.[147] Nearby, a flag with the words "Liberty and No Excise" embroidered on it flew from a so-called liberty pole, a symbol of defiance to federal authority.[148] Sitting on stumps and fallen trees, the delegates debated a course of action. Some, including Washington County militia officer James Marshall, renounced "all connection with the Government" and favored "opposition by violence, without further appeals to Congress." Other delegates remained

"The New Jerusalem"

unwilling to secede from the new nation but approved the use of armed resistance to regulate the federal government. Husband allied with a third faction that urged delegates "to submit to the national will rather than hazard the convulsions of a civil contest." This so-called moderate party ultimately convinced the assembly to elect a committee to revise some of Marshall's extreme resolutions.[149] Husband, along with moderates Hugh Brackenridge and Albert Gallatin and firebrand David Bradford, were chosen for the task.[150]

The next morning, the redrafting committee turned its attention to Marshall's most controversial resolution, to create a committee of public safety authorized to raise troops "to repel any hostile attempts . . . made against the rights of the citizens."[151] Bradford urged the committee to adopt the resolution, but Gallatin refused, viewing the proposal as a declaration of war. During the ensuing heated debate, Brackenridge, who also opposed the resolution, attempted to divert Bradford's attention by asking Husband to explain his vision of the New Jerusalem. While this was simply a ploy to diffuse the situation, Husband interpreted Brackenridge's request as sincere and produced a pamphlet from his pocket for Gallatin to read out loud.[152] Unamused, Bradford told Brackenridge "to be serious" and returned to Marshall's proposal.[153] The committee ultimately voted down the resolution but appeased Bradford and other militants by agreeing to form a standing committee empowered to take only "temporary measures in case of sudden emergency."[154]

Shortly after approving revisions to Marshall's resolutions, the committee unexpectedly received word that three federal commissioners—James Ross, Jasper Yeates, and William Bradford—were at a house near Parkinson's Ferry and wished to negotiate with the whiskey rebels. Much to Hamilton's delight, the attack on Neville's estate and the demonstration at Braddock's Field had convinced Washington that western Pennsylvanians were engaged in rebellion against the federal government. On August 7, Washington issued a proclamation calling for the mobilization of militia to quell the protest movement and ordering insurgents to disperse and return home by September 1.[155] He also dispatched Ross, Yeates, and Bradford to western Pennsylvania to deliver a copy of the proclamation to a local politician.[156] The commissioners pledged that they would grant amnesty to protestors who agreed to no longer obstruct the execution of the whiskey tax.[157]

Many delegates and spectators alike greeted Washington's proclamation with disdain. "It had a bad effect," Brackenridge recalled, and "seemed to produce anger; the idea of draughting the militia, and the charge of being guilty of treason, seemed to make them suppose it necessary to arm themselves."[158] Nonetheless, the commissioners' promise to pardon past transgressions convinced most attendees to now support "the adoption of pacific measures."[159] The delegates approved the redrafting committee's resolutions, which were more moderate in tone than Marshall's original proposals, and elected sixty men, including Husband, to meet with the three federal commissioners later that month at Redstone Old Fort in Fayette County.[160] Confident that peace was at hand, Husband returned home to western Bedford County.

On August 28, members of the so-called committee of sixty assembled at Redstone Old Fort under the shade of a hastily constructed wooden canopy to cast their vote for war or peace. Days earlier, a negotiating committee had met with the federal commissioners in Pittsburgh to reach a preliminary peace settlement. The commissioners refused to entertain a repeal of the whiskey tax and warned that the president would use military force if citizens continued to resist the law. However, they promised that Washington would forgive past offences and refrain from sending in troops on two conditions. First, the committee of sixty would have to vote unanimously "to submit to the Laws of the United States," denounce the use of violence, and pledge to support the whiskey tax.[161] Moreover, each western township would be required to hold a referendum on whether to support the terms proposed by the commissioners.[162] The negotiating committee agreed to present the president's conditions to the committee of sixty at Redstone Old Fort.

Some attendees of the Redstone Old Fort conference vehemently opposed the peace terms. David Bradford took the most radical position, urging the assembly to vote against them and create an independent government. "He proposed killing the first army that came against us, and supplying ourselves with arms and ammunition," William Findley remembered. "This harangue did not contain sufficient good sense to be relished, even by many of his admirers, though it excited their inflammation, and still more intimidated the Committee."[163] Husband—one of the leaders of the moderate faction—heatedly called Bradford "a mad man for giving the people such advice to oppose the Government" and advised the delegates "to accept the terms of the commissioners as the best they could do at that time, and after the government was reconciled with the western people, then to petition for the repeal of such laws as they thought wrong."[164] But the results of the secret-ballot vote hardly constituted a mandate for peace. Delegates favoring submission to the president's conditions won, but only by a slim majority—thirty-four to twenty-three.[165]

The close vote convinced the federal commissioners that all hopes for a peaceful reconciliation were now gone. Unbeknownst to them, however, the Washington administration had already begun planning for war. Weeks earlier, after reading the commissioners' report on the Parkinson's Ferry conference, President Washington had called an emergency cabinet meeting, certain that peace negotiations would come to naught. With Hamilton and Randolph, Washington decided to mobilize militia units from the states of Pennsylvania, New Jersey, Maryland, and Virginia.[166] Militiamen from

Virginia and Maryland, they agreed, would meet at Cumberland, Maryland, and proceed west along Braddock's Road to western Pennsylvania. The other troops would gather at Carlisle, Pennsylvania, before marching to Pittsburgh via Forbes's Road.[167] Washington and his cabinet pledged to keep these plans secret until after the Redstone Old Fort meeting, so it would appear that the administration was making every attempt to resolve the situation without military intervention. When Washington received news of the vote at Redstone Old Fort, he promptly "ordered all militia units to march to their rendezvous."[168]

Meanwhile, Husband continued to advocate for moderation from his home in Bedford County and was dismayed by the disaffection that had spread throughout the county. In late August, approximately two hundred residents marched into the town of Bedford and erected a liberty pole near the courthouse.[169] Shortly thereafter, disgruntled farmers raised another pole in Brunerstown, just miles from Husband's residence at Berlin.[170] "There is a dale of People much Displeased with the [committee of sixty]," Robert Philson wrote on September 6, explaining why many locals had begun to reject moderation and take more drastic measures. They "are determined . . . to have every oppressive Law Repealed at all Events."[171] An alarmed Husband attempted to intervene, organizing a meeting at Berlin in mid-September.[172] He made it clear to the group that he was disappointed with the Washington administration, accusing the president of "ruling with an iron rod" and "imposing worse laws upon the people than Britain did or intended." But Husband also urged the audience to seek redress through constitutional means. "The People," he reminded the assembly, had every "right to petition in a vigorous manner." Following Husband's speech, Philson asked the audience to sign a petition (perhaps written by Husband) demanding the repeal of the excise law and the creation of a convention to form a new state constitution for Pennsylvania.[173] This move was not radical enough for the militants in the audience, who, following the Berlin meeting, viewed Husband as "a friend to the excise law" and even considered tarring and feathering him.[174]

For the next month, Husband remained on his farm in the Glades, waiting for the arrival of Washington's army, not realizing that he was already a wanted man. In late September, revenue commissioner Tench Coxe had received depositions from collectors Philip Reagan and Benjamin Wells, both of whom identified Husband, along with Robert Philson and David Bradford, as principal leaders of the protest movement.[175] These depositions are no longer extant, and so the motivations of the authors are uncertain. Perhaps they believed that Husband's pamphlets had inspired westerners to protest against the federal government. Or maybe they reported that

Husband had committed sedition at the Parkinson's Ferry meeting. Whatever the reasons, Husband would soon find himself in a Philadelphia jail.

On October 19, the northern wing of the army, about seven thousand strong, reached Bedford, finding the town quiet.[176] That evening, thirty soldiers rode into Berlin, where they captured Philson and "the notorious Harmon Husband." The two men were escorted back to the Bedford jail with suspected rebels George Wisecarver and George Lucas.[177] Two days later, the prisoners learned that they would be immediately transported to Philadelphia to stand trial. Before departing on October 22, Husband hastily penned a letter to Emey, reassuring her that he would be well. "A prison seems the safest place for one of my age and profession," he wrote. "Make yourselves easy about me, for I am so rejoiced that at times, old as I am, I can scarcely keep from dancing and singing, for which I cannot account. All my wish is that you ... enjoy all the happiness you can with industry and frugality which are my favorite principles."[178] The prisoners arrived in Philadelphia on October 29; Husband would never return to his beloved western country.[179]

By early November, both wings of Washington's army had crossed over the Allegheny Mountains and taken positions throughout Fayette, Washington, Allegheny, and Westmoreland Counties.[180] Over the next several days, Hamilton, federal attorney William Rawle, and federal judge Richard Peters conducted preliminary investigations, rounding up witnesses and collecting testimony.[181] On the morning of November 13, cavalry soldiers conducted a dragnet operation in the four counties, arresting several hundred men, though in the end only seventeen of them would be transported to Philadelphia for trial.[182] On Christmas Day, after a month-long march through mud and snow, the weary prisoners entered the nation's capital and were paraded in front of twenty thousand spectators before joining Husband in jail.[183] From his residence, Washington watched the procession, no doubt relieved that the protest movement was over.[184]

Husband remained imprisoned for the next six months. According to legend, David Caldwell, the Presbyterian minister who had tried to broker a last-minute peace agreement before the Battle of Alamance, arrived in Philadelphia around the same time that Husband was imprisoned and received a petition from Husband's family and friends requesting a pardon for the former Quaker. Although the story claims that Caldwell secured Husband's release from captivity in May 1795 after convincing two North Carolina senators (Alexander Martin and Timothy Bloodworth) and the famous Philadelphia physician Benjamin Rush to support the petition, in reality, his release would not come until June and was not the result of the petition, if one ever existed.[185]

In May, federal attorney William Rawle attempted to indict Husband for treason, but the grand jury ruled that there was insufficient evidence to charge the prisoner with that crime.[186] Rawle did secure an indictment against Husband on the lesser charge of sedition for participating in the Parkinson's Ferry meeting, and on June 3, Husband and Robert Philson stood trial.[187] Witnesses testified that neither man had committed sedition at the Parkinson's Ferry conference, recalling that Husband advocated for peace and had urged delegates to use only constitutional methods to enact reform.[188] Even prosecution witnesses, though testifying that Husband had denounced the Washington administration, conceded that he preached against violence during and after the Parkinson's Ferry meeting. Based on those testimonies, the jury found the men innocent.[189]

Husband's acquittal proved to be his last victory over the "Horn of the Beast."[190] Released from custody, he began his journey back to Bedford County, but seven months in prison had weakened the seventy-year-old's health. Husband barely reached the outskirts of Philadelphia before collapsing from pneumonia. He was taken to a nearby tavern, where on June 18, 1795, he succumbed to the infection, the final casualty of the Whiskey Rebellion.[191] Husband's body was laid to rest in an unknown grave the next day.[192] His vision of the New Jerusalem would never become a reality.

Conclusion

Making Sense of Husband's World

> It will be readily granted, that the task of an Historian is a difficult one, and that because of its being almost impossible to obtain good, and proper information ... [and] from an aptness in Men to inform us, not of the facts as they are in themselves ... but of the impressions made upon their minds, by the effects of civil and political conduct.... But however difficult the task, the advantage of having even an imperfect History is so great as to be a sufficient counterpoise, and determine them, who have it in their power, to inform their Country, fully as they can.
> —Herman Husband, *A Fan for Fanning*

THROUGHOUT HERMAN HUSBAND'S LIFETIME, new religious, economic, political, and intellectual forces contributed to the transformation of American society. Radical Protestantism emboldened many ordinary folk to question religious authorities, commercial capitalism sanctified values that promoted individual self-interest and economic liberty, republicanism encouraged a growing number of common people to assert that they had a right to govern themselves, and Enlightenment ideas convinced some citizens that they possessed the ability to create a better future. These forces, intensified by the American Revolution, challenged the hierarchical, corporate world into which Husband was born and inspired him to advocate for fundamental changes in politics, religion, and the social order itself.

For Husband, the Revolution provided an opportunity to forge a more democratic society, one centered around a new republic that championed economic equality among white men. Husband believed that the so-called idle rich—bankers, lawyers, speculators, and professionals—would inevitably use their economic power to exploit the laboring citizenry—farmers, artisans, and wage earners—to retain control over the political system. He argued that government needed to work on behalf of common people by instituting laws that protected the property of those who had acquired it through labor and industry, made land readily available to western settlers, and ensured that wealth would not be concentrated in the hands of a few. Only then, Husband asserted, could ordinary white Americans achieve economic independence, retain their political rights, and redeem the young nation from tyranny.

Husband's radicalism, however, had its limits. He remained committed to the preservation of patriarchy, insisting that God had ordained men to oversee their households, which in turn prepared them to serve in public office. As he explained, "A Man who will make a good Mechanick, or a good Farmer, who can rule his Family well, is also capable, with a few Years Practice ... to make a good Assembly-man to rule the State."[1] Women, he charged, lacked the ability to effectively run their households, let alone government, declaring that "though a Wiked Man does often Abuse this Supream Power Given to him over a Private family, yet a wiked Wooman Would Abuse it far Worse."[2] Husband's views also reflected and perpetuated the racism prevalent in the period. He assumed that African Americans were incapable of becoming civilized participants in government. And though a critic of slavery, his opposition to the institution stemmed more from its impact on white farmers and laborers than a concern for the enslaved. Nor did he advocate for the abolition of private property, instead believing that every man was entitled to the land that his labor produced.

While far from egalitarian, Husband's vision for the new nation challenged the status quo and reflected the aspirations of many common people who opposed the political and economic inequalities of eighteenth-century America. His was one of countless other voices advocating for the expansion of political rights, the reduction of wealth inequality, and the creation of a just government. Ordinary activists like William Manning, a white Massachusetts farmer who rejected the idea that only the elite were fit for office, and Judith Sargent Murray, an accomplished writer who insisted that women had the ability to achieve economic independence, were often at odds with one another, but all viewed the Revolution as an opportunity "to begin the world anew."[3] Husband's experience ultimately illuminates the varied forces and events that converged to inspire this upsurge of radical sentiment.

Religious Influences

One resource that Husband and other common people drew upon to understand and shape their changing society was Protestant Christianity. In recent decades, scholars have emphasized the central role that religion played in the everyday lives of eighteenth-century Americans.[4] Despite the rise of Enlightenment rationalism, these historians argue, the worldview of most ordinary folk remained heavily influenced by religion. Although not always devout, these men and women relied on Protestantism to relieve their anxieties during times of crisis, maintain a sense of community, and explain the world. "Religion was that aspect of the culture that gave the highest level of meaning, order, and value to people's experience," Gordon S. Wood explains. "Indeed, for many of them religious belief made possible their social experience."[5] The vast majority of eighteenth-century Americans also continued to find inspiration in the Bible. "Its stories, images, and lessons supplied a common frame of reference," writes Marjoleine Kars. "It explained the present and gave clues to the future, suggesting the possibility of a better world."[6]

This religious vitality was reinforced and intensified by the Great Awakening. Most scholars agree that this evangelical movement disrupted "the staid world of religious hierarchy."[7] In part a response to Enlightenment secularism, the growth of consumerism, and increased economic inequality, the Great Awakening helped its followers make sense of the changes in their world and engendered within them an intense desire for spiritual independence. Believing in the power of the spirit within to achieve salvation, many evangelicals began to question church authorities and rely on their own judgment in religious matters. "The revivalists may not have been deliberate social levellers, but their words and actions had the effect of emphasizing individual values over hierarchical ones," Patricia U. Bonomi observes. "They insisted that there were choices, and that the individual was free to make them."[8] The evangelical message that "all stood equal before the cross of Christ" also inadvertently threatened to erode the racial, gender, and economic status quos.[9] According to Thomas S. Kidd, "Radical evangelicals ... opened up unprecedented, if ultimately limited, opportunities for African Americans, Native Americans, women, the uneducated, and the poor to assert individual religious, and even social authority."[10]

Husband came of age during this time of religious fervor and revival. As a teenager, he was naturally drawn to the Great Awakening, which allowed him to rebel against his Anglican upbringing and find his own meaning in life. In particular, the evangelical doctrine that any person could know God through the spirit within appealed to Husband, reassuring him that he would someday experience the New Birth and that he could trust his own decisions when seeking religious guidance. This faith ultimately convinced Husband that individual conscience trumped church authority. "The infallible Word of God is in the Heart of Man," he remarked, "and every Decree of Men ... is to be tried by this Evidence of God in the Conscience, and if it will not answer

Conclusion

thereunto, it is false and antichristian."[11] Like other converts, Husband had begun to embrace a new "defiant individualism" that—for the time being—confronted the tradition of hierarchy and deference in church affairs.[12]

The Great Awakening also sparked Husband's lifelong interest in millennialism. For many evangelical Protestants, the revivals of the 1730s and 1740s signaled the possible beginning of the Second Coming of Christ. Jonathan Edwards proclaimed in 1743: "'Tis not unlikely that this work of the God's Spirit ... is the dawning, or at least a prelude, of that glorious work of God, so often told in Scripture, which is the progress and issue of it, shall renew the world of mankind."[13] Revivalists like Edwards, influenced by the Enlightenment's belief in human progress, adhered to postmillennialism. Through prayer, preaching, and missionary work, they insisted, evangelicals would pave the way for Jesus Christ's return by spreading Christianity throughout the world and initiating a thousand-year period of justice and peace.[14] These men and women, however, were not yet political revolutionaries. As Ruth H. Bloch explains, "New Light millennialism during the Great Awakening did not contain a critique of the British government or any institutional social or political reforms. It invested its hopes for the world first and foremost in widespread spiritual regeneration."[15]

Along with the Great Awakening, postmillennialism intensified Husband's faith in the efficacy of human agency. Its "emphasis on the redemptive possibilities of human behavior" convinced him that all men—when guided by the spirit within—should play an active role in promoting the "Advancement of Christ's Church."[16] He believed that Christians had to take immediate action to reclaim their God-given right to act according to their consciences in religious matters from false churches claiming authority over them, and that only then could they restore the original "Apostolick Christian Church" and usher in the millennium.[17] "The Gospel Power is to free from all Powers but Christ himself in our own Hearts," he proclaimed. "Christ has purchased your Freedom with a Price, and you are no more to be the Servants of Men.... Stand fast in the Liberty wherewith he has made you free."[18] While critical of the Anglican Church, Husband's quest to redeem the world from spiritual tyranny did not at first translate into a call for political change. He and other evangelicals remained confident that the millennium would occur after Christians embraced the spirit within and reformed themselves. That stance would change during the 1760s.

Political Influences

Most historians agree that eighteenth-century Anglo-American political thought was heavily influenced by a fringe group of British writers known as the radical Whigs.[19] Drawing on classical republicanism and English republican theories from the previous century, these men—like most British political thinkers at the time—championed natural rights, social contract theory, and England's balanced constitution. However, while upholding such mainstream constitutional beliefs, radical Whigs remained unconvinced that liberty would continue to flourish, fearing that English institutions had again become morally corrupt. Power-hungry politicians and "popish Anglican bishops," they repeatedly warned, were conspiring together to undermine England's mixed constitution and enslave the populace.[20] The people thus had to remain vigilant to protect their political and religious freedoms. Ultimately, radical Whigs believed that government "could be, and reasonably should be, dismissed—overthrown—if it attempted to exceed its proper jurisdiction."[21]

Although making little headway in England, radical Whig ideology enjoyed widespread support among American colonists, especially by the 1760s. "Nowhere was its impact greater than in America," writes David Lefer. "Almost everything Americans learned about republicanism and the Whig tradition came from this body of writing, and in the years leading up to the American Revolution, it taught them to mistrust practically every action taken by the British government."[22] Such was the case in 1765, when the British Parliament enacted the Stamp Act, which many colonists perceived as a threat to their liberties as Englishmen and resisted by staging protests and boycotting British goods.

The Stamp Act crisis of 1765 came at a pivotal time in Husband's life. The previous year, his expulsion from the Quaker church had led him to conclude that the "best reformed society" had now fallen victim to spiritual tyranny.[23] The thirst for power, he bemoaned, had overtaken Quaker leadership, causing them to deny followers the natural right to use their consciences in religious matters. Convinced that all denominations had become morally bankrupt, Husband began to search for a new agent of reform that would help usher in the millennium.

It was in this context that Husband was exposed to the radical Whig ideology of Stamp Act protestors. In several ways, his religious convictions—shaped decades earlier by the Great Awakening—inclined him to embrace this political ideology. He already believed that men had the ability and God-given right to make decisions and act on them, felt that it was morally appropriate to resist authorities who abused their power, and viewed history as a constant battle between God (liberty) and the forces of Satan (tyranny). Husband's negative encounters with civil and religious officials in the North Carolina backcountry further made him receptive to radical Whig ideology, convincing the former Quaker that corrupt politicians sought to subjugate the region's inhabitants. These and other reasons left him confident that Stamp Act demonstrators were "Generally Inspired by the Same Spirit that we Relegeous Professors Called Christ" and caused him to become a proponent of radical Whig political thought.[24]

This development radically changed Husband's worldview. He no longer believed politics to be the "Province of Kings, Nobles, Learned Men, [and] Lawyers," and encouraged other Christians to do the same.[25] For generations, he now argued, Christians had been blind to the fact that civil and religious authorities often worked with one another to oppress them, and it was imperative that they begin to participate in the political sphere. "One reason why we have so few men who concern themselves properly in maintaining our rights, is a very capital error that prevails among most dissenting sects, that this [political activism] is a business that belongs to the [secular] world," he explained in 1770. "We lose our liberty by not asserting it properly."[26] Husband's embrace of political advocacy forced him to reevaluate his interpretation of biblical prophecy and view civil government—instead of organized religion—as the agent of reform.[27] "Outward Civill Government was as much the object and design of God and the authors who wrote the History of the Scriptures as the outside walls and roof of a house is the Object and Concern of the Master Builder," he insisted. "The Right Government of Passions by the Grace of God in Man's heart is originally the beginning of this kingdom of God."[28] He now believed that through political engagement, Christians could eradicate civil and religious oppression, create a just government, and bring about the millennium.

Husband was not alone in his convergence of radical Whig ideology and radical Protestantism. Mark A. Noll and other historians have discovered that these combined influences inspired a growing number of Americans in the 1760s and 1770s to engage in political activism and begin to question British authority.[29] "In the crisis atmosphere of the Revolution, the Whig struggle to preserve natural rights and the Christian struggle to protect God-given privileges often became the same thing," Noll explains. "Indeed, so deep was the mutual compatibility of ... Christianity and Whig ideology that over the course of the Revolutionary period it became increasingly difficult to discern where one left off and the other began."[30] The confluence of these two modes of thought helped to unite evangelicals, deists, and rationalists in the struggle against what they believed to be a corrupt British Parliament and Anglican Church conspiring to enslave them. Like Husband, many of them would embrace American independence, confident that this course of action would free them from civil and ecclesiastical oppression.

Economic Influences

Husband and his fellow North Carolina Regulators were part of a wave of agrarian protest movements that occurred before the American Revolution.

New Jersey settlers united throughout the 1740s and 1750s in opposition to proprietors' attempts to raise quitrents and evict squatters and delinquent tenants from their estates. In New York's Hudson Valley, small farmers revolted against the region's manor lords, demanding greater access to land ownership. During the 1760s, settlers from South Carolina launched a crusade to reform their colony's legal and land-tenure systems. Even as late as the early 1770s, farmers in the future state of Vermont confronted "speculators claiming title to the area through grants from New York authorities."[31]

These agrarian insurgents shared a number of beliefs that shaped their views on what an independent nation should be. Above all, they viewed land ownership as key to achieving economic autonomy. "When eighteenth-century Americans talked about independence, they invariably meant land ownership," Terry Bouton explains. "Land owners were thought to have been liberated from much of the dependency that characterized Europe, where landless tenants and serfs served landlords who commanded them and took a share of their crop as rent."[32] By midcentury, a growing number of colonists, including those living in the backcountry, found it more difficult to acquire land, leaving settlers frustrated and without resources. "Life on the frontier, where people had little capital, limited access to markets, often marginal land, and frequently poor health, was no Turnerian paradise," writes Gary B. Nash. "Even in the most fertile and commercially connected regions, such as Philadelphia's hinterland, the trend . . . was toward increasing landlessness, accelerating transiency, and growing rates of poverty."[33] Consequently, yeomen, tenants, and squatters remained on guard against laws that prevented them from gaining access to land, which would allow them to avoid a life of dependency.[34]

These protestors also drew upon the labor theory of value to counter absentee speculators' claims to the land. Influenced by Christianity and Lockean liberalism, they maintained that the labor they had performed in improving their property granted them rightful possession, an argument colonists had previously employed to justify the dispossession of Native American lands. "The Improvement," one New Jersey farmer explained in 1746, "of any part of [the earth] lying vacant, which is thereupon distinguished from the great common of Nature, and made the property of that Man, who bestowed his labour on it."[35] Some protestors went one step further, proclaiming that no man should possess more land than he could improve via his and his dependents' labor. As they saw it, undeveloped land on the estates of large proprietors was fair game for those individuals willing to make the effort to improve it.[36]

Moreover, agrarian agitators often identified as being members of the industrious community. Shared experiences, interests, and goals led many of them to conclude that they were different from men who profited from the labor of others. For them, white society was divided into two completing groups: the laboring many and the unworking few. The latter, they charged, used their wealth and political connections to manipulate the law to monopolize land and enslave the former. "Law has been ... used as a tool ... to cheat us out of the country, we have made vastly valuable by labour and expence of our fortunes," a New Hampshire farmer complained about absentee speculators in 1772. "Artful, wicked men ... seek our ruin ... to enrich themselves."[37] Protestors were not opposed to wealth per se but to the ways in which speculators, proprietors, and other moneyed men amassed their fortunes: by denying small producers the fruits of their labor.[38]

This set of beliefs influenced how yeomen, tenants, and squatters alike envisioned the proper role of government in society. They argued that state institutions had to work on behalf of the laboring many by protecting their property rights and making it easier for them to acquire land. Central to that goal was legislation that provided farmers with low interest loans, endorsed progressive taxation, favored settlers over speculators, and controlled the price of land. These laws would also help to curb what was, in their eyes, the greatest obstacle to land ownership: the concentration of property and—by extension—political power in the hands of the idle few. Most agrarians, however, stopped short of calling for the redistribution of land. They believed in the sanctity of private property and only sought to level the playing field by reducing wealth inequality in white society.[39]

It was within this context that Husband further embraced the North Carolina Regulation and, later, the American Revolution. Despite his affluence, he sympathized with agrarian protestors, viewing himself as a common farmer and member of the industrious community, a man who simply wanted to own land and enjoy the fruits of his labor. He also idealized the yeomanry as the backbone of a just and moral society. Well-versed in classical republicanism, Husband maintained that farmers with sufficient property acquired through the sweat of their own brows were best fit to participate in the political sphere. Economically independent, these men had the freedom to act according to their own consciences and would elect candidates who—like themselves—were unwilling to "sacrifice the true Interests of their Country to Avarice or Ambition."[40] This would allow them to serve as the voice of the common people and the protectors of liberty.

Like other agrarian agitators, Husband's faith in the common farmer brought him at odds with the unworking few, who he insisted betrayed both the Bible and the English constitution by depriving laborers of their natural right to own property and achieve economic autonomy. "The art of robbing and living on the labor of other men, are their talents and study," Husband argued. "This robbery ... of man's labor is ... provoking to God (and against which every honest enlightened mind will testify the greatest indignation)."[41] Through regressive taxes, high court fees, and pro-creditor laws, lawyers, merchants, and other moneyed men had rigged the political system in their favor in order to take away the property of small freeholders, while absentee speculators denied tenants and squatters the opportunity to acquire lands that they had worked to improve. "Who can justify," Husband complained in 1770, "the Conduct of any Government who have countenanced and encouraged so many Thousands of poor Families to bestow their All, and the Labour of many Years, to improve a Piece of waste Land, with full Expectation of a Title, to deny them Protection from being robbed of it all by a few roguish Individuals, who never bestowed a Farthing thereon."[42]

Embracing republicanism and liberalism, Husband envisioned the creation of a government that promoted the common good by securing the property rights of the laboring many. Like other agrarian reformers, Husband invoked the labor theory of value to defend farmers' claims to land and championed yeomen as the caretakers of liberty. He also believed that the accumulation of wealth and political power among the idle rich prevented ordinary white men from obtaining land and becoming economically independent. "I need not inform you, that a Majority of our Assembly is composed of Lawyers, Clerks, and others in Connection with them," Husband bemoaned. "We have not the least Reason to expect the Good of the Farmer, and consequently of the Community, will be consulted." To forge a just government, he endorsed laws that favored debtors, taxed residents based on "the profits of each man's estate," prohibited individuals from holding "unreasonable Quantities of waste Lands," and required absentee speculators to compensate squatters.[43] Such legislation would ultimately promote the widespread ownership of land by reducing wealth inequality and diminishing the political power of the idle few. While helping to lead Husband to embrace the North Carolina Regulation, these beliefs later convinced the former Quaker that the economic policies of the British Parliament threatened to impoverish the common farmer and pushed him to join the patriot cause. By 1776, he had concluded that by breaking free from England, Americans could establish a republic that protected the economic and—by extension—political rights of laboring white men.

Dashed Expectations

Throughout his life, Herman Husband would be continuously disappointed in the movements in which he placed his faith. The American Revolution was no different, and he was not alone in his dissatisfaction with the direction of the new republic. From Georgia to New Hampshire, countless farmers confronted high taxes, rising inflation, and the scarcity of money during the 1780s, preventing them from paying their debts, acquiring land, and supporting their families. "What are the present state of facts as they represent the yeomanry of this Commonwealth," a Massachusetts farmer complained in 1786. "Our taxes are so high, together with calls of a private nature, that our stock and cattle are greatly diminished.... The greater part then of those who gloriously supported our independence now find their moveables vanishing like empty shades, their lands sinking under their feet."[44] These disillusioned men and women blamed state leaders for their predicament and sought to reclaim—by force if necessary—what they believed the American Revolution had promised: the creation of a government that worked to preserve the economic and political independence of the common folk.[45]

It was this "radicalism of disappointment" that fueled Husband following the Revolution.[46] Even before the ratification of the U.S. Constitution in 1788, he had expressed concerns about the direction of the fledgling nation. Husband particularly viewed the "mercantile Part of Society" with suspicion, believing that their fiscal policies betrayed the American Revolution by promoting wealth inequality in white society.[47] Their endorsement of laws that favored creditors and speculators, required citizens to pay their debts and taxes in specie, and sanctioned private corporations such as the Bank of North America threatened to channel most of the nation's wealth and political power to the unworking few. Compared to yeomen and other members of the laboring community, Husband found such men, whose goal was to enrich themselves at the expense of the common people and the health of the republic, without virtue.

The economic plight of ordinary Americans during the 1780s hardened Husband's belief that corrupt leaders conspired to "create a nobility entailing misery and slavery on the bulk of the community."[48] Indeed, for a growing number of Americans, independence had not translated into economic prosperity. Unemployment and poverty steadily rose in many cities, causing the gap between rich and poor to widen. In Philadelphia, for instance, the richest 10 percent of the population held nearly 44 percent of the wealth in 1780. By 1795, that number had increased to 82 percent.[49] The situation was similarly bleak in the countryside. There, tenancy and landlessness continued to climb, even as unsettled lands in the frontier became—at least in theory—available to farmers. Where Husband lived in western Pennsylvania, "the percentage of rural landholders declined by 59 percent" between 1780 and 1795, "while absentee-owners from the East greatly enhanced their holdings."[50] This led him to conclude that large speculators and other moneyed men had begun to succeed in their quest to monopolize economic and political power.

However, it was not until the U.S. Constitution was ratified in 1788 that Husband completely lost faith in the new nation. The document's creation of large congressional districts particularly disgusted Husband, who feared that this method of election would prevent the "majority of the people [from having] any share or choice of their own," thereby allowing corrupt men to dominate the political arena and pass laws that benefited the few.[51] He saw evidence of such collusion in Congress's passage of the Funding Act in 1790, which he called an unjust law devised to further enrich speculators and creditors. Convinced that the nation's leaders had replanted the seed of tyranny and oppression, he complained, "It is clear to be seen that . . . the sole objects contemplated by the framers of the new constitution [are] national pomp and glory . . . which will sink a nation into want and misery as well as private families."[52]

Disenchanted, Husband turned to the one resource that had always guided him in times of crisis: the Bible. Its contents—which Husband called "our History"—reassured him.[53] "According to the scriptures," he proclaimed, the "divine spirit of God is to continue among men until it bruises the serpent's head, and until it finally prevails over the beast, the false prophet, and the great whore, all [of] which was to come to pass."[54] Still, Husband now believed that the New Jerusalem, as described in Ezekiel and promised in Revelation, would begin not in the thirteen states, as he once envisioned, but in "the everlasting Western hills, and mountainous land of the Columbian continent." There, settlers would carry out God's plan to perfect a government that worked on behalf of the laboring many and usher in the millennium. "The signs of this approaching summer [the millennium] appear as evident, as the signs of the common natural summer do, by the budding forth of the trees," he wrote in 1789. "God has set before us an open door, which no man shall ever shut any more."[55]

Other Americans also continued to rely on biblical scripture and prophecy to understand their changing world and relieve their anxieties. This was particularly true in the backcountry, where many farmers, struggling to achieve economic independence, felt betrayed by the outcomes of the Revolution. The religious rhetoric of Husband and other agrarian reformers appealed to these disappointed westerners, reminding them that they were God's chosen people and spurring them to defend their economic and political rights. As several historians have noted, agrarian unrest and radical Protestantism remained tightly linked during the 1780s and 1790s.[56] "Evangelicals encouraged men and women to follow their inner impulses, which led seekers concerned over the land conflict to a Christ who favored the settlers' struggle," Alan Taylor explains. "Visionary religion offered the resistance a style, a stock of symbols and arguments, borrowed and adapted by agrarians to define and

Conclusion

sustain their cause."[57] For many western Pennsylvanians, Husband was not "the crazy man of Bedford"—as the political elite dubbed him—but a spiritual leader whose words, at least in part, likely inspired them to support the Whiskey Rebellion.[58]

Husband's critics included members of the political establishment, who often made him the butt of their jokes, as well as other protestors. In the Whiskey Rebellion, as in the North Carolina Regulation, his refusal to resort to extralegal tactics to obtain change angered more radical participants. Like other agrarian and urban reformers, disgruntled western Pennsylvanians were divided over how far citizens in the new republic should go to regulate unresponsive governments.[59] For some, the Revolution had legitimized their right to use direct action protest and—if necessary—violence to oppose policies that they viewed as oppressive. Others, like Husband, warned that these forms of resistance were destined to fail and championed working within the existing political system. Husband urged his compatriots to seek redress at the ballot box, pointing out that their numerical supremacy ensured them victory. "This power to overcome [tyranny] has always been lodged in the body of the people, on account of their being ten to one, perhaps a hundred to one, more numerous than their governors," he explained. "A more peaceable way [to make government more responsive to ordinary folk] has taken place, to try our strength by a majority of voices, and elect all our rulers by the voice of the people."[60] Husband's call for moderation angered militant whiskey rebels but did not change federal officials' opinion that he was a rabble-rouser who needed to be brought to justice.

The Whiskey Rebellion and other agrarian protest movements were ultimately a reflection of small producers' disillusionment with the direction of commercial capitalism during the late eighteenth century.[61] Most historians agree that the Revolution hastened the advance of capitalism throughout the United States, a transition that was often painful for small producers. "The war experience greatly expanded the horizons of the merchant class, enabling them to trade in areas previously restricted by the British Navigation Acts," Eric Foner observes. "The need to supply the army and obtain assistance from France, the issuance of paper currency, and the creation of a national debt to finance the struggle stimulated the emergence of large-scale business ventures and the development of a national business class."[62] By 1790, the U.S. Congress and state governments had further promoted capitalist development by supporting a national banking system, encouraging freer trade, and endorsing market exchanges.

Many farmers, artisans, and other small producers were not opposed to all aspects of the nascent capitalist market economy. They often embraced free trade and the expansion of markets, confident that both would enable them to sell and purchase more goods, acquire additional land, and support their families. Husband shared this belief, remarking in 1783 that "life, liberty, property *and* freedom of trade are our inheritance, and no one, with impunity, can molest us in the enjoyment of them."[63] Husband and other farmers, however, criticized the emergence of an economic system in which moneyed men owned the means of production and forced ordinary people to sell their labor for wages. In their eyes, this was nothing short of slavery. Agrarian reformers like Husband ultimately sought not to completely eradicate capitalism but to sustain it "at a simple stage of development where households bought and sold the fruits of their labor without having to sell their labor itself."[64] Central to that goal was the creation of a government that allowed non-elite white men to retain control over the market and continue to reap the majority of its benefits.[65]

Husband's vision of a "new government of liberty" would never come to pass.[66] While common white men secured the right to participate in the political arena, their call for reducing economic inequality came to naught. In the decades following Husband's death, the federal and state governments continued down the path first paved by Alexander Hamilton and other founding fathers, implementing policies that channeled wealth to a burgeoning capitalist elite in the hopes of spurring economic development and pushing the economic populism championed by Husband and other like-minded revolutionaries to the margins of mainstream political discourse.[67] Nonetheless, opposition to disparities in wealth would continue to appear in American society throughout the nineteenth century and beyond. As rural and urban laborers found it increasingly difficult to maintain control over the means of production and achieve economic autonomy, workers of all races and genders protested against wealth inequality and demanded that the government protect the fruits of their labor.[68] Perhaps in their insistence that the health of the republic and democracy itself rested on this principle lies the most enduring legacy of Husband's critique of his world.

Notes

Abbreviations

AQA	Herman Husband, "Address to the Quakers in Assembly," in Christopher Marshall Papers, Historical Society of Pennsylvania
CIR	Henderson, "Hermon Husband's Continuation of the Impartial Relation"
CRNC	Saunders, *Colonial Records of North Carolina*
CWT	Powell, *Correspondence of William Tryon*
DAC	Husband, *Dialogue between an Assembly-Man and a Convention-Man*
FF	Husband, *Fan for Fanning*
IR	Husband, *Impartial Relation*
NGL	Ekirch, "'A New Government of Liberty'"
PA	*Pennsylvania Archives*
PAP	Husband, *Proposals to Amend and Perfect the Policy of the Government of the United States of America*
RNC	Powell, Huhta, and Farnham, *Regulators in North Carolina*
SBH	Husband, *Sermon to the Bucks and Hinds of America*
SPNT	Husband, *Second Part of the Naked Truth*
SRR	Husband, *Some Remarks on Religion*
UM	Herman Husband, Unpublished Manuscript, box 2, folder 4, Papers of the John Irwin Scull Family, Heinz History Center

Prologue

1. During his lifetime, Husband was referred to by many names in the press and by his contemporaries, most frequently as Harmon Husbands, Harmon Husband, Hermon Husbands, and Harman Husbands. Husband often signed his name as either Harmon Husband or Hermon Husband. I have elected to refer to him by the name that modern readers are familiar with, Herman Husband.

2. AQA.

3. *SBH*, 15.

4. Thomas Paine, "Common Sense," in Foner, *Complete Writings of Thomas Paine*, 1:45; Bailyn, *Ideological Origins of the American Revolution*, 230.

5. For a sample of scholarship on Africans Americans during the long American Revolution, see Gilbert, *Black Patriots and Loyalists*; Egerton, *Death or Liberty*; Sweet, *Bodies Politic*; Schama, *Rough Crossings*; Nash, *Forgotten Fifth*; Berlin, *Many Thousands Gone*; Frey, *Water from the Rock*; Davis, *Problem of Slavery in the Age of Revolution*; and Quarles, *Negro in the American Revolution*.

6. John Adams to Abigail Adams, April 14, 1776, in Hogan and Taylor, *My Dearest Friend*, 112.

7. For a sample of scholarship on women during the long American Revolution, see McMahon, *Mere Equality*; Zagarri, *Revolutionary Backlash*; Berkin, *Revolutionary Mothers*; Young, *Masquerade*; Gundersen, *To Be Useful*; Ulrich, *Midwife's Tale*; Kerber, *Women of the Republic*; and Norton, *Liberty's Daughters*.

8. For a sample of scholarship on common peoples' critique of economic inequality during the long American Revolution, see Fatovic, *America's Founding and the Struggle over Economic Inequality*; Cotlar, *Tom Paine's America*; Young, Nash, and Raphael, *Revolutionary Founders*; Holton, *Unruly Americans*; Bouton, *Taming Democracy*; Thompson, *Politics of Inequality*; Nash, *Unknown American Revolution*; and Richards, *Shays's Rebellion*.

ONE. "Like the Sun Breaking Out of Darkness"

1. William Husband was probably born sometime between 1650 and 1655. See Hoppin, *Washington Ancestry*, 2:282.

2. Hinke, "Report of the Journey of Francis Louis Michel," 16 (quotation); Middleton, *Tobacco Coast*, 3–37.

3. Hoppin, *Washington Ancestry*, 2:282.

4. Carr, Menard, and Walsh, *Robert Cole's World*, 15.

5. For examples, see Hall, *Narratives of Early Maryland*.

6. Alsop, *Character of the Province of Maryland*, 32–33, 56. For the most recent scholarship on indentured servitude in colonial America, see Wareing, *Indentured Migration and the Servant Trade from London to America*; Lawson, *Servants and Servitude in Colonial America*; Klepp and Smith, *Infortunate*; Morgan, *Slavery and Servitude in Colonial North America*; and Salinger, "To Serve Well and Faithfully."

7. Horn, "Servant Emigration to the Chesapeake in the Seventeenth Century," 75–76; Carr, "From Servant to Freeholder," 288.

8. Walsh and Menard, "Death in the Chesapeake"; Rutman and Rutman, "'Of Agues and Fevers'"; Earle, "Environment, Disease, and Mortality in Early Virginia"; Walsh, "'Till Death Us Do Part.'"

9. Miller, "Archaeological Perspective on the Evolution of Diet in the Colonial Chesapeake."

10. Horn, *Adapting to a New World*, 126.

11. Thomas Notley, St. Mary's City Men's Career Files, Abstract File no. 3075, MSA SC 5094; John Griggs, St. Mary's City Men's Career Files, Abstract File no. 1681, MSA SC 5094; William Husband, February 3, 1673, 589, reel SR 7358 Patents 17, 1670–75, Land Office (Patent Record), all Maryland State Archives.

12. Horn, *Adapting to a New World*, 10.

13. Carr, Menard, and Walsh, *Robert Cole's World*, 13. For additional information on colonial Maryland's tobacco trade and economy, see Russo and Russo, *Planting an Empire*; Bradburn and Coombs, *Early Modern Virginia*; Hahn, *Making Tobacco Bright*; Walsh, *Motive of Honor, Pleasure, and Profit*; Main, *Tobacco Colony*; Menard, "Economy and Society in Early Colonial Maryland"; Clemens, *Atlantic Economy and Colonial Maryland's Eastern Shore*; and Main, "Maryland and the Chesapeake Economy."

14. Horn, *Adapting to a New World*, 142.

15. Ibid.; brackets in original.

16. According to historian Lois Green Carr, 70 to 80 percent of Europeans who arrived in Maryland during the seventeenth century were initially indentured servants. See Carr, "From Servant to Freeholder," 289. For discussions on indentured servants in colonial Maryland, see Snyder, "'To Seeke for Justice'"; Carr, "From Servant to Freeholder"; Walsh, "Servitude and Opportunity in Charles County"; Carr, "Emigration and the Standard of Living"; and Menard, "From Servant to Freeholder."

17. Cronon, *Changes in the Land*, 48–52.

18. Boles, *South through Time*, 1:29.

19. For an excellent discussion on tobacco cultivation in seventeenth-century Maryland, see Carr, Menard, and Walsh, *Robert Cole's World*, 55–75.

20. Carr, "Emigration and the Standard of Living," 276–82; Carr, "From Servant to Freeholder," 289, 293, 295.

21. Carr, "From Servant to Freeholder," 289.

22. Menard, "From Servant to Freeholder," 50. See also Smith, "Indentured Servant and Land Speculation in Seventeenth-Century Maryland."

23. William Husband, February 3, 1673, 589, reel SR 7358 Patents 17, 1670–75, Land Office (Patent Record), Maryland State Archives.

24. Jonas, "Wages in Early Colonial Maryland"; Menard, "From Servant to Freeholder," 51.

25. Menard, "From Servant to Freeholder," 52; Carr, "From Servant to Freeholder," 297.

26. Menard, "Immigrants and their Increase."

27. Carr, Menard, and Walsh, *Robert Cole's World*, 13.

28. According to Lois Green Carr, "Around 1700, at least two thirds of heads of households owned freehold land." See Carr, "Emigration and the Standard of Living," 283.

29. William Beein (Bowen), St. Mary's City Men's Career Files, Abstract File no. 338, MSA SC 5094; Mary Beein (Bowen), St. Mary's City Men's Career Files, Abstract File no. 116, MSA SC 5094; William Husbands, St. Mary's City Men's Career Files, Abstract File no. 2186, MSA SC 5094, all Maryland State Archives; Opfer, "William Husband of Cecil County," 421.

30. William Bowin (Bowen), 1686, St. Mary's, liber 9, folios 27–29, Prerogative Court (Inventories and Accounts), Maryland State Archives; Cotton, "Notes from the Early Records of Maryland"; Hoppin, *Washington Ancestry*, 2:283. For more on women in seventeenth-century Maryland and Virginia, see Carr and Walsh, "Planter's Wife"; Brown, *Good Wives, Nasty Wenches, and Anxious Patriarchs*; Meyers, "Civic Lives of White Women in Seventeenth-Century Maryland"; and Sturtz, *Within Her Power*.

31. Mitchell, "Charles County, Maryland, Land Records," 11.

32. Hoppin, *Washington Ancestry*, 2:283.

33. Reavis, "The Maryland Gentry and Social Mobility," 424–26; Carr, "Emigration and the Standard of Living," 283; Walsh, "Servitude and Opportunity in Charles County," 122–26.

34. William Husbands, St. Mary's City Men's Career Files, Abstract File no. 2186, MSA SC 5094, Maryland State Archives; Hoppin, *Washington Ancestry*, 2:283–85.

35. Opfer, "William Husband of Cecil County," 421.

36. Carr, "Emigration and the Standard of Living," 283; Menard, "From Servant to Freeholder," 57–58.

37. Plowden, *Description of the Province of New Albion*, 16.

38. For more on Cecil County history, see Johnston, *History of Cecil County*; Miller, *Cecil County*; Wennersten, *Maryland's Eastern Shore*; and Blumgart, *At the Head of the Bay*.

39. Brown, *Abstracts of Cecil County, Maryland, Land Records, 1673–1751*, 117; Hoppin, *Washington Ancestry*, 2:286–88.

40. See William Husband Sr.'s inventory in Hoppin, *Washington Ancestry*, 2:290–92.

41. His children were John, a daughter (name unknown), James, William, and Thomas. Husband's son John and daughter predeceased him. See ibid., 2:292–95.

42. Ibid., 2:291.

43. For more on the rise of slavery in the Chesapeake, see Morgan, *American Slavery, American Freedom*; Menard, "From Servants to Slaves"; Clemens, *Atlantic Economy and Colonial Maryland's Eastern Shore*, 58–63; Main, *Tobacco Colony*, 97–139; Kulikoff, *Tobacco and Slaves*, 54–63; Greene, *Pursuits of Happiness*; Brown, *Good Wives, Nasty Wenches, and Anxious Patriarchs*; Morgan, *Slave Counterpoint*; Berlin, *Many Thousands Gone*; Menard, *Migrants, Servants, and Slaves*; Parent, *Foul Means*; Coombs, "Phases of Conversion"; and Coombs, "Beyond the 'Origins Debate.'"

44. Greene, *Pursuits of Happiness*, 178–79.

45. Carr, Menard, and Walsh, *Robert Cole's World*, 161.

46. For more on the declining opportunities of indentured servants and poor whites in colonial Maryland, see Menard, "From Servant to Freeholder," 57–64; Carr, "Emigration and the Standard of Living," 285–87; Walsh, "Servitude and Opportunity in Charles County," 118–28; Walsh, "The Development of Local Power Structures"; Carr and Menard, "Land, Labor, and Economies of Scale in Early Maryland"; and Carr, Menard, and Walsh, *Robert Cole's World*, 157–64.

47. William Jr. was born around 1697 in St. Mary's County. See Hoppin, *Washington Ancestry*, 2:293.

48. Husband Sr.'s estate was valued at £269, an amount higher than 84 percent of other farms in Maryland at the time. See ibid., 2:292; Land, "Planters of Colonial Maryland," 116; and Jones, "Herman Husband," 10.

49. Brown, *Abstracts of Cecil County, Maryland, Land Records, 1673–1751*, 116; Johnston, *History of Cecil County*, 189; Peden, *Early Anglican Church Records of Cecil County*, 4; Barnes, *Maryland Marriages*, 93; Peden and Peden, *Cecil County, Maryland, Marriage References*, 135.

50. Plummer, *Andrew and Mary (Husband) Dunbar of Octorara Hundred*, 2.

51. By the time of his death in 1767, William Jr. owned fifteen slaves. See William Husband, 1768, Cecil, liber 98, folios 131–36, Prerogative Court (Inventories and Accounts), Maryland State Archives; Brown, *Abstracts of Cecil County, Maryland, Land Records, 1673–1751*, 152, 187, 189, 510; and Brown, *Abstracts of Cecil County, Maryland, Land Records, 1734–1753*, 140, 167, 193, 232.

52. Clemens, *Atlantic Economy and Colonial Maryland's Eastern Shore*, 29–32, 168–205.

53. Blumgart, *At the Head of the Bay*, 49; Brown, *Abstracts of Cecil County, Maryland, Land Records, 1734–1753*, 48.

54. Harman Kankey (Kinkey), 1732, Cecil, liber 20, folios 653–55, Prerogative Court (Wills), Maryland State Archives; Brown, *Abstracts of Cecil County, Maryland, Land Records, 1673–1751*, 194–95.

55. Peden, *Inhabitants of Cecil County*, 15, 18, 19, 22.

56. Plummer, *Andrew and Mary (Husband) Dunbar of Octorara Hundred*, 1.

57. Since 1716, investors of the Principio Company, an iron-mining outfit in Cecil County, had seen their profits multiply. Perhaps inspired by the success of this operation, William Jr. decided to become part owner of the iron mine and -works in Baltimore County. See Jones, "Herman Husband," 51; William Husband, 1768, Cecil, liber 36, folios 282–84, Prerogative Court (Wills), Maryland State Archives; and "Joshua Husband," in *Biographical Record of Harford and Cecil Counties, Maryland*, 216. For more on the Principio Company and mining in colonial Maryland, see Heyl and Pearre, *Copper, Zinc, Lead, Iron, Cobalt, and Barite Deposits in the Piedmont Upland of Maryland*; Abbott, "Colonial Copper Mines"; Young, "Origins of the American Copper Industry"; Pearre, "Mining for Copper and Related Minerals in Maryland"; Diggins, "Principio"; and Nagy, "'Our Woods Are Full of Mine Hunters.'"

58. Plummer, *Andrew and Mary (Husband) Dunbar of Octorara Hundred*, 2; Hoppin, *Washington Ancestry*, 2:293. Although there is no evidence that William Jr. drank alcohol, given that the social mores of the day did not condemn its use, it is likely that he did. As the owner of a copper still, he certainly manufactured his own. See William Husband, 1768, Cecil, liber 98, folios 131–36, Prerogative Court (Inventories and Accounts), Maryland State Archives. For more on alcohol consumption and distilling in colonial America, see Salinger, *Taverns and Drinking in Early America*, and Meacham, *Every Home a Distillery*.

59. Burnard, *Creole Gentlemen*, 219.

60. Breen, "Horses and Gentlemen," 243. For more on entertainment and hospitality in the eighteenth-century Chesapeake, see Breslaw, "Chronicle as Satire"; Isaac, *Transformation of Virginia*, 118–19; Gorn, "'Gouge and Bite, Pull Hair and Scratch'"; Upton, *Holy Things and Profane*, 165–68; Brown, *Good Wives, Nasty Wenches, and Anxious Patriarchs*, 277–82; Fischer, *Albion's Seed*, 342–43, 360–62; Sommerville, *Tuesday Club of Annapolis*; and Struna, *People of Prowess*.

61. Peden, *Early Anglican Church Records of Cecil County*, 27. Herman Husband's siblings were Hannah (b. 1721), William (b. 1726), John (b. 1729), Thomas (b. 1731), a sister (b. 1732), Mary (b. 1734), Joseph (b. 1736), Catherine (b. 1738), Margery (b. 1741), Ann (b. 1745), and Sarah (b. 1748). See "Notes and Queries," 119.

62. *SRR*, 6–10, 18.

63. Fischer, *Albion's Seed*, 314–15. For more on childhood in colonial Virginia and Maryland, see Chudacoff, *Children at Play*, 19–38; Mintz, *Huck's Raft*, 32–52; Fischer, *Albion's Seed*, 311–20; Smith, *Inside the Great House*; Smith, "Autonomy and Affection"; Cable, *Little Darlings*, 29–58; and Morgan, *Virginians at Home*, 5–28.

64. Boyer, *Ship Passenger Lists*, 11; Peden, *Inhabitants of Cecil County*, 33.

65. Brown, *Abstracts of Cecil County, Maryland, Land Records, 1673–1751*, 116. For more on Augustine Herman, see Blumgart, *At the Head of the Bay*, 25–26; Kanskey, "Augustine Herman"; and Hall, *Narratives of Early Maryland*, 309–34.

66. *SRR*, 4.

67. Lazenby, *Herman Husband*, 4; Hoppin, *Washington Ancestry*, 2:286. For more on the Church of England and religion in colonial Maryland, see Carroll, "Maryland Quakers in the Seventeenth Century"; Carroll, "Eighteenth-Century Episcopalian Attack on Quaker and Methodist Manumission of Slaves"; Graham, "Churching the Unchurched"; Graham, "'Collapse of Equity'"; Voorst, *Anglican Clergy in Maryland*; Meyers, *Common Whores, Vertuous Women, and Loveing Wives*; and Coverdale, "'Flight on the Wings of Vanity.'"

68. As Husband complained about Anglican services in 1750, "It seem'd to me there was no true Worship in Spirit among them, he [the priest] deemed the best Fellow who first found the Place of the Book the Minister was in, and to answer him, and to know when to rise up and sit down." *SRR*, 4, 13; Isaac, *Transformation of Virginia*, 58–70, 120–21. Although evidence suggests that Herman's father viewed churchgoing mostly as an activity to display his status in the community, it is important to note that recent scholarship has begun to downplay the notion that most

Anglican gentlemen in the Chesapeake were irreligious. See Nelson, *Blessed Company*, and Winner, *Cheerful and Comfortable Faith*.

69. For more on Pietism and Theodorus Frelinghuysen, see Maze, *Theodorus Frelinghuysen's Evangelicalism*; Kidd, *Great Awakening*, 24–29; Lambert, *Inventing the "Great Awakening,"* 56–57; Longenecker, *Piety and Tolerance*; Balmer, *Perfect Babel of Confusion*, 103–16; and Tanis, *Dutch Calvinistic Pietism in the Middle Colonies*.

70. *SRR*, 4.

71. For more on dancing in eighteenth-century Virginia and Maryland, see Isaac, *Transformation of Virginia*, 80–87; Brown, *Good Wives, Nasty Wenches, and Anxious Patriarchs*, 277, 297, 298; and Fischer, *Albion's Seed*, 342–43.

72. *SRR*, 8–10.

73. For more on gambling in the eighteenth-century Chesapeake, see Breen, "Horses and Gentlemen," and Isaac, *Transformation of Virginia*, 118–19.

74. *SRR*, 4, 5, 8.

75. Hoffer, *Sensory Worlds in Early America*, 170.

76. Quoted in Lambert, *Inventing the "Great Awakening,"* 66.

77. Quoted in Hoffer, *Sensory Worlds in Early America*, 170.

78. For more on the Great Awakening in New England, see Winiarski, *Darkness Falls on the Land of Light*; Smith, *First Great Awakening*; Noll, *Rise of Evangelicalism*; Marsden, *Jonathan Edwards*; Conforti, *Jonathan Edwards, Religious Tradition, and American Culture*; Crawford, *Seasons of Grace*; Stout, *New England Soul*; and Tracy, *Jonathan Edwards, Pastor*.

79. Kidd, *Great Awakening*, 24.

80. Quoted in Sweet, *Revivalism in America*, 46.

81. Kidd, *Great Awakening*, 30–31. For more on Germans and Scots-Irish Presbyterians before and during the Great Awakening, see Stoeffler, *Continental Pietism and Early American Christianity*; Griffin, *People with No Name*; and Schmidt, *Holy Fairs*.

82. Lambert, *Inventing the "Great Awakening,"* 60.

83. For more on the Great Awakening in the middle colonies, see Kidd, *Great Awakening*; Smith, *First Great Awakening*; Noll, *Rise of Evangelicalism*; Ward, *Protestant Evangelical Awakening*, 241–73; Coalter, *Gilbert Tennent, Son of Thunder*; and Maxson, *Great Awakening in the Middle Colonies*.

84. Feist, "'A Stirring among the Dry Bones,'" 395.

85. Blumgart, *At the Head of the Bay*, 39–41; Miller, *Cecil County*, 23–24; Johnston, *History of Cecil County*, 152–54, 160–67, 275–76; Carroll, *Quakerism on the Eastern Shore*; Dunaway, *Scotch-Irish of Colonial Pennsylvania*, 50–53; McKenrich, "New Munster."

86. Perry, *Historical Collections Relating to the American Colonial Church*, 4:321.

87. Skaggs and Hartdagen, "Sinners and Saints."

88. Perry, *Historical Collections Relating to the American Colonial Church*, 4:296, 302–3, 310–11. See also Johnston, *History of Cecil County*, 218–22.

89. Leyburn, *Scotch-Irish*, 248–49; Wokeck, "Searching for Land."

90. These groups communicated regularly with Presbyterians in nearby Pennsylvania, many of whom had become more receptive to revivalism, especially after

evangelical pastor Samuel Blair—a graduate of revivalist William Tennent Sr.'s Log College seminary in Neshaminy, Pennsylvania—founded a seminary in Fagg's Manor in 1739. Kidd, *Great Awakening*, 31–32; Blumgart, *At the Head of the Bay*, 41; Miller, *Cecil County*, 23–24, 142–44; Johnston, *History of Cecil County*, 275–78; Barker, *Background of the Revolution in Maryland*, 16, 20; Jones, *History of the Rock Presbyterian Church in Cecil County*.

91. A carryover from Scotland, this practice was known as the holy fair. See Kidd, *Great Awakening*, 30–31; Lambert, *Inventing the "Great Awakening,"* 29–30; Blethen and Wood Jr., *From Ulster to Carolina*, 13, 36; and Schmidt, *Holy Fairs*.

92. Stout, *Divine Dramatist*, xvi. For other biographies of George Whitefield, see Kidd, *George Whitefield*, and Lambert, *"Pedlar in Divinity."*

93. Lambert, *Inventing the "Great Awakening,"* 93.

94. Quoted in Kidd, *Great Awakening*, 43.

95. Hoffer, *Sensory Worlds in Early America*, 171.

96. Kidd, *Great Awakening*, 43–50, 47 (quotation).

97. Johnston, *History of Cecil County*, 276.

98. *SRR*, 11–12.

99. Ibid.

100. Kidd, *Great Awakening*, 67; Lambert, *Inventing the "Great Awakening,"* 132.

101. Coalter, *Gilbert Tennent, Son of Thunder*, 64; Kidd, *Great Awakening*, 59–60.

102. Among other things, Tennent decried Old Side ministers who had not experienced the New Birth as "hypocritical Varlets"; "dead Dogs, that can't bark"; "moral Negroes"; "murderous Hypocrites"; and "Swarms of Locusts." See Kidd, *Great Awakening*, 60, and Tennent, *Danger of an Unconverted Ministry*.

103. Blumgart, *At the Head of the Bay*, 41–42; Feist, "'A Stirring among the Dry Bones,'" 394; Jones, "Herman Husband," 29; Johnston, *History of Cecil County*, 277–78; Miller, *Cecil County*, 142–44.

104. *SRR*, 13.

105. Jones, "Herman Husband," 25–26.

106. *SRR*, 12, 13–14.

107. Ibid., 14, 21, 22, 13.

108. Bloch, *Visionary Republic*, 13–15; Kidd, *Great Awakening*, 234–52.

109. For the best discussion on the radicalism of the evangelical movement, see Isaac, *Transformation of Virginia*.

110. Burnard, *Creole Gentlemen*, 225.

111. James Rigbie, a member of an elite Maryland family, also left the Anglican Church for the same reason. Like Husband, he would eventually become a Quaker. See Forman, "Narrative of Colonel James Rigbie."

112. For more on Quakers in Cecil County and elsewhere in colonial America, see Johnston, *History of Cecil County*, 90–91, 153, 205, 264; Carroll, *Quakerism on the Eastern Shore*; Miller, *Cecil County*, 23, 147; Crabtree, *Holy Nation*; Crothers, *Quakers Living in the Lion's Mouth*; Smolenski, *Friends and Strangers*; and Levy, *Quakers and the American Family*.

113. *SRR*, 22.

114. Tolles, *Meeting House and Counting House*, 4.
115. *SRR*, 23.
116. Ibid., 23, 24.
117. Ibid., 27–28.
118. For more on Robert Barclay, see Trueblood, *Robert Barclay*.
119. Barclay, *Apology for the True Christian Divinity*, 71, 67. For a history of Quakers in England during the seventeenth century, see Hinds, *George Fox and Early Quaker Culture*, and Ingle, *First among Friends*.
120. Barclay, *Apology for the True Christian Divinity*, 71, 67, 74.
121. *SRR*, 28.
122. *SPNT*, 44.
123. *SRR*, 32, 25.
124. Unlike postmillennialists, premillennialists believe that the second coming of Christ will occur prior to the millennium. Bloch, *Visionary Republic*, xi; Connors and Gow, "Anglo-American Millennialism," xiv.
125. For more on postmillennialism in colonial America, see Bloch, *Visionary Republic*; Connors and Gow, *Anglo-American Millennialism*; Jones, "Herman Husband"; Davidson, *Logic of Millennial Thought*; Beam, "Millennialism and American Nationalism"; Tuveson, *Redeemer Nation*; and Miller, "From the Covenant to the Revival."
126. Quoted in Heimert and Miller, *Great Awakening*, 154.
127. *UM*, 3, 4.
128. *SRR*, 28.
129. Ibid., 32–33, 29, 37.
130. *SPNT*, 17.

TWO. *"A New Government of Liberty"*

1. Quoted in Tolles, *Meeting House and Counting House*, 53.
2. For an excellent discussion the Quaker economic ethic, see ibid., 45–62.
3. *Pennsylvania Gazette*, September 13, 1753; *Maryland Gazette*, October 25, 1753; Hatchett, *Some Neglected History Concerning Harmon Husband*, 23.
4. The name of Husband's first wife and the year of her death remain unknown. We do know that she gave birth to John and Herman Jr. She was also likely the mother of Mary and James. See Jones, "Herman Husband," 48; Hatchett, *Some Neglected History Concerning Harmon Husband*, 4–5; and Hoppin, *Washington Ancestry*, 2:293.
5. For a discussion of Quaker communities and slavery in the West Indies during the colonial period, see Menard, *Sweet Negotiations*; Block, *Ordinary Lives in the Early Caribbean*; Gragg, *Quaker Community on Barbados*; Amussen, *Caribbean Exchanges*; Bridenbaugh and Bridenbaugh, *No Peace beyond the Line*; Dunn, *Sugar and Slaves*; Durham, *Caribbean Quakers*; and Tolles, *Quakers and the Atlantic Culture*.
6. "Commission Book, 82," 345.
7. Nottingham Monthly Meeting Minutes, p. 313, M-661, Maryland State Archives.

8. For an excellent discussion on Bridgetown, see Welch, *Slave Society in the City.*
9. Equiano, *Interesting Narrative of the Life of Olaudah Equiano,* 29.
10. Rediker, *Slave Ship,* 252–53.
11. Quoted in Beckles, *History of Barbados,* 47–48.
12. *SPNT,* 40.
13. *NGL,* 641.
14. For more on Quakers' support for or tolerance of slavery, see Carey and Plank, *Quakers and Abolition;* Crothers, "Quaker Merchants and Slavery in Early National Alexandria"; Soderlund, *Quakers and Slavery;* Drake, *Quakers and Slavery in America;* and Weeks, *Southern Quakers and Slavery.*
15. Plank, *John Woolman's Path to the Peaceable Kingdom,* 100.
16. For more on the rise of antislavery sentiment within the Quaker community, see Carey and Plank, *Quakers and Abolition;* Carey, *From Peace to Freedom;* Plank, *John Woolman's Path to the Peaceable Kingdom;* Slaughter, *Beautiful Soul of John Woolman;* Soderlund, *Quakers and Slavery;* Nash, "Slaves and Slaveholders in Colonial Philadelphia"; and Drake, *Quakers and Slavery in America.*
17. Crothers, "Quaker Merchants and Slavery in Early National Alexandria," 52.
18. Quoted in Weeks, *Southern Quakers and Slavery,* 200.
19. For more on the so-called Quaker Reformation, see Crabtree, *Holy Nation;* Levy, *Quakers and the American Family;* Marrietta, *Reformation of American Quakerism;* James, *People among Peoples;* and Tolles, *Meeting House and Counting House.*
20. Coverdale, "'Flight on the Wings of Vanity,'" 210–12.
21. *SRR,* 25 (quotation); *SPNT,* 9–13.
22. Nottingham Monthly Meeting Minutes, pp. 346, 351, 353, 354, 356, 359, 360, 362, 366, 367, 368, 369, 371, 372, 382, 396, M-661, Maryland State Archives; *SPNT,* 18–21; Jones, "Herman Husband," 54; Peden, *More Marylanders to Carolina,* 66.
23. James, *People among Peoples,* 9.
24. With his father, Husband also made millstones in Cecil County. See *Maryland Gazette,* October 25, 1753, and *Pennsylvania Gazette,* September 13, 1753.
25. Lemon, *Best Poor Man's Country.* For a discussion on economic hardship in eighteenth-century America, see Smith, *Down and Out in Early America.*
26. Between those decades, the price of land in Lancaster County rose from £1.10 per acre to £3.10 per acre. See Lemon, *Best Poor Man's Country,* 67–68.
27. Husband named his property Herman's Ramble. See Peden, *Inhabitants of Cecil County,* 12, 103.
28. Quoted in Merrens, *Colonial North Carolina in the Eighteenth Century,* 35.
29. For more on the North Carolina backcountry before the American Revolution, see Ramsey, *Carolina Cradle;* Ekirch, "Poor Carolina"; Cross et al., *Southern Colonial Backcountry;* Kars, *Breaking Loose Together;* and Merrens, *Colonial North Carolina in the Eighteenth Century.*
30. Kars, *Breaking Loose Together,* 29–30. For more on the Granville District, see Watt, *Granville District.*
31. Troxler, *Farming Dissenters,* 3. Husband believed that land in Pennsylvania was "more then double the price" of lands in North Carolina. See *NGL,* 638.

32. Hatchett, *Some Neglected History Concerning Harmon Husband*, 5; Weeks, *Southern Quakers and Slavery*, 179.

33. NGL, 638; Jones, "Herman Husband," 60. Husband's brother John may have been living in Anson County, North Carolina, at the time. See Jones, "Herman Husband," 73.

34. Husband arrived in Orange County in mid-October. See NGL, 639. For more on the Great Wagon Road and settlement in the Valley of Virginia, see Hofstra, "Searching for Peace and Prosperity," and Ramsey, *Carolina Cradle*.

35. NGL, 638; brackets in original.

36. The exact number of acreage was 1,920. Ibid., 641. For land purchased by Husband, see Weeks, *Register of Orange County, North Carolina, Deeds*, 4; Bennett, *Orange County Records*, 2:12; Bennett, *Orange County Records*, 3:102; and Jones, "Herman Husband," 73.

37. Quoted in Kars, *Breaking Loose Together*, 15.

38. Arthur Dobbs to Board of Trade, November 9, 1754, in CRNC, 5:149.

39. Kars, *Breaking Loose Together*, 16.

40. NGL, 639, 640; brackets in original. For more on James Carter, see Ramsey, "James Carter."

41. Only 5.6 percent of Orange County residents owned slaves in 1755. See ibid., 636, 641. In 1755, "perhaps as few as 450 blacks lived" in the entire North Carolina backcountry, "as opposed to about 12,000 whites. By 1767, a little more than 3,000 African Americans lived in the same area, with over 37,000 European Americans." See Kars, *Breaking Loose Together*, 22.

42. NGL, 641–42.

43. It remains unclear if Husband owned slaves. The only extant source concerning the matter comes from North Carolina governor William Tryon's expenditure receipt following the Battle of Alamance, which recorded Jobe Jackson as having received £2 for "taking Husband's Negro" in May 1771. Given the lack of additional evidence and his aversion to slavery, however, Husband was likely not a slaveholder, though he certainly viewed African Americans as inferior to whites. See "List of Expenditures of Governor Tryon on Hillsborough Expedition, April 24–June 20, 1771," in *RNC*, 484.

44. Kars, *Breaking Loose Together*, 107.

45. NGL, 636. See also "An Act, for Appointing Parishes and Vestries," in Clark, *State Records of North Carolina*, 25:298–304.

46. NGL, 644 (quotation); *SPNT*, 6–7, 29, 31.

47. Quoted in Kars, *Breaking Loose Together*, 107. See also Herman Husband to Lord Granville, 1756, M-Z.5.4n, Papers from the Marquis of Bath's Library in Longleat, Warminster, Wiltshire, England, English Records, 1729–80, State Archives of North Carolina.

48. NGL, 646.

49. For a discussion of evangelicals in the North Carolina backcountry, see Conser and Cain, *Presbyterians in North Carolina*; Rohrer, *Hope's Promise*; Sparks, *Roots of Appalachian Christianity*; Heyrman, *Southern Cross*; Denson, "Diversity, Religion,

and the North Carolina Regulators"; Conkin, "Church Establishment in North Carolina"; Paschal, *History of the North Carolina Baptists*; and Morgan, "Great Awakening in North Carolina."

50. For an excellent discussion of evangelicals' antiauthoritarian beliefs in the North Carolina backcountry, see Kars, *Breaking Loose Together*, 79–129.

51. Fries, *Records of the Moravians in North Carolina*, 1:191–92.

52. Hooker, *Carolina Backcountry on the Eve of the Revolution*, 78.

53. NGL, 643, 641. See also Jones, "Herman Husband," 65–66.

54. NGL, 646.

55. Along with purchasing two lots in Hillsborough and 1,920 acres of land near Sandy Creek, Husband also secured warrants for 5,080 acres of land in the Granville District by the fall of 1755. See Weeks, *Register of Orange County, North Carolina, Deeds*, 2; Bennett, *Orange County Records*, 2:12; Bennett, *Orange County Records*, 3:102; and Bennett, *Orange County Records*, 1:1, 8, 9, 12, 13.

56. Sparks, *Roots of Appalachian Christianity*, 34–54, 55–63.

57. Troxler, *Farming Dissenters*, 48–50.

58. Jones, "Herman Husband," 75.

59. Husband joined the Cane Creek Monthly Meeting of Friends in December 1755. Mary Pugh's family had been in the region since the 1750s. See Cane Creek Monthly Meeting, Minutes, December 6, 1755, Friends Historical Collection, Hege Library (hereafter Cane Creek Monthly Meeting).

60. Hatchett, *Some Neglected History Concerning Harmon Husband*, 5; Peden, *Marylanders to Carolina*, 90.

61. For a discussion of the Fountain Company and Husband's relationship to it, see Nagy, "'Our Woods Are Full of Mine Hunters'"; *Maryland Gazette*, December 11, 1760; and Ninian Hamilton to Herman Husband, June 24, 1760, box 1, and "Minutes and Accounts of 'Fountain Company,' 1744–1764," box 2, both MS 61, Bond Family Papers, 1749–1844, H. Furlong Baldwin Library.

62. On July 24, 1761, Husband "requested a certificate of removal to Cane Creek, North Carolina." See Peden, *Marylanders to Carolina*, 90. For Husband's marriage to Mary Pugh, see Cane Creek Monthly Meeting, July 3, 1762; Hatchett, *Some Neglected History Concerning Harmon Husband*, 7; and Hoppin, *Washington Ancestry*, 2:293.

63. Cane Creek Monthly Meeting, January 3, February 7, April 4, May 2, 1761.

64. For more on John and Rachel Wright, see Newlin, *Charity Cook*, 1–23. For additional information on female ministers in colonial America, see Larson, *Daughters of Light*; Brekus, *Strangers and Pilgrims*; and Bacon, *Mothers of Feminism*.

65. Cane Creek Monthly Meeting, April 4, 1761.

66. *SPNT*, 60–62.

67. Western Quarterly Meeting, Minutes, May 2, August 8, 1761, Friends Historical Collection, Hege Library (hereafter Western Quarterly Meeting).

68. *SPNT*, 60–62.

69. Cane Creek Monthly Meeting, December 5, 1761.

70. Rachel's son John requested a certificate in February. It is unknown exactly when Rachel requested a certificate. See Cane Creek Monthly Meeting, February 2, 1762, and Troxler, *Farming Dissenters*, 54.

71. For additional scholarship on the Rachel Wright affair, see Weeks, *Southern Quakers and Slavery*, 180–81; White, "A Church Quarrel and What Resulted"; Newlin, *Charity Cook*, 25–32; Jones, "Herman Husband," 84–90; Kars, *Breaking Loose Together*, 114–17; and Troxler, *Farming Dissenters*, 50–58.

72. *SPNT*, 21–24.

73. Western Quarterly Meeting, November 13, 1762; May 14, 1763.

74. Ibid., November 12, 1763.

75. *SPNT*, 62–79.

76. Cane Creek Monthly Meeting, January 7, 1764.

77. Western Quarterly Meeting, February 11, 1764.

78. Cane Creek Monthly Meeting, November 10, 1764. It was not until March 1767 that the Cane Creek Monthly Meeting granted Wright her certificate. See Cane Creek Monthly Meeting, March 7, 1767.

79. Convinced that he had behaved justly, Husband did challenge the committee charged with drawing up his expulsion papers, threatening to sue in civil court for libel if members recorded his offense as acting "Contrary to the Truth," which implied that he had defied God's word. The committee, according to Husband, acquiesced, opting instead to use the phrase "Contrary to Right Seeing." See AQA.

80. *SPNT*, 9, 6, 15, 12, 54.

81. For a further discussion of Husband's possible motives for leading the anti-Wright faction, see Troxler, *Farming Dissenters*, 57–58.

82. Comly and Comly, *Friends' Miscellany*, 12:258.

83. Husband was forty-one years old at the time of his third marriage. Emey was twenty-two.

84. Cane Creek Monthly Meeting, February 2, 1767; Jones, "Herman Husband," 105; Kars, *Breaking Loose Together*, 116; Troxler, *Farming Dissenters*, 59.

85. Nelson, *William Tryon and the Course of Empire*, 1–17.

86. For scholarship on North Carolina during the Stamp Act crisis, see Nelson, *William Tryon and the Course of Empire*, 39–50; Lee, *Crowds and Soldiers in Revolutionary North Carolina*, 35–45; and Spindel, "Law and Order." For an overview of the Stamp Act crisis throughout the American colonies, see Morgan and Morgan, *Stamp Act Crisis*.

87. *SRR*, 25.

88. *UM*, 5, 6.

89. Ekirch, "Poor Carolina," 176–77; Kars, *Breaking Loose Together*, 33–34; Nelson, *William Tryon and the Course of Empire*, 21–22.

90. Kars, *Breaking Loose Together*, 40.

91. Troxler, *Farming Dissenters*, 7–9; Nelson, *William Tryon and the Course of Empire*, 22; Kars, *Breaking Loose Together*, 34–54; Lee, *Crowds and Soldiers in Revolutionary North Carolina*, 28–35; Kay, "North Carolina Regulation," 83.

92. For more on the McCullohs, see Sellers, "Private Profits and British Colonial Policy."

93. Kars, *Breaking Loose Together*, 38.

94. When he left North Carolina in 1771, Fanning had accumulated over ten thousand acres of land and had purchased "twenty-nine valuable lots in various towns." For more on Fanning, see Kars, *Breaking Loose Together*, 40, 45, 47, 52, 53; Troxler, *Farming Dissenters*, 15–18; Whittenburg, "Planters, Merchants, and Lawyers," 230–31; and Jones, *General Edmund Fanning*.

95. Hudson, "Songs of the North Carolina Regulators," 477.

96. Whittenburg, "Planters, Merchants, and Lawyers," 228–30.

97. Troxler, *Farming Dissenters*, 10–15; Kars, *Breaking Loose Together*, 68–71; Watson, "Appointment of Sheriffs in Colonial North Carolina."

98. For a small sample of scholarship on colonial backcountry farmers' relationship with the market economy, see Hofstra, *Planting of New Virginia*; Kulikoff, *From British Peasants to Colonial American Farmers*; Bushman, "Markets and Composite Farms in Early America"; Merrill, "Putting 'Capitalism' in Its Place"; Thorp, *Moravian Community in Colonial North Carolina*; and Mitchell, *Commercialism and Frontier*.

99. *Virginia Gazette*, July 4, 1771, in *RNC*, 489; *NGL*, 632; Jones, "Herman Husband," 75.

100. Merrens, *Colonial North Carolina in the Eighteenth Century*, 108–15, 134–41; Kars, *Breaking Loose Together*, 61; Thorp, "Doing Business in the Backcountry."

101. Whittenburg, "Planters, Merchants, and Lawyers," 222–24; Kars, *Breaking Loose Together*, 61–63; Thorp, "Doing Business in the Backcountry."

102. Ekirch, "*Poor Carolina*," 10; Nelson, *William Tryon and the Course of Empire*, 59–61; Kars, *Breaking Loose Together*, 65–67.

103. Kars, *Breaking Loose Together*, 67 (quotation); Ekirch, "*Poor Carolina*," 182; Denson, "Diversity, Religion, and the North Carolina Regulators," 33; Kay, "Payment of Provincial and Local Taxes in North Carolina"; Kay, "Provincial Taxes in North Carolina during the Administrations of Dobbs and Tryon."

104. Nelson, *William Tryon and the Course of Empire*, 23–30; Kars, *Breaking Loose Together*, 108–9.

105. Kars, *Breaking Loose Together*, 62.

106. Ekirch, "*Poor Carolina*," 180.

107. According to historian James P. Whittenburg, this number likely represents only a fraction of total cases. See Whittenburg, "Planters, Merchants, and Lawyers," 226, 232, and Kars, *Breaking Loose Together*, 71.

108. Kars, *Breaking Loose Together*, 71, 72–73.

109. Sims, "Address to the People of Granville County," 182, 183, 186, 190–91.

110. *CIR*, 50.

111. *NGL*, 643 (quotation); *IR*, 91–92.

112. *FF*, 30.

113. *IR*, 92.

114. Whittenburg, "Planters, Merchants, and Lawyers."

115. These men were Jonathan Cell, William Cox, Isaac Vernon, Joseph Maddock, William Marshall, John Marshall, William Massett, and Thomas Branson. See Troxler, *Farming Dissenters*, 59; Kars, *Breaking Loose Together*, 115; and Jones, "Herman Husband," 105.

116. *IR*, 8–10; *FF*, 17–18; "Regulator Advertisement, No. 11," May 21, 1768, in *RNC*, 117.

117. "Regulator Advertisement, No. 1," August 1766, in *RNC*, 35.

118. *FF*, 21; "Regulator Advertisement, No. 11," May 21, 1768, in *RNC*, 117.

119. *FF*, 20–23; "Regulator Advertisement, No. 1," August 1766, in *RNC*, 36.

120. *IR*, 12; Jones, "Herman Husband," 108.

121. "Regulator Advertisement, No. 11," May 21, 1768, in *RNC*, 117.

122. "Regulator Advertisement, No. 3," October 10, 1766, in ibid., 36–37.

123. *IR*, 13.

124. Ibid.; *FF*, 17 (quotation).

125. "Regulator Advertisement, No. 11," May 21, 1768, in *RNC*, 118.

126. *IR*, 14.

127. NGL, 643.

THREE. *"Shew Yourselves to Be Freemen"*

1. *IR*, 42.

2. Lee, *Crowds and Soldiers in Revolutionary North Carolina*, 51.

3. *IR*, 21 (quotation); John Gray to Edmund Fanning, April 9, 1768, in *RNC*, 80–81; Edmund Fanning to Simon Dixon, May 1768, in *RNC*, 104; "The King vs. Hermon Husband," May 1, 1768, in *RNC*, 107–8.

4. *IR*, 15 (quotation); "Regulator Advertisement, No. 11," May 21, 1768, in *RNC*, 117–19.

5. This fee was two shillings eight pence. *FF*, 29; *IR*, 15–16; Tyree Harris announcement, in *CRNC*, 7:771–72.

6. *IR*, 16.

7. Nelson, *William Tryon and the Course of Empire*, 54–57; Dill, *Governor Tryon and His Palace*.

8. Kars, *Breaking Loose Together*, 162.

9. Kay, "Payment of Provincial and Local Taxes in North Carolina," 220–21.

10. Quoted in Troxler, *Farming Dissenters*, 20.

11. "Regulator Advertisement, No. 5," March 22, 1768, in *RNC*, 79.

12. *IR*, 16 (quotations); *FF*, 31–32.

13. *IR*, 16; "Regulator Advertisement, No. 4," January 1768, in *RNC*, 76.

14. "Regulator Advertisement, No. 8," April 30, 1768, in ibid., 97; "Regulator Advertisement, No. 11," May 21, 1768, in ibid., 119; *IR*, 21–22; *FF*, 37–39.

15. Ralph McNair to Herman Husband, May or June 1768, in *RNC*, 122; brackets in original.

16. Edmund Fanning to John Gray, April 13, 1768, in ibid., 81.

17. Francis Nash and Thomas Hart to Edmund Fanning, April 17, 1768, in ibid., 82.
18. Samuel Spencer to William Tryon, April 28, 1768, in ibid., 92–96.
19. Edmund Fanning to William Tryon, April 23, 1768, in ibid., 84, 86.
20. Samuel Spencer to William Tryon, April 28, 1768, in ibid., 92–96.
21. William Tryon to William Petty, 2nd Earl of Shelburne, July 8, 1767, in *CRNC*, 7:501.
22. William Tryon to Edmund Fanning, April 27, 1768, in *RNC*, 91.
23. "Council Minutes," April 27, 1768, in ibid., 88–89; "Governor Tryon's Orders to Regimental Officers," April 27, 1768, in ibid., 89–90; William Tryon to Edmund Fanning, April 27, 1768, in ibid., 90–91; William Tryon to Samuel Spencer, May 1768, in ibid., 100–102.
24. "The King vs. Herman Husband," May 1, 1768, in ibid., 107–8.
25. *IR*, 42 (quotation); *FF*, 38–40; "Thomas Lloyd to Keeper of the Public Gaol of the District of Newbern," May 2, 1768, in *RNC*, 109.
26. *IR*, 42–45 (quotations); *CIR*, 67–69.
27. "Regulator Advertisement, No. 11," May 21, 1768, in *RNC*, 120.
28. *IR*, 23; Edmund Fanning to William Tryon, May 3, 1768, in *RNC*, 109–10; William Tryon to Wills Hill, 1st Earl of Hillsborough, June 16, 1768, in *CWT*, 2:135.
29. Foote, *Sketches of North Carolina*, 55 (quotations); Caruthers, *Sketch of the Life and Character of the Rev. David Caldwell*, 123.
30. Hudson, "Songs of the North Carolina Regulators," 480.
31. *IR*, 23–24.
32. Ibid., 24; "Regulator Advertisement, No. 11," May 21, 1768, in *RNC*, 115.
33. *IR*, 25, 26–27. This committee consisted of John Lowe, James Hunter, Rednap Howell, Harmon Cox, John Marshall, William Cox, William Moffitt, and George Hendry. See "Regulator Advertisement, No. 10," May 21, 1768, in *RNC*, 113–14, and "Regulator Advertisement, No. 11," May 21, 1768, in *RNC*, 121.
34. "Regulator Advertisement, No. 11," May 21, 1768, in *RNC*, 115 (quotations); "Regulator Advertisement, No. 9 [Petition of the Inhabitants of Orange County to William Tryon and the Council]," May 21–30?, 1768, in *CWT*, 2:110–13; "Regulator Advertisement, No. 10," May 21, 1768, in *RNC*, 113–14; *IR*, 26–28; Regulators to William Tryon, June 1768, in *RNC*, 124.
35. "Regulator Advertisement, No. 11," May 21, 1768, in *RNC*, 116.
36. *IR*, 27–29.
37. Regulators to William Tryon, August 1, 1768, in *RNC*, 155–57.
38. "Deposition of Tyree Harris," August 3, 1768, in ibid., 152–53.
39. *FF*, 58–59; *IR*, 32–33.
40. *IR*, 33–36.
41. Ibid., 38.
42. "Insurgents to Governor Tryon," August 1768, in *RNC*, 149.
43. *IR*, 41.
44. "Regulator's Advertisement, No. 11," May 21, 1768, in *RNC*, 120; *CIR*, 68.
45. William Tryon to Lord Hillsborough, December 24, 1768, in *RNC*, 215.
46. *IR*, 45.

47. CIR, 69.
48. Ibid., 70.
49. Ibid., 71.
50. *IR*, 45.
51. CIR, 71.
52. Ibid., 74.
53. *IR*, 47.
54. Ibid., 47–48; CIR, 72.
55. *IR*, 49.
56. "Proceedings and Resolutions of Council of War Hillsborough," September 22–23, 1768, in *RNC*, 166–68; *IR*, 41–42.
57. *IR*, 39.
58. "Court Records of Orange County," September 26, 1768, in *CRNC*, 7:843.
59. *IR*, 50, 54–56.
60. CIR, 52; "Court Records of Orange County," September 27, 1768, in *CRNC*, 7:844.
61. These Regulators were William Few, Samuel Allen, William Butler, John Butler, James Hunter, Ninian Hamilton, Issac Jackson, John Philip Hartso, William Moffitt, John Pile, and Francis Dossett. See "Court Records of Orange County," September 27, 29, 30, 1768, in *CRNC*, 7:844–46; *IR*, 56–57; and William Tryon to Lord Hillsborough, December 24, 1768, in *CRNC*, 7:885.
62. *IR*, 56–57; "Court Records of Orange County," September 29, 30, 1768, in *CRNC*, 7:845–46; William Tryon to Lord Hillsborough, December 24, 1768, in *CRNC*, 7:885.
63. *IR*, 58; "Court Records of Orange County," September 27, 1768, in *CRNC*, 7:844; William Tryon to Lord Hillsborough, December 24, 1768, in *CRNC*, 7:884.
64. Tyree Harris to William Tryon, October 29, 1768, in *RNC*, 194. These twelve men were Peter Craven, Malachi Fyke, Solomon Gross, Matthew Hamilton, Ninian Hamilton, Ninian Bell Hamilton, James Hunter, Isaac Jackson, William Moffitt, Christopher Nation, John O'Neill, and William Payne. In March 1769, these men were either pardoned or, as in Husband's case, acquitted for insurgency in court. See "Proclamation of the Governor," October 3, 1768, in *CWT*, 2: 199; "Council Minutes," October 1, 1768, in *RNC*, 185–86; Lord Hillsborough to William Tryon, March 1, 1769, in *CRNC*, 8:17; and "Diary of Waightstill Avery," March 27, 1769, in *RNC*, 218. For information on disbanding the militia, see "William Tryon's Journal," October 2, 1768, in *CWT*, 2:159–60.
65. William Tryon to Lord Hillsborough, December 24, 1768, in *RNC*, 214.
66. "Petition of Citizens of Rowan and Orange Counties," October 4, 1768, in ibid., 187–89.
67. Kars, *Breaking Loose Together*, 162–63; Kay, "North Carolina Regulation," 91–93.
68. "The Humble Petition and Remonstrance of the Assembly of North Carolina," December 5, 1768, in *CRNC*, 7:981.
69. Kay, "North Carolina Regulation," 92; Kars, *Breaking Loose Together*, 166–67.

70. There were only a few cases of violence being committed by Regulators in 1769. See Lee, *Crowds and Soldiers in Revolutionary North Carolina*, 65–66.

71. *IR*, 70; "Diary of Waightstill Avery," March 28, 1769, in *RNC*, 218; "Indictment against Fanning," August 6, 1770, in *CRNC*, 8:225–26.

72. Born in Pennsylvania, Frohock moved to Rowan County in 1753. Elected to the North Carolina assembly in 1760, he incurred the wrath of local residents by working with Henry Eustace McCulloh to evict squatters from the absentee landlord's estate. Kars, *Breaking Loose Together*, 38–40, 45, 47, 53; *IR*, 69; Regulators to Herman Husband, September 14, 1769, in *CRNC*, 8:68–70.

73. According to Husband, "Some . . . apply'd to [Hooper], and made Information against the Clerk of the Inferior Court for taking . . . [excessive] Fee on a Common Attachment. [Hooper] told them he must have the Informations in Writing.—They found a Clerk, and carries it in writing.—Then [Hooper] wanted a Date, or name, and then something else, till at length they got one almost right; but had gone from Office to Office so often, that one the clerks D——d them for a pack of Sons of B——s, and denied serving them." See *IR*, 72, 69.

74. Ibid., 58; "Indictment against Fanning," August 6, 1770, in *CRNC*, 8:225–26; Regulators to Herman Husband, September 14, 1769, in *CRNC*, 8:68–70.

75. Regulators to Herman Husband, September 14, 1769, in *CRNC*, 8:70.

76. Kars, *Breaking Loose Together*, 170.

77. According to legend, Franklin "used to send Husbands pamphlets and Wilcox as he went every half-year to Philadelphia was the bearer of those papers but he said that for fear of detection they never committed anything to writing." See "Memorandum from the Superior Court at Hillsborough," July 5, 1819, in *RNC*, 565–66. For the Regulator song praising Husband, see Hudson, "Songs of the North Carolina Regulators," 483.

78. *IR*, 64–69.

79. Husband won 642 votes, while Pryor received 455 votes. Fanning won 314 votes. See *CIR*, 65.

80. Troxler, *Farming Dissenters*, 78–79; Kars, *Breaking Loose Together*, 170–71.

81. Henry Eustace McCulloh to John Harvey, March 30, 1770, in *CRNC*, 8:183.

82. Jones, "Herman Husband," 145.

83. Ekirch, *"Poor Carolina,"* 176.

84. "The Petition of the Inhabitants of Anson County," October 9, 1769, in *CRNC*, 8:77; "The Humble Petition of Us Inhabitants of Orange and Rowan Countys," October 1769, in *CRNC*, 8:81.

85. "The Humble Petition of Us Inhabitants of Orange and Rowan Countys," October 1769, in ibid., 8:81, 84; Kars, *Breaking Loose Together*, 171. For a discussion of the growing concern among colonial Americans about accountability in government, see Maloy, *Colonial American Origins of Modern Democratic Thought*.

86. "The Petition of the Inhabitants of Anson County," October 9, 1769, in *CRNC*, 8:76–77, 78.

87. "The Humble Petition of Us Inhabitants of Orange and Rowan Countys," October 1769, in ibid., 8:83.

88. "The Petition of the Inhabitants of Anson County," October 9, 1769, in ibid., 8:77–78.

89. *IR*, 77; Kars, *Breaking Loose Together*, 173 (quotation).

90. "The Petition of the Inhabitants of Anson County," October 9, 1769, in *CRNC*, 8:76 (quotation); "The Humble Petition of Us Inhabitants of Orange and Rowan Countys," October 1769, in *CRNC*, 8:82.

91. Kay, "North Carolina Regulation," 94; "The Humble Petition of Us Inhabitants of Orange and Rowan Countys," October 1769, in *CRNC*, 8:83. For more on these petitions, see Kars, *Breaking Loose Together*, 171–74; Troxler, *Farming Dissenters*, 79–81; and Jones, "Herman Husband," 145–49.

92. Quoted in Nelson, *William Tryon and the Course of Empire*, 77–78.

93. "Legislative Journals," October 27, 1769, in *CRNC*, 8:111–12.

94. *IR*, 75.

95. "Legislative Journals," October 26, 1769, in *CRNC*, 8:110–11.

96. "The Humble Petition of Us Inhabitants of Orange and Rowan Countys," October 1769, in ibid., 8:84.

97. Kay, "North Carolina Regulation," 97.

98. *IR*, 73.

99. Murray, *Sermons to Asses*, 16.

100. *IR*, 89–90.

101. CIR, 64, 68.

102. Kars, *Breaking Loose Together*, 179–80.

103. Maurice Moore to William Tryon, March 13, 1770, in *CWT*, 2:431.

104. Troxler, *Farming Dissenters*, 84–85; Kars, *Breaking Loose Together*, 182.

105. "Petition of the Inhabitants of Orange County," September 1770, in *CRNC*, 8:234.

106. CIR, 52–53, 74, 53–54; Jones, "Herman Husband," 152.

107. CIR, 66, 54.

108. Ibid., 76. The "Horn of the Beast" is "an allusion to the monster" that "accompanies the Antichrist in Revelation." Jones, "Herman Husband," 163.

109. These leaders included James Hunter, William Butler, Ninian Bell Hamilton, Jeremiah Fields, Matthew Hamilton, Ely Branson, Peter Craven, John Fruit, Abraham Teague, and Samuel Parks. See "Deposition of Ralph McNair," October 9, 1770, in *RNC*, 261, and "Orange County Court Records," September 22, 1770, in *CRNC*, 8:235.

110. Theodorus Swaine Drage to Benjamin Franklin, March 2, 1771, in Willcox et al., *Papers of Benjamin Franklin*, 18:43–46.

111. Richard Henderson to William Tryon, September 29, 1770, in *RNC*, 245.

112. *Virginia Gazette*, October 25, 1770, in ibid., 251 (quotation); Richard Henderson to William Tryon, September 29, 1770, in ibid., 245–46.

113. *Virginia Gazette*, October 25, 1770, in ibid., 251.

114. These officials were William Hooper, Thomas Hart, Alexander Martin, Michael Holt, and John Sitterell. See *Virginia Gazette*, October 25, 1770, in ibid., 252, and Richard Henderson to William Tryon, September 29, 1770, in ibid., 246.

115. Richard Henderson to William Tryon, September 29, 1770, in ibid., 246.
116. Ibid., 247.
117. *Boston Evening Post*, November 12, 1770, in ibid., 255.
118. William Tryon's Proclamation, October 18, 1770, in CRNC, 8:253–54; Thomas McGuire to William Tryon, October 18, 1770, in CRNC, 8:251–52.
119. "Council Journal," October 18, 1770, in ibid., 8:253; Thomas McGuire to William Tryon, October 18, 1770, in ibid., 8:252. See also William Tryon to Lord Hillsborough, October 20, 1770, in RNC, 273–74; William Tryon to the Colonels of the Orange and Rowan Regiments, October 19, 1770, in RNC, 272; and William Tryon to Colonels of Provincial Regiments, October 19, 1770, in RNC, 273.
120. "Council Journal," November 19, 1770, in CRNC, 8:258–59.
121. John Simpson to William Tryon, December 3, 1770, in ibid., 8:262.
122. "Authorization for Election of Hillsborough Representative to General Assembly," July 9, 1770, in RNC, 242–44.
123. Kars, *Breaking Loose Together*, 186; Troxler, *Farming Dissenters*, 92.
124. William Tryon to Robert Howe, November 20, 1770, in RNC, 274; William Tryon to Richard Caswell, November 20, 1770, in RNC, 275. See also William Tryon to John Hinton, November 1770, in RNC, 275–76, and William Tryon to John Simpson, November 20, 1770, in RNC, 276.
125. William Tryon to the General Assembly, December 5, 1770, in ibid., 288–90.
126. "Herman Husband," in RNC, 585; and Nash, "Herman Husbands," in Ashe, Weeks, and Noppen, *Biographical History of North Carolina*, 2:191.
127. "Assembly Resolution," December 20, 1770, in ibid., 295; Troxler, *Farming Dissenters*, 93. The author of this letter was actually James Hunter.
128. "Assembly Resolution," December 20, 1770, in RNC, 296. Before being expelled, Husband did manage to introduce two petitions from disgruntled Orange and Granville County residents. See "Legislative Journals," December 8, 10, 1770, in CRNC, 8:309.
129. William Tryon to Lord Hillsborough, January 31, 1771, in RNC, 337 (quotation); "Council Journals," December 20, 1770, in CRNC, 8:269–70.
130. William Tryon to Lord Hillsborough, January 31, 1771, in RNC, 337.
131. Quoted in Lee, *Crowds and Soldiers in Revolutionary North Carolina*, 72.
132. William Tryon to the General Assembly, December 31, 1770, in RNC, 298–99.
133. "An Act for Preventing Tumultuous and Riotous Assemblies," January 15, 1771, in ibid., 327–32; Kars, *Breaking Loose Together*, 187–88; Troxler, *Farming Dissenters*, 92–93; Lee, *Crowds and Soldiers in Revolutionary North Carolina*, 72–73.
134. Nelson, *William Tryon and the Course of Empire*, 80. For a more thorough discussion on the reforms passed by the assembly in the winter of 1770–71, see Kars, *Breaking Loose Together*, 189–91.
135. "Legislative Journals," December 17, 20 1770, in CRNC, 8:293–95; Troxler, *Farming Dissenters*, 92; Kars, *Breaking Loose Together*, 190; Jones, "Herman Husband," 173.
136. William Tryon to Lord Hillsborough, January 31, 1771, in RNC, 337.
137. "Deposition of Waightstill Avery," March 8, 1771, in ibid., 358–60.

138. "Council Minutes," February 20, 1771, in ibid., 348; "Council Minutes," February 7, 1771, in ibid., 339.

139. Theodorus Swaine Drage to Benjamin Franklin, March 2, 1771, in Willcox et al., *Papers of Benjamin Franklin*, 18:49.

140. Rednap Howell to James Hunter, February 16, 1771, in *CRNC*, 8:537. For an excellent discussion on how Husband's arrest made many eastern North Carolinians sympathetic to the Regulators, see Lee, *Crowds and Soldiers in Revolutionary North Carolina*, 74.

141. William Tryon to Lord Hillsborough, January 31, 1771, in *RNC*, 336–38; William Tryon to Edmund Fanning, February 2, 1771, in *RNC*, 338–39; "Council Minutes," February 7, 1771, in *RNC*, 339–40; William Tryon to Edmund Fanning, February 7, 1771 in *RNC*, 340–41; William Tryon to the Colonels of the Dobbs, Johnston, and Wake Regiments, February 7, 1771, in *RNC*, 341; William Tryon to Richard Henderson, February 7, 1771, in *RNC*, 342; William Tryon to John Ashe, February 7, 1771, in *RNC*, 343; William Tryon to William Cray, February 7, 1771, in *RNC*, 343; William Tryon to John Simpson, February 7, 1771, in *RNC*, 343–44; William Tryon to Joseph Leech, February 8, 9, 1771, in *RNC*, 344–45; William Tryon to William Thomson, February 9, 1771, in *RNC*, 345.

142. Lee, *Crowds and Soldiers in Revolutionary North Carolina*, 74.

143. Herman Husband to William Butler and James Hunter, February 13, 1771, in *RNC*, 346.

144. "Council Minutes," February 20, 1771, in ibid., 348; Thomas McGuire to William Tryon, February 27, 1771, in *CRNC*, 8:695–96.

145. "Deposition of Waightstill Avery," March 8, 1771, in *RNC*, 359.

146. John Frohock and Alexander Martin to William Tryon, March 18, 1771, in ibid., 371–72; "Minutes of the Regulator Meeting in Rowan County," March 7, 1771, in ibid., 357–58.

147. William Tryon to John Frohock and Alexander Martin, April 5, 1771, in ibid., 394–95.

148. "Crown Prosecutions List," March 11, 1771, in ibid., 360–62; "Court Minutes," March 11–15, 1771, in ibid., 367–68; "Council Journal," March 18, 1771, in ibid., 374–75.

149. Kars, *Breaking Loose Together*, 196–97.

150. Ibid., 198–99; Troxler, *Farming Dissenters*, 97–101; Lee, *Crowds and Soldiers in Revolutionary North Carolina*, 84–85.

151. "Petition of Inhabitants of Orange County," May 15, 1771, in *RNC*, 453, 454.

152. Troxler, *Farming Dissenters*, 107; Kars, *Breaking Loose Together*, 199–201.

153. Caruthers, *Sketch of the Life and Character of the Rev. David Caldwell*, 153.

154. William Tryon to the Regulators, May 16, 1771, in *RNC*, 456.

155. Caruthers, *Sketch of the Life and Character of the Rev. David Caldwell*, 152, 148.

156. Troxler, *Farming Dissenters*, 108–16; Kars, *Breaking Loose Together*, 201; Lee, *Crowds and Soldiers in Revolutionary North Carolina*, 86–87.

157. Kars, *Breaking Loose Together*, 201.

158. William Tryon to Lord Hillsborough, May 18, 1771, in *RNC*, 458–59.

159. "Journal of the Expedition against the Insurgents," May 17, 1771, in *CWT*, 2:722; William Tryon to Lord Hillsborough, August 1, 1771, in *CWT*, 2: 818.

160. "Journal of the Expedition against the Insurgents," May 21, 1771, in ibid., 2: 724; "Letter," [1771], in *RNC*, 151.

161. "Journal of the Expedition against the Insurgents," May 21, 1771, in *CWT*, 2:724; "Return of the Army whilst Encamp'd at Hermon Husbands on Sandy Creek," May 22, 1771, in *CWT*, 2:747; William Tryon to Hugh Waddell, May 23, 1771, in *CWT*, 2:749.

162. *Virginia Gazette*, July 4, 1771, in *RNC*, 489 (quotation); Troxler, *Farming Dissenters*, 115–16; Kars, *Breaking Loose Together*, 203–4.

163. "Governor Tryon's Proclamation," May 17, 1771, in *RNC*, 457; Kars, *Breaking Loose Together*, 204.

164. "Governor Tryon's Proclamation," June 9, 1771, in *RNC*, 473.

165. Kars, *Breaking Loose Together*, 211.

FOUR. *"Perfecting a Free Government"*

1. For more on Gilpin, see Jordan, *Colonial and Revolutionary Families of Pennsylvania*, 1:608.

2. Bruner, *Recollections of Somerset County's Earliest Years*, 2. Gilpin married Husband's younger sister Margery.

3. Ibid., 114–15.

4. Ibid., 115–16.

5. Ibid., 116.

6. Caruthers, *Sketch of the Life and Character of the Rev. David Caldwell*, 166.

7. Fries, *Records of the Moravians in North Carolina*, 1:457–58.

8. Bruner, *Recollections of Somerset County's Earliest Years*, 2–3.

9. Harper, *Transformation of Western Pennsylvania*, 5; Cassady, *Somerset Outline*, 102, 109.

10. Hinderaker and Mancall, *At the Edge of Empire*, 92–93; Ward, *Breaking the Backcountry*; Dowd, *War under Heaven*, 33–41; Calloway, *New Worlds for All*, 144–45; McConnell, *Country Between*, 5–20; McClure, "Ends of the American Earth," 1:4–7; Downes, *Council Fires of the Upper Ohio*, 8–20; Buck and Buck, *Planting of Civilization in Western Pennsylvania*, 25–30; Cassady, *Somerset Outline*, 75–79.

11. Hinderaker and Mancall, *At the Edge of Empire*, 92–93; Ward, *Breaking the Backcountry*, 22–24; McClure, "Ends of the American Earth," 1:7–9; Volwiler, *George Croghan and the Westward Movement*; Downes, *Council Fires of the Upper Ohio*, 20–21.

12. Hinderaker and Mancall, *At the Edge of Empire*, 94–97; Ward, *Breaking the Backcountry*, 24–29; McClure, "Ends of the American Earth," 1:9–17; Volwiler, *George Croghan and the Westward Movement*, 75–84; Buck and Buck, *Planting of Civilization in Western Pennsylvania*, 46–56.

13. Crist, "Cumberland Country," 107–8; Blessing, "Upper Juniata Valley," 155; Buck and Buck, *Planting of Civilization in Western Pennsylvania*, 135–41.

14. Ward, *Breaking the Backcountry*, 33.

15. Hinderaker and Mancall, *At the Edge of Empire*, 98–112; Ward, *Breaking the Backcountry*, 29–45; Downes, *Council Fires of the Upper Ohio*, 53–74; Buck and Buck, *Planting of Civilization in Western Pennsylvania*, 67–82.

16. Ward, *Breaking the Backcountry*, 49–90; Buck and Buck, *Planting of Civilization in Western Pennsylvania*, 75–95.

17. Hinderaker and Mancall, *At the Edge of Empire*, 117–24, 134–37; Ward, *Breaking the Backcountry*, 219–54; Dowd, *War under Heaven*; Downes, *Council Fires of the Upper Ohio*, 75–122; Buck and Buck, *Planting of Civilization in Western Pennsylvania*, 96–114.

18. Blessing, "Upper Juniata Valley," 155; Harper, *Transformation of Western Pennsylvania*, 7; Buck and Buck, *Planting of Civilization in Western Pennsylvania*, 141–42.

19. This migration intensified after the Iroquois Confederacy, which also claimed jurisdiction over southwestern Pennsylvania, ceded that territory to the British at the Treaty of Fort Stanwix in 1768. See Harper, *Transformation of Western Pennsylvania*, 7–10; Volwiler, *George Croghan and the Westward Movement*, 221–25; Buck and Buck, *Planting of Civilization in Western Pennsylvania*, 143–45; and Griffin, *American Leviathan*, 72–94.

20. Buck and Buck, *Planting of Civilization in Western Pennsylvania*, 144; Downes, *Council Fires of the Upper Ohio*, 123–51.

21. McMurry, *From Sugar Camps to Star Barns*, 3; Harper, *Transformation of Western Pennsylvania*, 7.

22. Cassady, *Somerset Outline*, 38.

23. Bruner, *Recollections of Somerset County's Earliest Years*, 3–4.

24. Ibid., 4–7, 15.

25. Ibid., 7–9, 10–11, 14–15, 12.

26. Ibid., 13, 14.

27. Ibid., 15–16.

28. Kars, *Breaking Loose Together*, 206–7; Troxler, *Farming Dissenters*, 117. For more on James Pugh, see Compton, "'James Pugh,' Regulator Sharpshooter."

29. Caruthers, *Sketch of the Life and Character of the Rev. David Caldwell*, 165–66.

30. *Massachusetts Spy*, July 25, 1771.

31. *Pennsylvania Journal*, July 11, 1771. For more information on American colonists' reaction to the Battle of Alamance and its aftermath, see Kars, *Breaking Loose Together*, 208–10; Ekirch, "Poor Carolina," 200–202; and Maier, *From Resistance to Revolution*, 195–98.

32. Bruner, *Recollections of Somerset County's Earliest Years*, 15–16.

33. Ibid., 4, 17–20, 22.

34. Cassady, *Somerset Outline*, 124.

35. Bruner, *Recollections of Somerset County's Earliest Years*, 24–25.

36. These children included Husband's sons from his first marriage, John and Herman Jr.; his son with Mary Pugh, William; and his son with Emey, David. Following the birth of Isaac Tuscape in 1772, Husband and Emey would have two daughters, Emey and Phoebe. See Hoppin, *Washington Ancestry*, 2:293–94, and Hatchett, *Some Neglected History Concerning Harmon Husband*, 42.

37. Bruner, *Recollections of Somerset County's Earliest Years*, 24–26; Hatchett, *Some Neglected History Concerning Harmon Husband*, 23.

38. By now, Husband owned seventeen cows, two colts, and several dozen hogs. See Bruner, *Recollections of Somerset County's Earliest Years*, 28, 30.

39. Ibid., 30; Jones, "Herman Husband," 205–6.

40. Harper, *Transformation of Western Pennsylvania*, 9.

41. "Warrantees of Land in the County of Bedford, 1771–1893," in *PA*, 3rd ser., 25:530, 492; Hatchett, *Some Neglected History Concerning Harmon Husband*, 23–24. Husband also secured patents for Samuel Gilpin, John Stump, and other relatives in Maryland. See Jones, "Herman Husband," 205–6.

42. Jones, "Herman Husband," 203.

43. Delafield, "Notes on the Woods Family," 335–36; Kussart, "Colonel George Woods," 73–75.

44. Specht, "Finding Aid to Lukens Family Papers."

45. Jones, "Herman Husband," 208.

46. Kussart, "Colonel George Woods," 76; "Warrantees of Land in the County of Cumberland, 1750–1874," in *PA*, 3rd ser., 24:777–81; Jones, "Herman Husband," 208.

47. By 1776, Woods had purchased three additional lots in the town of Bedford and issued warrants totaling 788 acres in Bedford County. Three years later, he owned 1,355 acres, 7 horses, and 19 cattle in Bedford County. See "Warrantees of Land in the County of Bedford, 1771–1893," in *PA*, 3rd ser., 25:654–55, and "A Return of Property of the County of Bedford, for the Year 1779," in *PA*, 3rd ser., 22:159.

48. Delafield, "Notes on the Woods Family," 336; Kussart, "Colonel George Woods," 74–77; Jones, "Herman Husband," 209.

49. Jones, *Pair of Lawn Sleeves*, 1–22, 78–83; Konkle, *Life and Times of Thomas Smith*, 26–36; Jones, "Herman Husband," 210.

50. By 1776, Thomas had purchased a lot in the town of Bedford and issued warrants totaling four hundred acres in Bedford County. Three years later, he owned 1,309 acres in Bedford County. See "Warrantees of Land in the County of Bedford," in *PA*, 3rd ser., 25:621–23; "A Return of Property of the County of Bedford," in *PA*, 3rd ser., 22:159; Jones, *Pair of Lawn Sleeves*, 83–84; Jones, "Herman Husband," 210; and Konkle, *Life and Times of Thomas Smith*, 36–41.

51. Jones, *Pair of Lawn Sleeves*, 133–34.

52. Konkle, *Life and Times of Thomas Smith*, 42–49; Smith, *James Wilson*, 47; Jones, "Herman Husband," 211.

53. Smith, *St. Clair Papers*, 1:1–6, 12.

54. Ibid., 1:6–9; Smith, *James Wilson*, 47; Jones, "Herman Husband," 211–12.

55. The Woods faction also included Bedford attorneys Davis Espy and Bernard Dougherty. Espy was the son-in-law of George Woods. Dougherty, "an original lot owner in Bedford, received a justice commission in 1771, and served as a trustee who oversaw construction of the county courthouse and goal." See Jones, "Herman Husband," 212; and Espy, *History and Genealogy of the Espy Family in America*, 25.

56. Hatchett, *Some Neglected History Concerning Harmon Husband*, 23; Smith, *Bedford County, Pennsylvania, Quarter Sessions*, 46–48.

57. For a discussion of American colonists' reaction to the Tea Act, see Carp, *Defiance of the Patriots*.

58. The next highest bond was £500. See Smith, *Bedford County, Pennsylvania, Quarter Sessions*, 47.

59. Hatchett, *Some Neglected History Concerning Harmon Husband*, 23; Smith, *Bedford County, Pennsylvania, Quarter Sessions*, 46–48; Jones, "Herman Husband," 222.

60. Bouton, *Taming Democracy*, 16–30, 24 (quotation).

61. Ibid., 31–51, 35 (quotation).

62. Carp, *Defiance of the Patriots*, 192–200.

63. *Pennsylvania Journal*, July 20, 1775.

64. Middlekauff, *Glorious Cause*, 221–73; Selsam, *Pennsylvania Constitution of 1776*, 49–93; Thayer, *Pennsylvania Politics and the Growth of Democracy*, 153–73.

65. Foner, *Tom Paine and Revolutionary America*, 71–106.

66. Bouton, *Taming Democracy*, 52. The resolution recommended "to the colonies that where no government sufficient to the exigencies of their affairs existed, such a government should be adopted." See Ousterhout, *State Divided*, 133.

67. Ousterhout, *State Divided*, 103–39; Hogeland, *Founding Finance*, 42–71; Brunhouse, *Counter-Revolution in Pennsylvania*, 10–17; Hawke, *In the Midst of a Revolution*, 111–50; Selsam, *Pennsylvania Constitution of 1776*, 94–135; Thayer, *Pennsylvania Politics and the Growth of Democracy*, 175–97.

68. Bouton, *Taming Democracy*, 53, 55.

69. Quoted in Nash, *Unknown American Revolution*, 275.

70. Quoted in Bouton, *Taming Democracy*, 52.

71. For more on Pennsylvania's 1776 constitution, see Bouton, *Taming Democracy*, 51–57; Nash, *Unknown American Revolution*, 272–77; Selsam, *Pennsylvania Constitution of 1776*, 136–204; and Hawke, *In the Midst of a Revolution*, 181–200.

72. AQA.

73. *PAP*, 32.

74. *SBH*, ii.

75. AQA.

76. Baldwin, *Duty of Rejoicing*, 38.

77. Quoted in Foner, *Tom Paine and Revolutionary America*, 114.

78. Paine, "Common Sense," 1:45.

79. Strong, *Sermon*, 11.

80. For more on millennialism during the American Revolution, see Kidd, *God of Liberty*; Bloch, "Religion and Ideological Change in the American Revolution"; Smith, "'Promised Day of the Lord'"; Marini, "Uncertain Dawn"; Cherry, *God's New Israel*; Clark, *Language of Liberty*; Bloch, *Visionary Republic*, 53–93; Hatch, *Sacred Cause of Liberty*; Beam, "Millennialism and American Nationalism"; Tuveson, *Redeemer Nation*; and Miller, "From the Covenant to the Revival."

81. For more on loyalists, see Allen, *Tories*.

82. Ousterhout, *State Divided*, 148–49; Brunhouse, *Counter-Revolution in Pennsylvania*, 40–44.

83. Sadlier, "Prelude to the American Revolution?"; Kars, *Breaking Loose Together*, 212–14; Troxler, *Farming Dissenters*, 121–24.

84. "Memorandum from Superior Court at Hillsborough," in *RNC*, 566.

85. *PAP*, 17, 7.

86. Quoted in Selsam, *Pennsylvania Constitution of 1776*, 248.

87. For more on Republicans' opposition to the test oath and other clauses in the 1776 Pennsylvania Constitution, see Brunhouse, *Counter-Revolution in Pennsylvania*, 53–60, and Selsam, *Pennsylvania Constitution of 1776*, 205–64.

88. Thomas Smith to Arthur St. Clair, August 22, 1776, in Smith, *St. Clair Papers*, 1:373–74.

89. Thomas Smith to Arthur St. Clair, August 3, 1776, in ibid., 1:371. For more on Republicans' opposition to white male suffrage, see Selsam, *Pennsylvania Constitution of 1776*, 206–12.

90. Selsam, *Pennsylvania Constitution of 1776*, 205–54; Brunhouse, *Counter-Revolution in Pennsylvania*, 21–22, 27–38.

91. Of those four Republicans, three—Barnard Dougherty, David Espy, and Henry Rhoads—were known members of the Woods faction. See *Pennsylvania Evening Post*, November 23, 1776, and Brunhouse, *Counter-Revolution in Pennsylvania*, 27.

92. *Pennsylvania Journal*, March 19, 1777.

93. Jones, "Herman Husband," 234; Blackburn and Welfley, *History of Bedford and Somerset Counties*, 1:97.

94. "Committee of Correspondence of Bedford to President [Thomas] Wharton," October 2, 1777, in *PA*, 2nd ser., 3:113–14.

95. Robert Galbraith to Thomas Smith, September 29, 1777, in ibid., 1st ser., 5:638; "Deposition of Robert Galbraith," 1777, in ibid., 5:638; Robert Galbraith to Thomas Wharton, October 31, 1777, in ibid., 5:730–31; "Warrant for Arrest of Prothonotary of Bedford County," November 17, 1777, in ibid., 6:12; Brunhouse, *Counter-Revolution in Pennsylvania*, 36; Konkle, *Life and Times of Thomas Smith*, 89, 93–94; Jones, "Herman Husband," 235.

96. *Pennsylvania Evening Post*, March 15, 1777; *Pennsylvania Journal*, March 19, 1777; Konkle, *Life and Times of Thomas Smith*, 89–90; Hillegas, *Journals of the House of Representatives of the Commonwealth of Pennsylvania*, 129.

97. Hillegas, *Journals of the House of Representatives of the Commonwealth of Pennsylvania*, 131.

98. Brunhouse, *Counter-Revolution in Pennsylvania*, 46.

99. The other men were Charles Cisna, William McCoombe, John Burd, John Stephens, and John Stewart. See Hillegas, *Journals of the House of Representatives of the Commonwealth of Pennsylvania*, 161; "Election Returns, Bedford County, 1777–1789," in *PA*, 6th ser., 11:14; *Pennsylvania Evening Post*, September 19, 1776; *Pennsylvania Packet*, September 24, 1776; Selsam, *Pennsylvania Constitution of 1776*, 85–88; Whisker, *Bedford County, Pennsylvania, Archives*, 5:29; and Jones, "Herman Husband," 227–28, 236.

100. Brunhouse, *Counter-Revolution in Pennsylvania*, 46.

101. Husband took the test oath and assumed his seat in the assembly on December 17, 1777. See Hillegas, *Journals of the House of Representatives of the Commonwealth of Pennsylvania*, 174.

102. Jones, "Herman Husband," 238.

103. Ousterhout, *State Divided*, 145–73; Brunhouse, *Counter-Revolution in Pennsylvania*, 38–50.

104. Hillegas, *Journals of the House of Representatives of the Commonwealth of Pennsylvania*, 186.

105. Society of Friends, *A Collection of Memorials Concerning Divers, Deceased Ministers*, 433.

106. AQA.

107. Hillegas, *Journals of the House of Representatives of the Commonwealth of Pennsylvania*, 186.

108. AQA.

109. *Laws Enacted in the Second General Assembly*, 79–80; Hillegas, *Journals of the House of Representatives of the Commonwealth of Pennsylvania*, 177.

110. *Laws Enacted in the Second General Assembly*, 127–30; Hillegas, *Journals of the House of Representatives of the Commonwealth of Pennsylvania*, 186, 188; Ousterhout, *State Divided*, 145–78; Brunhouse, *Counter-Revolution in Pennsylvania*, 47–50.

111. Cooper, *Two Centuries of Brothersvalley Church of the Brethren*, 145–50, 168–70.

112. Hillegas, *Journals of the House of Representatives of the Commonwealth of Pennsylvania*, 193; Jones, "Herman Husband," 247.

113. Bezanson, *Prices and Inflation during the American Revolution, Pennsylvania*; Brunhouse, *Counter-Revolution in Pennsylvania*, 51–52.

114. *Laws Enacted in the Second General Assembly*, 125 (quotations); Hillegas, *Journals of the House of Representatives of the Commonwealth of Pennsylvania*, 177, 197, 203.

115. Duane, *Extracts from the Diary of Christopher Marshall*, 171. In 1778, Husband also had copies of his monetary plan published in Lancaster. The only extant copy of his 1778 scheme is included in Husband's *Proposals to Amend and Perfect*. See Husband, "A Proposal, or a General Plan and Mode of Taxation, throughout the American States," in *PAP*, 22–27.

116. *PAP*, 23, 22.

117. Ibid., 25.

118. Duane, *Extracts from the Diary of Christopher Marshall*, 171.

119. Brunhouse, *Counter-Revolution in Pennsylvania*, 53–60.

120. Robert Galbraith to Thomas Wharton, February 6, 1778, in *PA*, 1st ser., 6:238.

121. Robert Galbraith to Thomas Wharton, May 16, 1778, in ibid., 6:511 (quotation); Robert Galbraith to Thomas Wharton, February 6, 1778, in ibid., 6:238–39.

122. Robert Galbraith to James Martin, July 20, 1777, in Hoenstine, *History of Bedford, Somerset, and Fulton Counties*, 87 (quotation); Robert Galbraith to Thomas Wharton, May 16, 1778, in *PA*, 1st ser., 6:512. See also Robert Galbraith to Thomas Wharton, February 6, 1778, in *PA*, 1st ser., 6:238–39.

123. Hugh Davison to Council, May 15, 1778, in *PA*, 1st ser., 6:505.

124. The other men in Bedford County elected to the assembly were Henry Rhoads, Bernard Dougherty, Hugh Davison, and John Burd. Rhoads, Dougherty, and Davison were Republicans and members of the Woods faction. See "Election Returns, Bedford County, 1777–1789," in *PA*, 6th ser., 11:16, and Hillegas, *Journals of the House of Representatives of the Commonwealth of Pennsylvania*, 232.

125. For more on the frontier war in Pennsylvania, see Hinderaker and Mancall, *At the Edge of Empire*, 173–76; Garbarino, *Indian Wars along the Upper Ohio*; McClure, "Ends of the American Earth," 2:342–476; Thwaites and Kellogg, *Frontier Defense on the Upper Ohio*; Knouff, "Soldiers and Violence on the Pennsylvania Frontier"; Knouff, "'An Arduous Service'"; Buck and Buck, *Planting of Civilization in Western Pennsylvania*, 175–276; and Downes, *Council Fires of the Upper Ohio*, 179–276.

126. "Memorial of Inhabitants of Bedford County," May 19, 1778, in *PA*, 2nd ser., 3:168.

127. Jones, "Herman Husband," 265.

128. John Piper to Joseph Reed, August 6, 1780, in Hoenstine, *History of Bedford, Somerset, and Fulton Counties*, 94.

129. George Woods to Thomas Urie, July 4, 1779, in *PA*, 1st ser., 7:534.

130. Downes, *Council Fires of the Upper Ohio*, 274.

131. Bruner, *Recollections of Somerset County's Earliest Years*, 54–56; Jones, "Herman Husband," 279–80.

132. Brunhouse, *Counter-Revolution in Pennsylvania*, 88–91; Main, *Sovereign States*, 391.

133. "Transmitted by Tench Coxe from the Treasury Department, May 12, 1781," in Catanzariti and Ferguson, *Papers of Robert Morris*, 6:63 (quotation); Rappleye, *Robert Morris*, 242–43.

134. Main, *Sovereign States*, 253.

135. Ferguson, *Power of the Purse*, 113.

136. Brunhouse, *Counter-Revolution in Pennsylvania*, 96–97; Rappleye, *Robert Morris*, 244.

137. Bouton, *Taming Democracy*, 80–83; Rappleye, *Robert Morris*, 244.

138. *PAP*, 17–18. In other words, Husband believed that Republicans were acting contrary to the moral economy. For more on the moral economy, see Bogin, "Petitioning and the New Moral Economy of Post-Revolutionary America"; Nash, *Urban Crucible*; and Thompson, "Moral Economy of the English Crowd in the Eighteenth Century."

139. *PAP*, 17–21, 20, 21 (quotations).

140. For more on the forty-for-one funding measure, see Ver Steeg, *Robert Morris*, 45–46; Lefer, *Founding Conservatives*, 235; Rappleye, *Robert Morris*, 211–12; Main, *Sovereign States*, 251–52; and Ferguson, *Power of the Purse*, 51–52.

141. *PAP*, 29–30.

142. Ibid., 3–4 (quotation), 7–8.

143. Ibid., 4–10, 4, 10 (quotations).

144. Holton, *Unruly Americans*, 172.

145. Husband, *XIV Sermons*, vi.

146. *PAP*, 15, 8.

147. Spero, "Americanization of the Pennsylvania Almanac," 44.

148. For more on almanacs during the American Revolution, see Spero, "Revolution in Popular Publications"; Waldstreicher, *In the Midst of Perpetual Fetes*, 45–50; Raymond, "To Reach Men's Minds"; and Greenough, "New England Almanacs, 1766–1776, and the American Revolution."

149. Ellicott, *Maryland, Delaware, Pennsylvania, Virginia, and North-Carolina Almanack and Ephemeris, for the Year of our Lord, 1781*, 6–7 (quotation); Rittenhouse, *Continental Almanac, for the Year of our Lord, 1780*, 4; Rittenhouse, *Continental Almanac, for the Year of our Lord, 1781*, 2.

150. Jones, "Herman Husband," 266.

151. See Morrison, *Travels in the Confederation*, 292, and Hunter, "John Badollet's 'Journal of the Time I Spent in Stony Creek Glades,'" 175.

152. Ellicott, *Maryland, Delaware, Pennsylvania, Virginia, and North-Carolina Almanack and Ephemeris, for the Year of our Lord, 1781*, 7.

153. Ellicott, *Pennsylvania, Delaware, Maryland, and Virginia Almanack and Ephemeris, for the Year of our Lord, 1782*, 7.

154. Ellicott, *Pennsylvania, Delaware, Maryland, and Virginia Almanack and Ephemeris, for the Year of our Lord, 1783*, 6.

155. Ellicott, *Pennsylvania, Delaware, Maryland, and Virginia Almanack and Ephemeris, for the Year of our Lord, 1784*, 28.

156. AQA.

157. *PAP*, 32, 14.

FIVE. *"The New Jerusalem"*

1. Morrison, *Travels in the Confederation*, 292.

2. Ibid., 293. In 1780, Husband wrote a letter to the American Philosophical Society in Philadelphia disputing Burnet's theory. See Herman Husband to Lewis Nicola, April 26, 1780, RG IIa, 1743–1806, American Philosophical Society Archives.

3. Morrison, *Travels in the Confederation*, 292–93.

4. Ibid., 293–94.

5. *PAP*, 35; Husband, *XIV Sermons*, iv.

6. See Ezekiel, chaps. 40–48.

7. Husband, *XIV Sermons*, vi; Brackenridge, *Incidents of the Insurrection in the Western Parts of Pennsylvania*, 1:95.

8. *PAP*, 35; Revelation, chap. 21.

9. *PAP*, 36–37.

10. Husband, *XIV Sermons*, 23; *SBH*, ii (quotation).

11. *SBH*, 19; *PAP*, 11.

12. Bouton, "Tying Up the Revolution," 175–76.

13. Quoted in Bouton, *Taming Democracy*, 105.

14. "On the eve of independence [in Pennsylvania] . . . there had been approximately $5.30 per person in government paper in circulation. By comparison, in 1786

there was only about $1.90. At the end of 1790, the amount of currency stood at a mere 30 cents per person." Ibid., 91.

15. Quoted in ibid., 89–90.

16. For more on the economic troubles plaguing Pennsylvanians and other Americans during the 1780s, see Bouton, *Taming Democracy*; Holton, *Unruly Americans*; Richards, *Shays's Rebellion*; Lee, *Price of Nationhood*; Brown, *Redeeming the Republic*; Taylor, *Liberty Men and Great Proprietors*; Nadelhaft, *Disorders of War*; Szatmary, *Shays' Rebellion*; Flannagan, "Trying Times"; and Maganzin, "Economic Depression in Maryland and Virginia."

17. For more on Pennsylvanians' opposition to the Bank of North America, see Rappaport, *Stability and Change in Revolutionary Pennsylvania*.

18. Bouton, *Taming Democracy*, 79–80.

19. Carey, *Debates and Proceedings of the General Assembly*, 65–66.

20. Bouton, *Taming Democracy*, 83–87. For more on the bond speculation, see Holton, *Unruly Americans*; Brown, *Redeeming the Republic*; and Ferguson, *Power of the Purse*.

21. Bouton, *Taming Democracy*, 129–44.

22. *Carlisle [PA] Gazette*, February 22, 1786.

23. *Pennsylvania Gazette*, April 18, 1787.

24. *PAP*, 21, 20; *SBH*, 8.

25. Husband, *XIV Sermons*, 20, 23, 21, 19, 34–35 [1st pagination], 17 [2nd pagination].

26. "Transmitted by Tench Coxe from the Treasury Department, May 12, 1781," in Catanzariti and Ferguson, *Papers of Robert Morris*, 6:63.

27. For more on Robert Morris and economic conservatism during the 1780s, see Smith, *Robert Morris's Folly*; Rappleye, *Robert Morris*; Bouton, *Taming Democracy*; Holton, *Unruly Americans*; Brown, *Redeeming the Republic*; Lefer, *Founding Conservatives*; and Ferguson, *Power of the Purse*.

28. Bouton, *Taming Democracy*, 105–24, 145–67, 197–215.

29. Smith, *Bedford County, Pennsylvania, Quarter Sessions*, 199; David Jones to John Nicholson, January 19, 1787, roll 5, General Correspondence (1786–87), RG 4, Records of the Office of the Comptroller General, Pennsylvania State Archives.

30. *Gazette of the State of South Carolina*, May 6, 1784, quoted in Brown, *Redeeming the Republic*, 78.

31. See Holton, *Unruly Americans*; Lee, *Price of Nationhood*; Brown, *Redeeming the Republic*; Bellesiles, *Revolutionary Outlaws*; Nadelhaft, *Disorders of War*; Flannagan, "Trying Times"; and Maganzin, "Economic Depression in Maryland and Virginia."

32. Richards, *Shays's Rebellion*.

33. Edmund Randolph, May 29, 1787, in Farrand, *Records of the Federal Convention of 1787*, 1:26.

34. Robert Morris to Alexander Hamilton, August 28, 1782, in Catanzariti and Ferguson, *Papers of Robert Morris*, 6:271.

35. Alexander Hamilton, June 18, 1787, in Farrand, *Records of the Federal Convention of 1787*, 1:301.

36. Holton, *Unruly Americans*, 5.
37. Alexander Hamilton, "Conjectures about the New Constitution," September 17–30, 1787, in Syrett, *Papers of Alexander Hamilton*, 4:275.
38. James Madison to Thomas Jefferson, October 24, 1787, in Rutland et al., *Papers of James Madison*, 10:212.
39. See U.S. Constitution, art. I, sec. 8.
40. See U.S. Constitution, art. I, sec. 10.
41. Edmund Randolph, May 29, 1787, in Farrand, *Records of the Federal Convention of 1787*, 1:26.
42. James Madison, June 6, 1787, in ibid., 1:136. See also Bouton, *Taming Democracy*, 176–80.
43. *SBH*, iii. For more on American postmillennialism during the so-called Critical Period, see Bloch, *Visionary Republic*, 94–115, and Marini, "Uncertain Dawn."
44. *SBH*, iii; *DAC*, 6 (quotation).
45. *PAP*, 11.
46. *SBH*, 9, 11, 13, 14–15, 18–19.
47. AQA. These pamphlets were *A Sermon to the Bucks and Hinds of America* (1788), *XIV Sermons on the Characters of Jacob's Fourteen Sons* (1789), and *A Dialogue between an Assembly-Man and a Convention-Man* (1790).
48. Holton, *Unruly Americans*, 172; *DAC*, 6.
49. *SBH*, 14.
50. *DAC*, 5; *SBH*, 14, 15.
51. *SBH*, 14, 15.
52. Ibid., 12–14; *DAC*, 5–6.
53. *DAC*, 9–10. Under Husband's plan, ten townships would be combined to create a district, and three districts would be combined to create a county.
54. *PAP*, 14.
55. Husband, *XIV Sermons*, vi.
56. *SBH*, 21.
57. *DAC*, 6.
58. *SBH*, 21–22.
59. Ibid., 23, 30–31.
60. Ibid., 23–25.
61. Ibid., 2; Husband, *XIV Sermons*, 34.
62. *SBH*, 25–26, 28–29; *XIV Sermons*, 32–33.
63. *SBH*, 23–24; Jones, "Herman Husband," 306 (quotation).
64. *SBH*, 24.
65. Ibid., 23.
66. Whittenburg, "'Common Farmer (Number 2),'" 650; *SBH*, 23.
67. *PAP*, 12 (quotation); *SBH*, 23–24.
68. Husband, *XIV Sermons*, ix; *DAC*, 9.
69. This was particularly true with *XIV Sermons on the Characters of Jacob's Fourteen Sons*.
70. Husband, *XIV Sermons*, 17–18; *SBH*, iii (quotation).

71. Husband, *XIV Sermons*, 21, 29, 12; *SBH*, 19.
72. Husband, *XIV Sermons*, 33; *SBH*, 15.
73. Quoted in Young, *Liberty Tree*, 203–4.
74. Jones, "Herman Husband," 294.
75. Brunhouse, *Counter-Revolution in Pennsylvania*, 200–211; Bouton, *Taming Democracy*, 180–84.
76. *SBH*, 14.
77. Husband, *XIV Sermons*, 25. For more on James Wilson, see Smith, *James Wilson*.
78. Wilson, "Oration Delivered on the Fourth of July 1788, at the Procession Formed at Philadelphia," in McCloskey, *Works of James Wilson*, 2:774–75.
79. Husband, *XIV Sermons*, 31.
80. Ibid., v.
81. UM, 147.
82. Husband, *XIV Sermons*, 45–46, 22; *SBH*, 25–26.
83. Brackenridge, *Incidents of the Insurrection in the Western Parts of Pennsylvania*, 1:95.
84. Morrison, *Travels in the Confederation*, 295.
85. Writing to Thomas Jefferson in 1805, Gallatin also called Husband "the Pennsylvania madman." See Albert Gallatin to Hannah Gallatin, May 15, 1795, Papers of Albert Gallatin, roll 3 (January 3, 1794–May 23, 1798), New-York Historical Society; Testimony of Albert Gallatin, June 3, 1795, *United States v. Robert Philson and Harman Husbands*, folder 120, Court Cases, 1765–1808, William Paterson Papers, Askew Library; and Albert Gallatin to Thomas Jefferson, April 23, 1805, in Adams, *Writings of Albert Gallatin*, 1:229.
86. Hunter, "John Badollet's 'Journal of the Time I Spent in Stony Creek Glades,'" 173.
87. Testimony of Robert Smilie, June 3, 1795, *United States v. Robert Philson and Harman Husbands*, folder 120, William Paterson Papers, Askew Library. See also Holt, "New Jerusalem," 260.
88. Testimony of James Wells, June 3, 1795, *United States v. Robert Philson and Harman Husbands*, folder 120, William Paterson Papers, Askew Library.
89. Testimony of James Wilson, ibid.
90. Testimony of James Wells, ibid.; Husband, *XIV Sermons*, 21.
91. Smith, *Bedford County, Pennsylvania, Quarter Sessions*, 103, 112, 129, 133, 167, 172, 180, 199; Herman Husband to Thomas Mifflin, January 1, 1793, "Hermon Husband's Papers" folder, Internal Improvements File, RG 26, Records of the Department of State, Pennsylvania State Archives; Minutes of the Bedford County Commissioner's Records, Pioneer Library, Bedford County Historical Society; Holt, "New Jerusalem," 260; Jones, "Herman Husband," 266, 329.
92. *Minutes of the First Session of the Fourteenth General Assembly of the Commonwealth of Pennsylvania*, 38; *Carlisle Gazette*, January 6, 1790.
93. The complete proposed amendment read as follows: "After the first enumeration required by the first Article of the Constitution, there shall be one Representative

for every thirty thousand, until the number shall amount to one hundred, after which, the proportion shall be so regulated by Congress, that there shall be no less than one hundred Representatives, nor less than one Representative for every forty thousand persons, until the number of Representatives shall amount to two hundred, after which the proportion shall be so regulated by Congress, that there shall not be less than two hundred Representatives, nor more than one Representative for every fifty thousand persons." See Keller, "Pennsylvania's Role in the Origin and Defeat of the First Proposed Amendment on Representation," 73–74.

94. *Pennsylvania Packet*, December 18, 1787.

95. *Pittsburgh Gazette*, September 27, 1788.

96. Keller, "Pennsylvania's Role in the Origin and Defeat of the First Proposed Amendment on Representation," 98.

97. *DAC*, 4–5.

98. Quoted in Keller, "Pennsylvania's Role in the Origin and Defeat of the First Proposed Amendment on Representation," 99.

99. Richard Peters to James Madison, March 31, 1790, reel 4, series 1: General Correspondence, James Madison Papers, Library of Congress.

100. Jones, "Herman Husband," 340.

101. *Minutes of the Third Session of the Fourteenth General Assembly of the Commonwealth of Pennsylvania*, 295.

102. This article would not be ratified by the states until 1992. See Keller, "Pennsylvania's Role in the Origin and Defeat of the First Proposed Amendment on Representation," 73.

103. *DAC*, 7–8.

104. Roark et al., *Understanding the American Promise*, 232.

105. For more on Hamilton's first "Report on Public Credit," see Hogeland, *Founding Finance*, 160–76; Wright, *One Nation under Debt*, 131–35; Ferguson, *Power of the Purse*, 292–305; Rappleye, *Robert Morris*, 470–74; Brown, *Redeeming the Republic*, 236–40; and Holton, *Unruly Americans*, 258–62.

106. *DAC*, 11. For more on the policy of discrimination, see Wright, *One Nation under Debt*, 135–40; Holton, *Unruly Americans*, 258–61; and Ferguson, *Power of the Purse*, 297–305.

107. *DAC*, 11; Holton, *Unruly Americans*, 259–60.

108. *DAC*, 11.

109. Ibid., 12. The Funding Act also created a national bank. One year later, Congress passed the Revenue Act of 1791, which imposed excise taxes on domestically distilled whiskey and other luxuries.

110. Bouton, *Taming Democracy*, 195, 204, 208. For more on the 1790 state constitutional convention, see ibid., 194–96, and Brunhouse, *Counter-Revolution in Pennsylvania*, 221–27.

111. *DAC*, 2–3.

112. AQA.

113. Bouton, *Taming Democracy*, 195.

114. *Independent Gazetteer* (Philadelphia), September 11, 1790.

115. *Minutes of the Third Session of the Fourteenth General Assembly of the Commonwealth of Pennsylvania*, 301–2.
116. UM, 59, 80–81.
117. Ellicott, *Ellicott's Maryland and Virginia Almanac, and Ephemeris, for the Year Our Lord, 1791*, 17–18.
118. UM, 1.
119. Ibid., 6–8.
120. Jones, "Herman Husband," 345.
121. UM, 9–13, 14–16, 31–34, 12, 18 (quotations).
122. Ibid., 20, 47 (1st quotation), 131, 137, 1 (2nd quotation), 80–81, 59 (third quotation), 147–55, 148 (fourth quotation). Husband predicted that final accomplishment of the fifth kingdom in the western backcountry would occur between 1814 and 1844. For more on Husband's interpretation of Daniel's visions in the Old Testament, see Jones, "Herman Husband," 344–50.
123. *National Gazette* (Philadelphia), November 28, 1792; Alexander Hamilton to George Washington, September 9, 1792, in Syrett, *Papers of Alexander Hamilton*, 12:345; Alexander Hamilton to George Washington, September 1, 1792, in Syrett, *Papers of Alexander Hamilton*, 12:311–44; Alexander Hamilton to Tench Coxe, September 1, 1792, in Syrett, *Papers of Alexander Hamilton*, 12:305–10.
124. "Minutes of the Meeting at Pittsburgh," August 22, 1792, in *PA*, 2nd ser., 4:30–31. For more on the economic importance of whiskey distillation in Pennsylvania and other parts of the American frontier during the eighteenth century, see Slaughter, *Whiskey Rebellion*; Baldwin, *Whiskey Rebels*; Fennell, "From Rebelliousness to Insurrection"; Barksdale, "Our Rebellious Neighbors"; Crow, "The Whiskey Rebellion in North Carolina"; and Tachau, "New Look at the Whiskey Rebellion."
125. Brackenridge, *Incidents of the Insurrection in the Western Parts of Pennsylvania*, 3:14.
126. "Minutes of the Meeting at Pittsburgh," September 7, 1791, in *PA*, 2nd ser., 4:20–22.
127. Alexander Hamilton to George Washington, September 1, 1792, in Syrett, *Papers of Alexander Hamilton*, 12:312.
128. *National Gazette*, November 28, 1792; Baldwin, *Whiskey Rebels*, 87–90.
129. Bouton, *Taming Democracy*, 231–32.
130. *National Gazette*, November 28, 1792.
131. For more on resistance to the excise law and other federal policies in southwestern Pennsylvania before 1792, see Bouton, *Taming Democracy*, 197–215; Baldwin, *Whiskey Rebels*, 76–109; and Slaughter, *Whiskey Rebellion*, 109–57.
132. Findley, *Review of the Revenue System*, 125.
133. Bouton, *Taming Democracy*, 197–215; Baldwin, *Whiskey Rebels*, 76–109; Slaughter, *Whiskey Rebellion*, 109–57.
134. Findley, *Review of the Revenue System*, 128.
135. Alexander Hamilton to George Washington, September 1, 1792, in Chase et al., *Papers of George Washington*, 11:60.

136. Edmund Randolph to Alexander Hamilton, September 8, 1792, in Syrett, *Papers of Alexander Hamilton*, 12:336–40.

137. "Proclamation," September 15, 1792, in Chase et al., *Papers of George Washington*, 11:122–23. For more on Washington's decision to issue a proclamation, see Kohn, "Washington Administration's Decision to Crush the Whiskey Rebellion."

138. For more on Tom the Tinker, see Baldwin, *Whiskey Rebels*, 102–3; Slaughter, *Whiskey Rebellion*, 184–85; and Hogeland, *Whiskey Rebellion*, 130–32.

139. Davis, "Guarding the Republican Interest"; Sioli, "Democratic Republican Societies at the End of the Eighteenth Century."

140. For an excellent description of the gunfight, see Bouton, *Taming Democracy*, 230–34.

141. For more on the meeting at Braddock's Field, see Baldwin, *Whiskey Rebels*, 146–55; Slaughter, *Whiskey Rebellion*, 185–87; and Hogeland, *Whiskey Rebellion*, 172–78.

142. George Clymer to Alexander Hamilton, October 10, 1792, in Syrett, *Papers of Alexander Hamilton*, 12:541.

143. Findley, *History of the Insurrection in the Four Western Counties of Pennsylvania*, 107–9.

144. Rupp, *Early History of Western Pennsylvania*, appendix, 275. For more on the growing opposition to the whiskey tax in Bedford County, see John Webster to John Neville, August 2, 1794, John Neville Papers, Craig Manuscript Collection, William R. Oliver Special Collections Room, Carnegie Library.

145. Testimony of David Wright, June 3, 1795, *United States v. Robert Philson and Harman Husbands*, folder 120, William Paterson Papers, Askew Library.

146. Testimony of William Dunn, June 3, 1795, ibid.; James Ross, Jasper Yeates, and William Bradford to Edmund Randolph, August 17, 1794, in *PA*, 2nd ser., 4:163.

147. The delegates represented Bedford, Washington, Fayette, Westmoreland, and Allegheny Counties in southwestern Pennsylvania, and Ohio County in northwestern Virginia. See Baldwin, *Whiskey Rebels*, 174–75, and Hogeland, *Whiskey Rebellion*, 182.

148. Testimony of Albert Gallatin, June 3, 1795, *United States v. Robert Philson and Harman Husbands*, folder 120, William Paterson Papers, Askew Library; Baldwin, *Whiskey Rebels*, 103, 169–70.

149. James Ross, Jasper Yeates, and William Bradford to Edmund Randolph, August 17, 1794, in *PA*, 2nd ser., 4:163–66.

150. For more on events during the first day of the Parkinson's Ferry meeting, see Baldwin, *Whiskey Rebels*, 174–77. For more on David Bradford, see McClure, "Let Us Be Independent."

151. Findley, *History of the Insurrection in the Four Western Counties of Pennsylvania*, 114.

152. Brackenridge, *Incidents of the Insurrection in the Western Parts of Pennsylvania*, 1:94; Testimony of Albert Gallatin, June 3, 1795, *United States v. Robert Philson and Harman Husbands*, folder 120, William Paterson Papers, Askew Library.

153. Brackenridge, *Incidents of the Insurrection in the Western Parts of Pennsylvania*, 1:95.

154. Baldwin, *Whiskey Rebels*, 180.

155. Ibid., 180–81; Slaughter, *Whiskey Rebellion*, 196–97.

156. Kohn, "Washington Administration's Decision to Crush the Whiskey Rebellion," 575–76.

157. Baldwin, *Whiskey Rebels*, 180–81.

158. Brackenridge, *Incidents of the Insurrection in the Western Parts of Pennsylvania*, 3:139.

159. Gallatin, *Speech of Albert Gallatin*, 16.

160. The "resolutions adopted by the assembly were conciliatory, rather than provocative. Delegates protested attempts to bring citizens to trial outside their neighborhood. They appointed a committee to petition Congress for repeal of the excise law and substitution of a 'less odious tax'; and pledged that such attacks 'will be cheerfully paid by the people of these counties.' They committed themselves to 'support of the municipal laws of the respective states,' but declined to guarantee compliance with all federal laws." See Slaughter, *Whiskey Rebellion*, 189.

161. "Propositions Submitted by the U.S. Commissioners," August 22, 1794, *PA*, 2nd ser., 4:192.

162. "Resolutions at Red Stone Old Fort," ibid., 211–12.

163. Findley, *History of the Insurrection in the Four Western Counties of Pennsylvania*, 124–25.

164. Smith, *Great Whiskey Rebellion*, 101.

165. Slaughter, *Whiskey Rebellion*, 201.

166. Kohn, "Washington Administration's Decision to Crush the Whiskey Rebellion," 578–79.

167. Baldwin, *Whiskey Rebels*, 225.

168. Kohn, "Washington Administration's Decision to Crush the Whiskey Rebellion," 579, 581.

169. Jasper Yeates and William Bradford to Secretary of State, September 5, 1794, container 1, Pennsylvania Whiskey Rebellion Collection, Library of Congress.

170. Smith, *Great Whiskey Rebellion*, 99. In November 1794, the Bedford County Court of Quarter Sessions charged 124 residents with riot and treason for raising these liberty poles. See Smith, *Bedford County, Pennsylvania, Quarter Sessions*, 228–36.

171. Robert Philson to Albert Gallatin, September 6, 1794, Papers of Albert Gallatin, roll 3, New-York Historical Society.

172. Testimony of James Wells, June 3, 1795, *United States v. Robert Philson and Harman Husbands*, folder 120, William Paterson Papers, Askew Library. See also Testimony of George Burchart, June 3, 1795, *United States v. Robert Philson and Harman Husbands*, folder 120, William Paterson Papers, Askew Library.

173. Testimony of James Wells, June 3, 1795, ibid. See also testimonies of Robert Smilie, George Burchart, William Fitzhman, Thomas Kennedy, James Wilson, Thomas Miffin, and Philip King, June 3, 1795, all ibid.

174. Testimony of Abel Faith, June 3, 1795, ibid.

175. Tench Coxe to William Rawle, October 1, 1794, roll 1, M414 (May 11, 1792–December 19, 1795), Letters Sent by the Commissioner of the Revenue and the Revenue Office, 1792–1802, RG 58, Records of the Internal Revenue Service, National Archives II.

176. Dorland, "The Second Troop Philadelphia City Cavalry," 154.

177. *Connecticut Journal*, November 6, 1794 (quotation); *Gazette of the United States* (Philadelphia), October 28, 1794. For more on Husband's capture, see *New York Daily Advertiser*, October 29, 1794; *New Jersey State Gazette*, October 29, 1794; *Independent Gazetteer*, November 1, 1794; Dorland, "The Second Troop Philadelphia City Cavalry," 154; Robert Philson to William Rawle, October 21, 1794, box 5, folder 4, series 1c, Rawle Family Papers, Historical Society of Pennsylvania; Findley, *History of the Insurrection in the Four Western Counties of Pennsylvania*, 151–52, 212–13; Dallas, *Life and Writings of Alexander James Dallas*, 42; and George Washington, diary, October 20, 1794, in Fitzpatrick, *Diaries of George Washington*, 4:223.

178. Quoted in Smith, *Great Whiskey Rebellion*, 100.

179. *Philadelphia General Advertiser*, October 30, 1794; *Washington Spy*, November 4, 1794; Parsons, *Extracts from the Diary of Jacob Hiltzheimer*, 209; George Washington to Alexander Hamilton, October 31, 1794, in Fitzpatrick, *Writings of George Washington*, 34:10.

180. Baldwin, *Whiskey Rebels*, 235–36; Slaughter, *Whiskey Rebellion*, 216–17.

181. Baldwin, *Whiskey Rebels*, 241.

182. "A total of 64 men were eventually jailed or faced with criminal charges as a result of the Rebellion (including 22 from Franklin, Northumberland, and Cumberland Counties in the east, four from Bedford, and one from Ohio County, Virginia). Only two of this whole group would ever be convicted of any crime resulting from the Rebellion." See Holt, "Whiskey Rebellion of 1794," 74.

183. Brackenridge, *History of the Western Insurrection in Western Pennsylvania*, 330.

184. Slaughter, *Whiskey Rebellion*, 219.

185. Caruthers, *Sketch of the Life and Character of the Rev. David Caldwell*, 168.

186. *United States v. Robert Philson and Harmon Husbands*, May 11, 1795, roll 1, M-986, "Criminal Case Files of the U.S. Circuit Court for the Eastern District of Pennsylvania, 1791–1840," RG 21, Records of District Courts of the United States, National Archives Regional Office, Philadelphia.

187. *United States v. Robert Philson and Harmon Husbands*, June 3, 4, 1795, roll 1, M-932, "Engrossed Minutes, 1792–1808," "Minutes of the U.S. Circuit Court for the Eastern District of Pennsylvania," RG 21, Records of District Courts of the United States, National Archives Regional Office, Philadelphia.

188. Testimony of William Fitzhman, June 3, 1795, *United States v. Robert Philson and Harman Husbands*, folder 120, William Paterson Papers, Askew Library.

189. *United States v. Robert Philson and Harmon Husbands*, June 4, 1795, roll 1, M-932, "Engrossed Minutes, 1792–1808," "Minutes of the U.S. Circuit Court for the Eastern District of Pennsylvania," RG 21, Records of District Courts of the United States, National Archives Regional Office, Philadelphia; Holt, "New Jerusalem," 271.

190. CIR, 76

191. The exact date of Husband's death remains a mystery. Given that he was buried on June 19, he likely passed away the previous day. It also remains unclear if Emey was present when he died. According to Eli Caruthers in 1842, she was "with him in his final hours," but there is no evidence to support this claim. Given that his body was not taken back to Bedford County, she was likely not with him. See Caruthers, *Sketch of the Life and Character of the Rev. David Caldwell*, 168.

192. Biddle, *Extracts from the Journal of Elizabeth Drinker*, 269.

Conclusion

1. *PAP*, 10.
2. UM, 124.
3. Nelson, *Thomas Paine*, 335 (quotation); Merrill and Wilentz, *Key of Liberty*; Skemp, "America's Mary Wollstonecraft."
4. For a sample of this scholarship, see Wood, "Religion and the American Revolution"; Bonomi, *Under the Cope of Heaven*; Kars, *Breaking Loose Together*; Kidd, *Great Awakening*; and Butler, *New World Faiths*.
5. Wood, "Religion and the American Revolution," 181.
6. Kars, *Breaking Loose Together*, 82.
7. Kidd, *God of Liberty*, 21. For a sample of this scholarship, see Bonomi, *Under the Cope of Heaven*; Isaac, *Transformation of Virginia*; Kars, *Breaking Loose Together*; Bloch, *Visionary Republic*; Kidd, *Great Awakening*; Heimert, *Religion and the American Mind*; Bushman, *From Puritan to Yankee*; and Smith, *First Great Awakening*.
8. Bonomi, *Under the Cope of Heaven*, 147.
9. Kidd, *American Colonial History*, 222.
10. Kidd, *Great Awakening*, 323.
11. *SPNT*, 56.
12. Bonomi, *Under the Cope of Heaven*, 158.
13. Quoted in Marsden, *Jonathan Edwards*, 264.
14. Connors and Gow, "Anglo-American Millennialism," xv. For more on postmillennialism and the secular belief in human progress, see Bloch, *Visionary Republic*; Brekus, *Sarah Osborn's World*, 301–5; Davidson, *Logic of Millennial Thought*, 31–33; and Tuveson, *Redeemer Nation*, 38–39. Tuveson downplays the influence of the Enlightenment on postmillennial thought.
15. Bloch, *Visionary Republic*, 18.
16. Ibid.; *SRR*, 30.
17. *SPNT*, 52; UM, 4 (quotation).
18. *SPNT*, 54.
19. The two best works on radical Whigs remain Caroline Robbins's *Eighteenth-Century Commonwealthman* and Bernard Bailyn's *Ideological Origins of the American Revolution*.
20. Bloch, *Visionary Republic*, 5.
21. Bailyn, *Ideological Origins of the American Revolution*, 47.

22. Lefer, *Founding Conservatives*, 18.

23. *SRR*, 25.

24. *UM*, 5.

25. Ibid.

26. *IR*, 89–90.

27. Like most colonial Americans who embraced radical Whig ideology, Husband did not seek to abolish government but to eradicate the corruption that existed within it. He was not averse to the creation of a strong, activist government that remained beholden to the people and worked for the common good. In other words, Husband's support for radical Whig ideology did not prevent him from viewing government as a vehicle for reform. For a recent discussion on patriots' endorsement of an activist government, see Novak and Pincus, "Revolutionary State Formation."

28. *UM*, 6.

29. For a sample of this scholarship, see Noll, *America's God*; Noll, *Christians in the American Revolution*; Byrd, *Sacred Scripture, Sacred War*; Clark, *Language of Liberty*; Kidd, *God of Liberty*; Bloch, *Visionary Republic*; Bonomi, *Under the Cope of Heaven*; Hatch, *Sacred Cause of Liberty*; and Kars, *Breaking Loose Together*.

30. Noll, *Christians in the American Revolution*, 56–57, 52.

31. For more on these agrarian protest movements, see Kim, *Landlord and Tenant in Colonial New York*; Countryman, "'Out of the Bounds of the Law'"; Klein, *Unification of a Slave State*; Shalhope, *Bennington and the Green Mountain Boys*; McConville, *These Daring Disturbers of the Public Peace*; Kulikoff, *From British Peasants to Colonial American Farmers*; Humphrey, *Land and Liberty*; Johnson, "Regulation Reconsidered"; and Norton et al., *People and a Nation*, 113 (quotation).

32. Bouton, *Taming Democracy*, 14.

33. Nash, "Poverty and Politics in Early American History," 13.

34. For more on the decline in the fortunes of colonial farmers, see Smith, *Down and Out in Early America*, and Smith, "Poverty and Economic Marginality in Eighteenth-Century America."

35. Quoted in McConville, *These Daring Disturbers of the Public Peace*, 168.

36. For an excellent discussion on the labor theory of value in colonial America, see Huston, *Securing the Fruits of Labor*.

37. Shalhope, *Bennington and the Green Mountain Boys*, 85.

38. For more on the formation of class identity in colonial America, see Young and Nobles, *Whose American Revolution Was It?* especially 192–223; Middleton and Smith, *Class Matters*; Young, *Liberty Tree*, especially 227–31; and Kulikoff, "American Revolution, Capitalism, and the Formation of the Yeoman Classes."

39. For more on farmers' critique of land and wealth inequality, see Huston, *Securing the Fruits of Labor*; Bouton, *Taming Democracy*; Thompson, *Politics of Inequality*; and Fatovic, *America's Founding and the Struggle over Economic Inequality*.

40. *IR*, 65–66.

41. Husband, *XIV Sermons*, 23.

42. *IR*, 77–78.

43. Ibid., 66, 85, 78.

44. Quoted in Szatmary, *Shays' Rebellion*, 36.

45. For more on these protest movements, see Bouton, *Taming Democracy*; Holton, *Unruly Americans*; Richards, *Shays's Rebellion*; Lee, *Price of Nationhood*; Brown, *Redeeming the Republic*; Taylor, *Liberty Men and Great Proprietors*; Nadelhaft, *Disorders of War*; Szatmary, *Shays' Rebellion*; Flannagan, "Trying Times"; Maganzin, "Economic Depression in Maryland and Virginia"; and Smith, *Freedoms We Lost*.

46. Young, *Liberty Tree*, 226.

47. "Transmitted by Tench Coxe from the Treasury Department, May 12, 1781," in Catanzariti and Ferguson, *Papers of Robert Morris*, 6:63.

48. Husband, *XIV Sermons*, 32.

49. Bouton, *Taming Democracy*, 101.

50. Slaughter, *Whiskey Rebellion*, 65–66.

51. *SBH*, 13.

52. Husband, *XIV Sermons*, 33.

53. UM, 156.

54. *SBH*, iii.

55. Husband, *XIV Sermons*, 13, 29–30 [2nd pagination].

56. For a sample of this scholarship, see Balik, "Persecuted in the Bowels of a Free Republic"; Young, Nash, and Raphael, *Revolutionary Founders*; Gross, *In Debt to Shays*; Taylor, *Liberty Men and Great Proprietors*; Hatch, *Democratization of American Christianity*; and Bloch, *Visionary Republic*.

57. Taylor, *Liberty Men and Great Proprietors*, 143.

58. Albert Gallatin to Hannah Gallatin, May 15, 1795, Papers of Albert Gallatin, roll 3, New-York Historical Society.

59. For scholarship on divisions within radical ranks over the use of extralegal protest and violence, see Bouton, "William Findley, David Bradford, and the Pennsylvania Regulation of 1794," and Young, *Liberty Tree*, 243–45.

60. Husband, *XIV Sermons*, 21.

61. Although I have elected to use the word "capitalism," it is important to note that the term was not commonly employed until the late nineteenth century. For a sample of scholarship on the nature and expansion of capitalism during and after the American Revolution, see Post, *American Road to Capitalism*; Smith, *Freedoms We Lost*; Lamoreaux, "Rethinking the Transition to Capitalism in the Early American Northeast"; Appleby, "Vexed Story of Capitalism Told by American Historians"; Kulikoff, *From British Peasants to Colonial American Farmers*; Gilje, *Wages of Independence*; Gilje, "Rise of Capitalism in the Early Republic"; Clark et al., "Transition to Capitalism in America"; Merrill and Wilentz, *Key of Liberty*; Rothenberg, *From Market Places to a Market Economy*; Merrill, "Putting 'Capitalism' in Its Place"; Clark, *Roots of Rural Capitalism*; Vickers, "Competency and Competition"; and McCoy, *Elusive Republic*.

62. Foner, *Tom Paine and Revolutionary America*, 26–27.

63. Ellicott, *Pennsylvania, Delaware, Maryland, and Virginia Almanack and Ephemeris, for the Year of our Lord, 1784*, 29; emphasis added. Seven years later, Husband would declare, "The American farmer has a constant demand for the fruits of

his labour—there is no fear of his industry meeting with an ample reward, while the ships of all nations are crouding to our ports, to purchase the various articles of our produce." See Ellicott, *Ellicott's Maryland and Virginia Almanac, and Ephemeris, for the Year of our Lord, 1791*, 17.

64. Taylor, *Liberty Men and Great Proprietors*, 8.

65. In other words, Husband and other agrarian reformers were neither "modern entrepreneurial capitalists in embryo" nor "backward-looking agrarians who resisted the economic transformations of the late eighteenth century." Influenced by Lockean liberalism and republicanism, they were a combination of both; they embraced the benefits of commercial capitalism while also hoping to maintain a moral economy. Cotlar, *Tom Paine's America*, 158. For more on the moral economy, see Bogin, "Petitioning and the New Moral Economy of Post-Revolutionary America"; Nash, *Urban Crucible*; and Thompson, "Moral Economy of the English Crowd in the Eighteenth Century."

66. NGL, 643.

67. Moreover, as Terry Bouton has argued, many ordinary white men, unable to achieve economic independence, ultimately doubled down on protecting the privileges that the Revolution had bestowed on them. By the nineteenth century, they increasingly directed their anger not at moneyed men but toward African Americans, women, and other groups who protested against white supremacy and patriarchy, the two institutions that allowed white men—regardless of their economic standing—to remain atop the social hierarchy. See Bouton, *Taming Democracy*, 263–65.

68. For more on economic populism during the nineteenth century, see Wilentz, "America's Lost Egalitarian Tradition"; Huston, *Securing the Fruits of Labor*; Thompson, *Politics of Inequality*; and Shankman, *Crucible of American Democracy*.

Bibliography

Unpublished Primary Sources

American Philosophical Society Archives, American Philosophical Society, Philadelphia
    Record Group IIA, 1743–1846

Askew Library, William Paterson University, Paterson, New Jersey
    William Paterson Papers, 1689–1841

Friends Historical Collection, Hege Library, Guilford College, Greensboro, North Carolina
    Cane Creek Monthly Meeting (Minutes), 1751–1796
    Western Quarterly Meeting (Minutes), 1760–1900

H. Furlong Baldwin Library, Maryland Historical Society, Baltimore
    Bond Family Papers, 1749–1844
    Cecil County (MD) Papers, 1739–1831
    Principio Company Papers, 1670–1913

Heinz History Center, Historical Society of Western Pennsylvania, Pittsburgh, Pennsylvania
    Papers of Robert Ayres, 1785–1837
    Papers of the John Irwin Scull Family, 1736–1956

Hillman Library, Special Collections, University of Pittsburgh
    Mary Elinor Lazenby Papers, 1933–1955

Historical Society of Pennsylvania, Philadelphia
    Christopher Marshall Papers, 1744–1971
    Rawle Family Papers, 1682–1921
    Jasper Yeates Papers, 1733–1876

Library of Congress, Washington, D.C.
    Christian Boerstler Papers, 1784–1915
    George Clymer Papers, 1781–1793
    James Madison Papers, 1723–1836
    Pennsylvania Whiskey Rebellion Collection, 1792–1796

Maryland State Archives, Annapolis
    Nottingham Monthly Meeting Minutes, 1730–1756
    Land Office (Patent Records), 1637–1975
    Prerogative Court (Inventories and Accounts), 1674–1718
    Prerogative Court (Wills), 1635–1777
    St. Mary's City Men's Career Files, n.d.

National Archives II, College Park, Maryland
    Domestic Letters of the Department of State, 1784–1906
    Records of the Internal Revenue Service, 1791–1996

National Archives Regional Office, Philadelphia
    Records of District Courts of the United States, 1685–1993

New-York Historical Society, New York City
    Papers of Albert Gallatin, 1258–1947

Pennsylvania State Archives, Harrisburg
    Luckens-Lenox Papers, 1702–1900
    Records of the Department of State, 1790–1902
    Records of the Office of the Comptroller General, 1776–1809
    Somerset County: Estate Papers, 1795–1857
    Somerset County: Register of Wills, 1795–1841

Pioneer Library, Bedford County Historical Society, Bedford, Pennsylvania
    Minutes of the Bedford County Commissioner's Records, 1785–1788

Southern Historical Collection, University of North Carolina at Chapel Hill
    Fanning and McCulloh Papers, 1758–1822
    Orange County (NC) Court Records, 1769–1771

State Archives of North Carolina, Raleigh
    English Records, 1729–1780

William R. Oliver Special Collections Room, Carnegie Library, Pittsburgh
    Craig Manuscript Collection, 1748–1808

Published Primary Sources

Adams, Henry, ed. *The Writings of Albert Gallatin*. 3 vols. Philadelphia: J. B. Lippincott, 1879.

Alsop, George. *A Character of the Province of Maryland*. London: Peter Dring, 1666.

Baldwin, Ebenezer. *The Duty of Rejoicing*. New York: Hugh Gaine, 1776.

Barclay, Robert. *An Apology for the True Christian Divinity: Being an Explanation and Vindication of the Principles of the People Called Quakers*. 1676; Dublin: L. Flin, 1780.

Barnes, Robert, ed. *Maryland Marriages, 1634–1777*. Baltimore: Genealogical Publishing, 1976.

Bennett, William D., ed. *Orange County Records*, vol. 1, *Granville Proprietary Land Office: Abstracts of Loose Papers*. Raleigh, NC: Privately published, 1987.

———. *Orange County Records*, vol. 2, *Deed Books 1 and 2: Abstracts*. Raleigh, NC: Privately published, 1989.

———. *Orange County Records*, vol. 3, *Deed Book 3: Abstracts*. Raleigh, NC: Privately published, 1990.

Biddle, Henry D., ed. *Extracts from the Journal of Elizabeth Drinker: From 1759–1807*. Philadelphia: J. B. Lippincott, 1889.

Boyer, Carl, III, ed. *Ship Passenger Lists: The South, 1538–1825*. Newhall, CA: Carl Boyer III, 1979.

Brackenridge, Hugh Henry. *Incidents of the Insurrection in the Western Parts of Pennsylvania, in the Year 1794*. 3 vols. Philadelphia: John M'Culloch, 1795.

Brown, June D., ed. *Abstracts of Cecil County, Maryland, Land Records, 1673–1751*. Berwyn Heights, MD: Heritage Books, 2003.

———. *Abstracts of Cecil County, Maryland, Land Records, 1734–1753*. Berwyn Heights, MD: Heritage Book, 2009.

Bruner, Ronald G., ed. *Recollections of Somerset County's Earliest Years*. Rockwood, PA: Somerset County Historical and Genealogical Society, 2005.

Carey, Mathew, ed. *Debates and Proceedings of the General Assembly, on the Memorial Praying a Repeal or Suspension of the Law Annulling the Charter of the Bank*. Philadelphia: Seddon and Pritchard, 1786.

Catanzariti, John, and E. James Ferguson, eds. *The Papers of Robert Morris, 1781–1784*, vol. 6, *July 22–October 31, 1782*. Pittsburgh: University of Pittsburgh Press, 1984.

Chase, Philander D., et al., eds. *The Papers of George Washington: Presidential Series*, vol. 11, *August 1792–January 1793*. Charlottesville: University Press of Virginia, 1987.

Clark, Walter, ed. *The State Records of North Carolina*, vol. 25, *Laws 1789–1790*. Goldsboro, NC: Nash Brothers, 1906.

Comly, John, and Isaac Comly, eds. *Friends' Miscellany*. Vol. 12. Philadelphia: J. Richards, 1839.

"Commission Book, 82." *Maryland Historical Magazine* 26 (September 1931): 138–58, 244–63, 342–61.

Cotton, Jane Baldwin, ed. "Notes from the Early Records of Maryland." *Maryland Historical Magazine* 16 (March 1921): 369–85.

Dallas, George Mifflin, ed. *The Life and Writings of Alexander James Dallas*. Philadelphia: J. B. Lippincott, 1871.

Dorland, W. A. Newman, ed. "The Second Troop Philadelphia City Cavalry." *Pennsylvania Magazine of History and Biography* 47, no. 2 (1923): 147–77.

Duane, William, ed. *Extracts from the Diary of Christopher Marshall, Kept in Philadelphia during the American Revolution, 1774–1781*. Albany, NY: J. Munsell, 1877.

Ekirch, A. Roger, ed. "'A New Government of Liberty': Hermon Husband's Vision of Backcountry North Carolina." *William and Mary Quarterly*, 3rd ser., 34 (October 1977): 632–46.

Ellicott, Andrew, ed. *Ellicott's Maryland and Virginia Almanac, and Ephemeris, for the Year of Our Lord, 1791*. Baltimore: John Hayes, 1790.

———. *The Maryland, Delaware, Pennsylvania, Virginia, and North-Carolina Almanack and Ephemeris, for the Year of Our Lord, 1781*. Baltimore: M. K. Goddard, 1780.

———. *The Pennsylvania, Delaware, Maryland, and Virginia Almanack and Ephemeris, for the Year of Our Lord, 1782*. Baltimore: M. K. Goddard, 1781.

———. *The Pennsylvania, Delaware, Maryland, and Virginia Almanack and Ephemeris, for the Year of Our Lord, 1783*. Baltimore: M. K. Goddard, 1782.

———. *The Pennsylvania, Delaware, Maryland, and Virginia Almanack and Ephemeris, for the Year of Our Lord, 1784*. Baltimore: M. K. Goddard, 1783.

———. *William Goddard's Pennsylvania, Delaware, Maryland, and Virginia Almanack and Ephemeris, for the Year of Our Lord, 1785*. Baltimore: William Goddard, 1784.

Equiano, Olaudah. *The Interesting Narrative of the Life of Olaudah Equiano*. Gloucester, MA: Dodo Press, 2008.

Farrand, Max, ed. *The Records of the Federal Convention of 1787*. Vol. 1. New Haven, CT: Yale University Press, 1966.

Findley, William. *A History of the Insurrection in the Four Western Counties of Pennsylvania*. Philadelphia: Samuel Harrison Smith, 1796.

———. *A Review of the Revenue System Adopted by the First Congress under the Federal Constitution*. Philadelphia: T. Dobson, 1794.

Fitzpatrick, John C., ed. *The Diaries of George Washington, 1748–1799*, vol. 4, *1789–1799*. Boston: Houghton Mifflin, 1925.

———, ed. *The Writings of George Washington from the Original Manuscript Sources, 1795–1799*, vol. 34, *October 11, 1794–March 29, 1796*. Washington, DC: Government Printing Office, 1940.

Foner, Philip S., ed. *The Complete Writings of Thomas Paine*. 2 vols. New York: Citadel Press, 1945.

Forman, Henry Chandlee, ed. "The Narrative of Colonel James Rigbie." *Maryland Historical Quarterly* 36 (March 1941): 39–49.

Fries, Adelaide L., ed. *Records of the Moravians in North Carolina*, vol. 1, *1752–1771*. Raleigh, NC: Edwards and Broughton, 1922.

Gallatin, Albert. *The Speech of Albert Gallatin . . . on the Important Question Touching the Validity of the Elections Held in the Four Western Counties of the State, on the 14th Day of October, 1794*. Philadelphia: William W. Woodward, 1795.

Hall, Clayton Colman, ed. *Narratives of Early Maryland, 1633–1684*. New York: Charles Scribner's Sons, 1910.

Heimert, Alan, and Perry Miller, eds. *The Great Awakening: Documents Illustrating the Crisis and Its Consequences*. Indianapolis: Bobbs-Merrill, 1967.

Henderson, Archibald, ed. "Hermon Husband's Continuation of the Impartial Relation." *North Carolina Historical Review* 18 (January 1941): 48–81.

Hillegas, Michael, ed. *Journals of the House of Representatives of the Commonwealth of Pennsylvania. Beginning the Twenty-Eighth Day of November, 1776, and Ending the Second Day of October, 1781. With the Proceedings of the Several Committees and Conventions, before and at the Commencement of the American Revolution*. Philadelphia: John Dunlap, 1782.

Hinke, William J., ed. "Report of the Journey of Francis Louis Michel from Berne, Switzerland to Virginia, October 2, 1701–December 1, 1702." *Virginia Magazine of History and Biography* 24 (April 1916): 1–43.

Hogan, Margaret A., and C. James Taylor, eds. *My Dearest Friend: Letters of Abigail and John Adams*. Cambridge, MA: Belknap Press of Harvard University Press, 2007.

Hooker, Richard J., ed. *The Carolina Backcountry on the Eve of the Revolution: The Journal and Other Writings of Charles Woodmason, Anglican Itinerant*. Chapel Hill: University of North Carolina Press, 1953.

Hunter, William A., ed. "John Badollet's 'Journal of the Time I Spent in Stony Creek Glades,' 1793–1794." *Pennsylvania Magazine of History and Biography* 104 (April 1980): 162–99.

Husband, Herman. *A Dialogue between an Assembly-Man and a Convention-Man, on the Subject of the State Constitution of Pennsylvania*. Philadelphia: William Spotswood, 1790.

———. *A Fan for Fanning and Touchstone to Tryon, Containing an Impartial Account of the Rise and Progress of the So Much Talked about Regulation in North-Carolina*. Boston: Daniel Kneeland, 1771.

———. *XIV Sermons on the Characters of Jacob's Fourteen Sons*. Philadelphia: William Spotswood, 1789.

———. *An Impartial Relation of the First Rise and Cause of the Recent Differences, in Publick Affairs, in the Province of North Carolina; and of the Past Tumults and Riots That Lately Happened in That Province*. New Bern, NC: Herman Husband, 1770.

———. *Proposals to Amend and Perfect the Policy of the Government of the United States of America*. Lancaster, PA: Herman Husband, 1782.

———. *The Second Part of the Naked Truth; or, Historical Account of the Actual Transactions of Quakers in Their Meetings of Business*. New Bern, NC: N.p., 1768.

———. *A Sermon to the Bucks and Hinds of America*. Philadelphia: Herman Husband, 1788.

———. *Some Remarks on Religion, with the Author's Experience in Pursuit Thereof*. Philadelphia: William Bradford, 1761.

Rutland, Robert A., et al., eds. *The Papers of James Madison*, vol. 10, *May 27–March 3, 1788*. Chicago: University of Chicago Press, 1977.

Jensen, Merrill, ed. *The Documentary History of the Ratification of the Constitution: Ratification of the Constitution by the States: Pennsylvania*. Madison: State Historical Society of Wisconsin, 1976.

Laws Enacted in the Second General Assembly of the Representatives of the Freemen of the Common-Wealth of Pennsylvania. Lancaster: John Dunlap, 1778.

McCloskey, Robert Green, ed. *The Works of James Wilson*. 2 vols. Cambridge, MA: Harvard University Press, 1967.

Minutes of the First Session of the Fourteenth General Assembly of the Commonwealth of Pennsylvania, Which Commenced at Philadelphia, on Monday, the Twenty-Sixth Day of October, in the Year of Our Lord One Thousand Seven Hundred and Eighty-Nine. Philadelphia: Hall and Sellers, 1789.

Minutes of the Third Session of the Fourteenth General Assembly of the Commonwealth of Pennsylvania, Which Commenced at Philadelphia, on Tuesday, the Fourth Day of August, in the Year of Our Lord One Thousand Seven Hundred and Ninety. Philadelphia: Hall and Sellers, 1790.

Mitchell, Carol Gehrs, ed. "Charles County, Maryland, Land Records: Deeds, 1743–1744." *Maryland Genealogical Society Bulletin* 26 (Winter 1985): 2–12.

Morrison, Alfred J., ed. *Travels in the Confederation, 1783–1784*. Philadelphia: William J. Campbell, 1911.

Murray, James. *Sermons to Asses*. Philadelphia: John Dunlap, 1770.

"Notes and Queries." *Pennsylvania Magazine of History and Biography* 10 (April 1886): 115–24.

Paine, Thomas. *Common Sense*. 1776; Philadelphia: W. and T. Bradford, 1791.

Parsons, Jacob Cox, ed. *Extracts from the Diary of Jacob Hiltzheimer, of Philadelphia: 1765–1798*. Philadelphia: William F. Fell, 1893.

Peden, Henry C., Jr., ed. *Early Anglican Church Records of Cecil County*. Westminster, MD: Family Line, 1990.

———. *Inhabitants of Cecil County, Maryland, 1649–1774*. Westminster, MD: Family Line, 1993.

———. *Marylanders to Carolina: Migration of Marylanders to North Carolina and South Carolina prior to 1800*. Westminster, MD: Family Line, 1994.

———. *More Marylanders to Carolina: Migration of Marylanders to North Carolina and South Carolina prior to 1800*. Westminster, MD: Willow Bend, 1999.

Peden, Henry C., Jr., and Veronica Clarke Peden, eds. *Cecil County, Maryland, Marriage References, 1674–1824*. Berwyn Heights, MD: Heritage Books, 2008.

Pennsylvania Archives. 138 vols. Philadelphia, 1838–1935.

Perry, William Stevens, ed. *Historical Collections Relating to the American Colonial Church*, vol. 4, *Maryland*. Hartford, CT: Church Press, 1878.

Plowden, Edward. *A Description of the Province of New Albion*. London: J. Maxon, 1650.

Powell, William S., ed. *The Correspondence of William Tryon and Other Selected Papers*. 2 vols. Raleigh: North Carolina Division of Archives and History, 1980.

Powell, William S., James K. Huhta, and Thomas J. Farnham, eds. *The Regulators in North Carolina: A Documentary History, 1759–1776*. Raleigh, NC: State Department of Archives and History, 1971.

Rittenhouse, David, ed. *The Continental Almanac, for the Year of Our Lord, 1780*. Philadelphia: Francis Bailey, 1779.

———. *The Continental Almanac, for the Year of Our Lord, 1781*. Philadelphia: Francis Bailey, 1780.

Saunders, William L., ed. *The Colonial Records of North Carolina*, vol. 5, 1752–1759. New York: AMS Press, 1968.

———, ed. *The Colonial Records of North Carolina*, vol. 7, 1765–1768. New York: AMS Press, 1968.

———, ed. *The Colonial Records of North Carolina*, vol. 8, 1769–1771. New York: AMS Press, 1968.

Sims, George. "An Address to the People of Granville County." In *Some Eighteenth Century Tracts Concerning North Carolina*, edited by William K. Boyd, 182–92. Raleigh, NC: Edwards and Broughton, 1927.

Smith, Gerald, ed. *Bedford County, Pennsylvania, Quarter Sessions, 1771–1801*. Westminster, MD: Heritage Books, 2010.

Smith, William Henry, ed. *The St. Clair Papers: The Life and Public Services of Arthur St. Clair*. 2 vols. Cincinnati: Robert Clarke, 1882.

Society of Friends. *A Collection of Memorials Concerning Divers, Deceased Ministers, and Others of the People Called Quakers, in Pennsylvania, New-Jersey, and Parts Adjacent, from the First Settlement Thereof*. Philadelphia: Joseph Chrukshank, 1787.

Strong, Nathan. *A Sermon*. Hartford, CT: Hudson and Goodwin, 1780.

Syrett, Harold C., ed. *The Papers of Alexander Hamilton*, vol. 12, *July 1792–October 1792*. New York: Columbia University Press, 1967.

Syrett, Harold C., and Jacob E. Cooke, eds. *The Papers of Alexander Hamilton*, vol. 4, *January 1787–May 1788*. New York: Columbia University Press, 1962.

Tennent, Gilbert. *The Danger of an Unconverted Ministry*. Philadelphia: Benjamin Franklin, 1740.

Weeks, Eve B., ed. *Register of Orange County, North Carolina, Deeds, 1752–1768, and 1793*. Danielsville, GA: Heritage Papers, 1984.

Whisker, James B., ed. *Bedford County, Pennsylvania, Archives*. Vol. 5. Apollo, PA: Closson Press, 1989.

Whittenburg, James P., ed. "'The Common Farmer (Number 2)': Herman Husband's Plan for Peace between the United States and the Indians, 1792." *William and Mary Quarterly*, 3rd ser., 34 (October 1977): 647–50.

Willcox, William B., et al., eds. *The Papers of Benjamin Franklin*, vol. 18, *January 1–December 31, 1771*. New Haven, CT: Yale University Press, 1974.

Secondary Sources

Abbott, Collamer M. "Colonial Copper Mines." *William and Mary Quarterly*, 3rd ser., 27 (April 1970): 295–309.

Allen, Thomas B. *Tories: Fighting for the King in America's First Civil War*. New York: HarperCollins, 2010.

Amussen, Susan Dwyer. *Caribbean Exchanges: Slavery and the Transformation of English Society, 1640–1700*. Chapel Hill: University of North Carolina Press, 2007.

Appleby, Joyce. "The Vexed Story of Capitalism Told by American Historians." *Journal of the Early Republic* 21 (Spring 2001): 1–18.

Ashe, Samuel A., Stephen B. Weeks, and Charles L. Van Noppen, eds. *Biographical History of North Carolina: From Colonial Times to the Present*. Vol. 2. Greensboro, NC: Charles L. Van Noppen, 1905.

Bacon, Margaret Hope. *Mothers of Feminism: The Story of Quaker Women in America*. San Francisco: Harper and Row, 1986.

Bailyn, Bernard. *The Ideological Origins of the American Revolution*. Cambridge, MA: Belknap Press of Harvard University Press, 1967.

Baldwin, Leland D. *Whiskey Rebels: The Story of a Frontier Uprising*. Pittsburgh: University of Pittsburgh Press, 1939.

Balik, Shelby M. "Persecuted in the Bowels of a Free Republic: Samuel Ely and the Agrarian Theology of Justice, 1768–1797." *Massachusetts Historical Review* 15 (2013): 89–123.

Balmer, Randall H. *A Perfect Babel of Confusion: Dutch Religion and English Culture in the Middle Colonies*. New York: Oxford University Press, 1989.

Barker, Charles Albro. *The Background of the Revolution in Maryland*. New Haven, CT: Yale University Press, 1967.

Barksdale, Kevin T. "Our Rebellious Neighbors: Virginia's Border Counties during the Pennsylvania's Whiskey Rebellion." *Virginia Magazine of History and Biography* 111, no. 1 (2003): 5–32.

Beam, Christopher M. "Millennialism and American Nationalism, 1740–1800." *Journal of Presbyterian History* 54 (Spring 1976): 182–99.

Beckles, Hilary. *A History of Barbados: From Amerindian Settlement to Nation-State*. Cambridge: Cambridge University Press, 1990.

Bellesiles, Michael. *Revolutionary Outlaws: Ethan Allen and the Struggle for Independence on the Early American Frontier*. Charlottesville: University Press of Virginia, 1993.

Berkin, Carol. *Revolutionary Mothers: Women in the Struggle for America's Independence*. New York: Knopf, 2005.

Berlin, Ira. *Many Thousands Gone: The First Two Centuries of Slavery in North America*. Cambridge, MA: Belknap Press of Harvard University Press, 1998.

Bezanson, Anne. *Prices and Inflation during the American Revolution, Pennsylvania, 1770–1790*. Philadelphia: University of Pennsylvania Press, 1951.

Biographical Record of Harford and Cecil Counties, Maryland. Westminster, MD: Family Line, 1989.

Blackburn, E. Howard, and William H. Welfley. *History of Bedford and Somerset Counties, Pennsylvania*. 3 vols. New York: Lewis, 1906.

Blessing, Tim H. "The Upper Juniata Valley." In *Beyond Philadelphia: The American Revolution in the Pennsylvania Hinterland*, edited by John B. Frantz and William Pencak, 153–70. University Park: Pennsylvania State University Press, 1998.

Blethen, H. Tyler, and Curtis W. Wood. *From Ulster to Carolina: The Migration of the Scotch Irish to Southwestern North Carolina.* Raleigh: North Carolina Division of Archives and History, 1998.

Bloch, Ruth H. "Religion and Ideological Change in the American Revolution." In *Religion and American Politics: From the Colonial Period to the Present,* edited by Mark A. Noll and Luke E. Harlow, 47–64. New York: Oxford University Press, 2007.

———. *Visionary Republic: Millennial Themes in American Thought, 1756–1800.* Cambridge: Cambridge University Press, 1985.

Block, Kristen. *Ordinary Lives in the Early Caribbean: Religion, Colonial Competition, and the Politics of Profit.* Athens: University of Georgia Press, 2012.

Blumgart, Pamela James, ed. *At the Head of the Bay: A Cultural and Architectural History of Cecil County, Maryland.* Crownsville: Maryland Historical Trust, 1996.

Bogin, Ruth. "Petitioning and the New Moral Economy of Post-Revolutionary America." *William and Mary Quarterly,* 3rd ser., 46 (July 1988): 391–425.

Boles, John B. *The South through Time: A History of an American Region.* 2 vols. Upper Saddle River, NJ: Pearson Education, 2004.

Bonomi, Patricia U. *Under the Cope of Heaven: Religion, Society, and Politics in Colonial America.* New York: Oxford University Press, 1986.

Bouton, Terry. *Taming Democracy: "The People," the Founders, and the Troubled Ending of the American Revolution.* New York: Oxford University Press, 2007.

———. "Tying Up the Revolution: Money, Power, and the Regulation in Pennsylvania, 1765–1800." Ph.D. dissertation, Duke University, 1996.

———. "William Findley, David Bradford, and the Pennsylvania Regulation of 1794." In *Revolutionary Founders: Rebels, Radicals, and Reformers in the Making of the Nation,* edited by Alfred F. Young, Gary B. Nash, and Ray Raphael, 233–72. New York: Knopf, 2001.

Brackenridge, Henry Marie. *History of the Western Insurrection in Western Pennsylvania, Commonly Called the Whiskey Insurrection: 1794.* Pittsburgh: W. S. Haven, 1859.

Bradburn, Douglas, and John C. Coombs, eds. *Early Modern Virginia: Reconsidering the Old Dominion.* Charlottesville: University of Virginia Press, 2011.

Breen, T. H. "Horses and Gentlemen: The Cultural Significance of Gambling among the Gentry of Virginia." *William and Mary Quarterly,* 3rd ser., 34 (April 1977): 239–57.

Brekus, Catherine A. *Sarah Osborn's World: The Rise of Evangelical Christianity in Early America.* New Haven, CT: Yale University Press, 2013.

———. *Strangers and Pilgrims: Female Preaching in America, 1740–1845.* Chapel Hill: University of North Carolina Press, 1998.

Breslaw, Elaine G. "The Chronicle as Satire: Dr. Hamilton's 'History of the Tuesday Club.'" *Maryland Historical Magazine* 70 (Summer 1975): 129–48.

Bridenbaugh, Carl, and Roberta Bridenbaugh. *No Peace beyond the Line: The English in the Caribbean, 1624–1690.* New York: Oxford University Press, 1972.

Brown, Kathleen. *Good Wives, Nasty Wenches, and Anxious Patriarchs: Gender, Race, and Power in Colonial Virginia.* Chapel Hill: University of North Carolina Press, 1996.

Brown, Roger H. *Redeeming the Republic: Federalists, Taxation, and the Origins of the Constitution*. Baltimore: Johns Hopkins University Press, 1993.

Brunhouse, Robert L. *The Counter-Revolution in Pennsylvania, 1776–1790*. New York: Octagon Books, 1971.

Buck, Solon J., and Elizabeth Hawthorn Buck. *The Planting of Civilization in Western Pennsylvania*. Pittsburgh: University of Pittsburgh Press, 1939.

Burnard, Trevor. *Creole Gentlemen: The Maryland Elite, 1691–1776*. New York: Routledge, 2002.

Bushman, Richard Lyman. *From Puritan to Yankee: Character and the Social Order in Connecticut, 1690–1763*. Cambridge, MA: Harvard University Press, 1967.

———. "Markets and Composite Farms in Early America." *William and Mary Quarterly*, 3rd ser., 55 (July 1998): 351–74.

Butler, Jon. *New World Faiths: Religion in Colonial America*. New York: Oxford University Press, 2008.

Byrd, James P. *Sacred Scripture, Sacred War: The Bible and the American Revolution*. New York: Oxford University Press, 2013.

Cable, Mary. *The Little Darlings: A History of Child Rearing in America*. New York: Charles Scribner's Sons, 1975.

Calloway, Colin G. *New Worlds for All: Indians, Europeans, and the Remaking of Early America*. Baltimore: Johns Hopkins University Press, 1997.

Carey, Brycchan. *From Peace to Freedom: Quaker Rhetoric and the Birth of Antislavery, 1657–1761*. New Haven, CT: Yale University Press, 2012.

Carey, Brycchan, and Geoffrey Plank, eds. *Quakers and Abolition*. Urbana: University of Illinois Press, 2014.

Carp, Benjamin L. *Defiance of the Patriots: The Boston Tea Party and the Making of America*. New Haven, CT: Yale University Press, 2010.

Carr, Lois Green. "Emigration and the Standard of Living: The Seventeenth-Century Chesapeake." *Journal of Economic History* 52 (June 1992): 271–91.

———. "From Servant to Freeholder: Daniel Clocker's Adventure." *Maryland Historical Magazine* 99 (Fall 2004): 286–311.

Carr, Lois Green, and Russell R. Menard. "Land, Labor, and Economies of Scale in Early Maryland: Some Limits to Growth in the Chesapeake System of Husbandry." *Journal of Economic History* 49 (June 1989): 407–18.

Carr, Lois Green, Russell R. Menard, and Lorena S. Walsh. *Robert Cole's World: Agriculture and Society in Early Maryland*. Chapel Hill: University of North Carolina Press, 1991.

Carr, Lois Green, and Lorena S. Walsh. "The Planter's Wife: The Experience of White Women in Seventeenth-Century Maryland." *William and Mary Quarterly*, 3rd ser., 34 (October 1977): 542–71.

Carroll, Kenneth L. "An Eighteenth-Century Episcopalian Attack on Quaker and Methodist Manumission of Slaves." *Maryland Historical Magazine* 80 (Summer 1985): 139–50.

———. "Maryland Quakers in the Seventeenth Century." *Maryland Historical Quarterly* 47 (December 1953): 81–96.

———. *Quakerism on the Eastern Shore.* Baltimore: Maryland Historical Society, 1970.

Caruthers, Eli W. *A Sketch of the Life and Character of the Rev. David Caldwell, D.D.* Greensboro, NC: Swaim and Sherwood, 1842.

Cassady, John C. *The Somerset Outline.* Scottdale, PA: Mennonite Publishing, 1932.

Cherry, Conrad, ed. *God's New Israel: Religious Interpretations of American Destiny.* Chapel Hill: University of North Carolina Press, 1998.

Chudacoff, Howard P. *Children at Play: An American History.* New York: New York University Press, 2007.

Clark, Christopher. *The Roots of Rural Capitalism: Western Massachusetts, 1780–1812.* Ithaca, NY: Cornell University Press, 1990.

Clark, Christopher, et al. "The Transition to Capitalism in America: A Panel Discussion." *History Teacher* 27 (May 1994): 263–88.

Clark, J. C. D. *The Language of Liberty, 1660–1832: Political Discourse and Social Dynamics in the Anglo-American World.* Cambridge: Cambridge University Press, 1994.

Clemens, Paul G. E. *The Atlantic Economy and Colonial Maryland's Eastern Shore: From Tobacco to Grain.* Ithaca, NY: Cornell University Press, 1980.

———. "Economy and Society on Maryland's Eastern Shore, 1689–1733." In *Law, Society, and Politics in Early Maryland,* edited by Aubrey C. Land, Lois Green Carr, and Edward C. Papenfuse, 153–70. Baltimore: Johns Hopkins University Press, 1977.

Coalter, Milton J. *Gilbert Tennent, Son of Thunder: A Case Study on Continental Pietism's Impact on the First Great Awakening in the Middle Colonies.* Westport, CT: Greenwood Press, 1986.

Compton, Stephen. "'James Pugh,' Regulator Sharpshooter: A Conundrum Unfolded." *North Carolina Historical Review* 90 (April 2013): 173–96.

Conforti, Joseph. *Jonathan Edwards, Religious Tradition, and American Culture.* Chapel Hill: University of North Carolina Press, 1995.

Conkin, Paul. "The Church Establishment in North Carolina, 1765–1776." *North Carolina Historical Review* 32 (January 1955): 1–30.

Connors, Richard, and Andrew Colin Gow. "Anglo-American Millennialism, from Milton to the Millerites." In *Anglo-American Millennialism, from Milton to the Millerites,* edited by Richard Connors and Andrew Colin Gow, vii–xviii. Leiden: Brill, 2004.

———, eds. *Anglo-American Millennialism, from Milton to the Millerites.* Leiden: Brill, 2004.

Conser, Walter H., Jr., and Robert J. Cain. *Presbyterians in North Carolina: Race, Politics, and Religious Identity in Historical Perspective.* Knoxville: University of Tennessee Press, 2012.

Coombs, John C. "Beyond the 'Origins Debate': Rethinking the Rise of Virginia Slavery." In *Early Modern Virginia: Reconsidering the Old Dominion,* edited by Douglas Bradburn and John C. Coombs, 239–78. Charlottesville: University of Virginia Press, 2011.

———. "The Phases of Conversion: A New Chronology for the Rise of Slavery in Early America." *William and Mary Quarterly*, 3rd ser., 69 (July 2011): 332–60.

Cooper, H. Austin. *Two Centuries of Brothersvalley Church of the Brethren, 1762–1962*. Westminster, MD: The Times, 1962.

Cotlar, Seth. *Tom Paine's America: The Rise and Fall of Transatlantic Radicalism in the Early Republic*. Charlottesville: University of Virginia Press, 2011.

Countryman, Edward. "'Out of the Bounds of the Law': Northern Land Rioters in the Eighteenth Century." In *The American Revolution: Explorations in the History of American Radicalism*, edited by Alfred F. Young, 37–70. DeKalb: Northern Illinois University Press, 1976.

Coverdale, Miles. "'Flight on the Wings of Vanity': Maryland Quakers' Struggle for Identity, 1715–1760." *Maryland Historical Magazine* 105 (Fall 2010): 197–222.

Crabtree, Sarah. *Holy Nation: The Transatlantic Quaker Ministry in an Age of Revolution*. Chicago: University of Chicago Press, 2015.

Cragg, Larry. *The Quaker Community on Barbados: Challenging the Culture of the Planter Class*. Jefferson City: University of Missouri Press, 2009.

Crawford, Michael. *Seasons of Grace: Colonial New England's Revival Tradition in Its British Context*. New York: Oxford University Press, 1991.

Crist, Robert G. "Cumberland County." In *Beyond Philadelphia: The American Revolution in the Pennsylvania Hinterland*, edited by John B. Frantz and William Pencak, 107–32. University Park: Pennsylvania State University Press, 1998.

Cronon, William. *Changes in the Land: Indians, Colonists, and the Ecology of New England*. New York: Hill and Wang, 1983.

Cross, David Colin, et al., eds. *The Southern Colonial Backcountry: Interdisciplinary Perspectives on Frontier Communities*. Knoxville: University of Tennessee Press, 1998.

Crothers, A. Glenn. "Quaker Merchants and Slavery in Early National Alexandria, Virginia: The Ordeal of William Hartshorne." *Journal of the Early Republic* 25 (Spring 2005): 47–77.

———. *Quakers Living in the Lion's Mouth: The Society of Friends in Northern Virginia, 1730–1865*. Gainesville: University of Florida Press, 2012.

Crow, Jeffrey J. "The Whiskey Rebellion in North Carolina." *North Carolina Historical Review* 66 (January 1989): 1–28.

Davidson, James West. *The Logic of Millennial Thought: Eighteenth-Century New England*. New Haven, CT: Yale University Press, 1977.

Davis, David Brion. *The Problem of Slavery in the Age of Revolution*. Ithaca, NY: Cornell University Press, 1975.

Davis, Jeffrey A. "Guarding the Republican Interest: The Western Pennsylvania Democratic Societies and the Excise Tax." *Pennsylvania History* 67 (Winter 2000): 43–62.

Delafield, Joseph L. "Notes on the Woods Family, of Bedford, Pennsylvania." *Pennsylvania Magazine of History and Biography* 32 (March 1903): 335–44.

Denson, Andrew C. "Diversity, Religion, and the North Carolina Regulators." *North Carolina Historical Review* 72 (January 1995): 30–53.

Diggins, Milt. "Principio." *Cecil Historical Journal* 1 (Fall 2000): 3–9.

Dill, Alonzo Thomas. *Governor Tryon and His Palace*. Chapel Hill: University of North Carolina Press, 1955.

Dowd, Gregory Evans. *War under Heaven: Pontiac, the Indian Nations, and the British Empire*. Baltimore: Johns Hopkins University Press, 2002.

Downes, Randolph C. *Council Fires of the Upper Ohio: A Narrative of Indian Affairs in the Upper Ohio Valley until 1795*. Pittsburgh: University of Pittsburgh Press, 1940.

Drake, Thomas E. *Quakers and Slavery in America*. New Haven, CT: Yale University Press, 1950.

Dunaway, Wayland F. *The Scotch-Irish of Colonial Pennsylvania*. Chapel Hill: University of North Carolina Press, 1944.

Dunaway, Wilma. *The First American Frontier: Transition to Capitalism in Appalachia, 1700–1860*. Chapel Hill: University of North Carolina Press, 1996.

Dunn, Richard. *Sugar and Slaves: The Rise of the Planter Class in the English West Indies*. New York: Norton, 1972.

Durham, Harriet. *Caribbean Quakers*. Hollywood, FL: Dukane Press, 1972.

Earle, Carville V. "Environment, Disease, and Mortality in Early Virginia." In *The Chesapeake in the Seventeenth Century: Essays on Anglo-American Society*, edited by Thad W. Tate and David L. Ammerman, 96–125. Chapel Hill: University of North Carolina Press, 1979.

Egerton, Douglas R. *Death or Liberty: African Americans and Revolutionary America*. New York: Oxford University Press, 2009.

Ekirch, A. Roger. *"Poor Carolina": Politics and Society in Colonial North Carolina, 1729–1776*. Chapel Hill: University of North Carolina Press, 1981.

Espy, Florence Mercy. *History and Genealogy of the Espy Family in America*. Fort Madison, IA: Pythian, 1905.

Fatovic, Clement. *America's Founding and the Struggle over Economic Inequality*. Lawrence: University Press of Kansas, 2015.

Feist, Timothy Philip. "'A Stirring among the Dry Bones': George Whitefield and the Great Awakening in Maryland." *Maryland Historical Magazine* 95 (Winter 2000): 388–408.

Fennell, Dorothy Elaine. "From Rebelliousness to Insurrection: A Social History of the Whiskey Rebellion." Ph.D. dissertation, University of Pittsburgh, 1981.

Ferguson, E. James. *The Power of the Purse: A History of American Public Finance, 1776–1790*. Chapel Hill: University of North Carolina, 1961.

Fischer, David Hackett. *Albion's Seed: Four British Folkways*. New York: Oxford University Press, 1989.

Flannagan, John H., Jr. "Trying Times: Economic Depression in New Hampshire, 1781–1789." Ph.D. dissertation, Georgetown University, 1972.

Foner, Eric. *Tom Paine and Revolutionary America*. New York: Oxford University Press, 1976.

Foote, William Henry. *Sketches of North Carolina, Historical and Biographical*. New York: Robert Carter, 1846.

Frey, Sylvia. *Water from the Rock: Black Resistance in a Revolutionary Age*. Princeton, NJ: Princeton University Press, 1991.

Garbarino, William M., Jr. *Indian Wars along the Upper Ohio: A History of the Indian Wars and Related Events along the Upper Ohio and Its Tributaries.* Midway, PA: Midway, 2001.

Gilbert, Alan. *Black Patriots and Loyalists: Fighting for Emancipation in the War for Independence.* Chicago: University of Chicago Press, 2012.

Gilje, Paul A. "The Rise of Capitalism in the Early Republic." *Journal of the Early Republic* 16 (Summer 1996): 159–81.

———, ed. *Wages of Independence: Capitalism in the Early Republic.* Madison, WI: Madison House, 1998.

Gorn, Elliot J. "'Gouge and Bite, Pull Hair and Scratch': The Social Significance of Fighting in the Southern Backcountry." *American Historical Review* 90 (February 1985): 18–43.

Gragg, Larry. *The Quaker Community on Barbados: Challenging the Culture of the Planter Class.* Jefferson City: University of Missouri Press, 2009.

Graham, Michael J. "Churching the Unchurched: The Establishment in Maryland, 1692–1724." *Maryland Historical Quarterly* 83 (Winter 1988): 297–309.

———. "'The Collapse of Equity': Catholic and Quaker Dissenters in Maryland, 1692–1720." *Maryland Historical Quarterly* 88 (Spring 1993): 5–25.

Greene, Jack P. *Pursuits of Happiness: The Social Development of Early Modern British Colonies and the Formation of American Culture.* Chapel Hill: University of North Carolina Press, 1988.

Greenough, Chester Noyes. "New England Almanacs, 1766–1776, and the American Revolution." *Proceedings of the American Antiquarian Society* 45 (October 1935): 288–316.

Griffin, Patrick. *American Leviathan: Empire, Nation, and Revolutionary Frontier.* New York: Hill and Wang, 2007.

———. *The People with No Name: Ireland's Ulster Scots, America's Scots Irish, and the Creation of a British Atlantic World, 1689–1764.* Princeton, NJ: Princeton University Press, 2001.

Gross, Robert A., ed. *In Debt to Shays: The Bicentennial of an Agrarian Revolution.* Charlottesville: University Press of Virginia, 1993.

Gundersen, Joan R. *To Be Useful: Women in Revolutionary America, 1740–1790.* New York: Twayne, 1996.

Hahn, Barbara M. *Making Tobacco Bright: Creating an American Commodity, 1617–1937.* Baltimore: Johns Hopkins University Press, 2011.

Hamm, Thomas D. *The Quakers in America.* New York: Columbia University Press, 2003.

Harper, R. Eugene. *The Transformation of Western Pennsylvania, 1770–1800.* Pittsburgh: University of Pittsburgh Press, 1991.

Hatch, Nathan O. *The Democratization of American Christianity.* New Haven, CT: Yale University Press, 1989.

———. *The Sacred Cause of Liberty: Republican Thought and the Millennium in Revolutionary New England.* New Haven, CT: Yale University Press, 1977.

Hatchett, George R. *Some Neglected History Concerning Harmon Husband Who Incited Battle against the British Long before the Boston Tea Party.* Privately published, 1936.

Hawke, David. *In the Midst of a Revolution.* Philadelphia: University of Pennsylvania Press, 1961.

Heimert, Alan. *Religion and the American Mind: From the Great Awakening to the Revolution.* Cambridge, MA: Harvard University Press, 1966.

Heyl, Allen V., and Nancy C. Pearre. *Copper, Zinc, Lead, Iron, Cobalt, and Barite Deposits in the Piedmont Upland of Maryland.* Baltimore: Maryland Geological Survey, 1965.

Heyrman, Christine Leigh. *Southern Cross: The Beginnings of the Bible Belt.* Chapel Hill: University of North Carolina Press, 1997.

Hinderaker, Eric, and Peter C. Mancall. *At the Edge of Empire: The Backcountry in British North America.* Baltimore: Johns Hopkins University Press, 2003.

Hinds, Hillary. *George Fox and Early Quaker Culture.* Manchester: Manchester University Press, 2011.

Hoenstine, Floyd G. *History of Bedford, Somerset, and Fulton Counties, Pennsylvania.* Chicago: Waterman, Watkins, 1884.

Hoffer, Peter Charles. *Sensory Worlds in Early America.* Baltimore: Johns Hopkins University Press, 2003.

Hofstra, Warren R. *The Planting of New Virginia: Settlement and Landscape in the Shenandoah Valley.* Baltimore: Johns Hopkins University Press, 2004.

———. "Searching for Peace and Prosperity: Opequon Settlement, Virginia, 1730s–1760s." In *Ulster to America: The Scots-Irish Migration Experience, 1680–1830*, edited by Warren R. Hofstra, 105–22. Knoxville: University of Tennessee Press, 2012.

Hogeland, William. *Founding Finance: How Debt, Speculation, Foreclosures, Protests, and Crackdowns Made Us a Nation.* Austin: University of Texas Press, 2012.

———. *The Whiskey Rebellion: George Washington, Alexander Hamilton, and the Frontier Rebels Who Challenged America's Newfound Sovereignty.* New York: Simon and Schuster, 2006.

Holt, Wythe. "The New Jerusalem: Herman Husband's Egalitarian Alternative to the United States Constitution." In *Revolutionary Founders: Rebels, Radicals, and Reformers in the Making of the Nation*, edited by Alfred F. Young, Gary B. Nash, and Ray Raphael, 253–72. New York: Knopf, 2001.

———. "The Whiskey Rebellion of 1794: A Democratic Working-Class Insurrection." Paper presented at the Georgia Workshop of Early American History and Culture, University of Georgia, Athens, September 23, 2004.

Holton, Woody. *Unruly Americans and the Origins of the Constitution.* New York: Hill and Wang, 2007.

Hoppin, Charles Arthur. *The Washington Ancestry and Records of the McClain, Johnson, and Forty Other Colonial American Families.* 2 vols. Greenfield, OH: Privately published, 1932.

Horn, James. *Adapting to a New World: English Society in the Seventeenth-Century Chesapeake*. Chapel Hill: University of North Carolina Press, 1994.

———. "Servant Emigration to the Chesapeake in the Seventeenth Century." In *The Chesapeake in the Seventeenth Century: Essays on Anglo-American Society*, edited by Thad W. Tate and David L. Ammerman, 51–95. Chapel Hill: University of North Carolina Press, 1979.

Hudson, Arthur Palmer. "Songs of the North Carolina Regulators." *William and Mary Quarterly*, 3rd ser., 4 (October 1947): 470–85.

Humphrey, Thomas J. *Land and Liberty: Hudson Valley Riots in the Age of Revolution*. DeKalb: Northern Illinois University Press, 2004.

Huston, James L. *Securing the Fruits of Labor: The American Concept of Wealth Distribution, 1765–1900*. Baton Rouge: Louisiana State University Press, 1998.

Ingle, H. Larry. *First among Friends: George Fox and the Creation of Quakerism*. New York: Oxford University Press, 1994.

Isaac, Rhys. *The Transformation of Virginia, 1740–1790*. Chapel Hill: University of North Carolina Press, 1982.

James, Sydney V. *A People among Peoples: Quaker Benevolence in Eighteenth-Century America*. Cambridge, MA: Harvard University Press, 1963.

Johnson, D. Andrew. "The Regulation Reconsidered: Shared Grievances in the Colonial Carolinas." *South Carolina Historical Magazine* 114 (Spring 2013): 132–54.

Johnston, George. *History of Cecil County, Maryland, and Early Settlements around the Head of the Chesapeake Bay and the Delaware River, with Sketches of Some of the Old Families of Cecil County*. Elkton, MD: George Johnston, 1881.

Jonas, Manfred. "Wages in Early Colonial Maryland." *Maryland Historical Magazine* 51 (March 1956): 27–38.

Jones, A. D. *General Edmund Fanning*. New York: Henry Miller, 1869.

Jones, J. H. *A History of the Rock Presbyterian Church in Cecil County, Maryland*. Oxford, PA: Oxford Press, 1872.

Jones, Mark H. "Herman Husband: Millenarian, Carolina Regulator, and Whiskey Rebel." Ph.D. dissertation, Northern Illinois University, 1982.

Jones, Thomas Firth. *A Pair of Lawn Sleeves: A Biography of William Smith, 1727–1803*. Philadelphia: Chilton, 1972.

Jordan, John W. *Colonial and Revolutionary Families of Pennsylvania: Genealogical and Personal Memoirs*. Vol. 1. New York: Lewis, 1911.

Kanskey, Karel J. "Augustine Herman: The Leading Cartographer on the Seventeenth Century." *Maryland Historical Magazine* 73 (December 1978): 352–59.

Kars, Marjoleine. *Breaking Loose Together: The Regulator Rebellion in Pre-Revolutionary North Carolina*. Chapel Hill: University of North Carolina Press, 2002.

Kay, Marvin L. Michael. "The North Carolina Regulation, 1766–1776: A Class Conflict." In *The American Revolution: Explorations in the History of American Radicalism*, edited by Alfred F. Young, 71–123. DeKalb: Northern Illinois University Press, 1976.

———. "The Payment of Provincial and Local Taxes in North Carolina, 1748–1771." *William and Mary Quarterly*, 3rd ser., 26 (April 1969): 218–40.

———. "Provincial Taxes in North Carolina during the Administrations of Dobbs and Tryon." *North Carolina Historical Review* 4 (October 1965): 440–53.

Keller, Clair W. "Pennsylvania's Role in the Origin and Defeat of the First Proposed Amendment on Representation." *Pennsylvania Magazine of History and Biography* 112 (January 1988): 73–102.

Kerber, Linda K. *Women of the Republic: Intellect and Ideology in Revolutionary America*. Chapel Hill: University of North Carolina Press, 1980.

Kidd, Thomas S. *American Colonial History: Clashing Cultures and Faiths*. New Haven, CT: Yale University Press, 2016.

———. *George Whitefield: America's Spiritual Founding Father*. New Haven, CT: Yale University Press, 2014.

———. *God of Liberty: A Religious History of the American Revolution*. New York: Basic Books, 2012.

———. *The Great Awakening: The Roots of Evangelical Christianity in Colonial America*. New Haven, CT: Yale University Press, 2007.

Kim, Sung Bok. *Landlord and Tenant in Colonial New York Manorial Society, 1664–1775*. Chapel Hill: University of North Carolina Press, 1978.

Klein, Rachel N. *Unification of a Slave State: The Rise of the Planter Class in the South Carolina Backcountry, 1760–1808*. Chapel Hill: University of North Carolina Press, 1990.

Klepp, Susan E., and Billy G. Smith, eds. *The Infortunate: The Voyage and Adventures of William Moraley, an Indentured Servant*. University Park: Pennsylvania State University Press, 2005.

Knouff, Gregory T. "'An Arduous Service': The Pennsylvania Backcountry Soldiers' Revolution." *Pennsylvania History* 61 (January 1994): 45–71.

———. "Soldiers and Violence on the Pennsylvania Frontier." In *Beyond Philadelphia: The American Revolution in the Pennsylvania Hinterland*, edited by John B. Frantz and William Pencak, 171–94. University Park: Pennsylvania State University Press, 1998.

Kohn, Richard H. "The Washington Administration's Decision to Crush the Whiskey Rebellion." *Journal of American History* 59 (December 1972): 567–84.

Konkle, Burton Alva. *The Life and Times of Thomas Smith, 1745–1809: A Pennsylvania Member of the Continental Congress*. Philadelphia: Campion, 1904.

Kulikoff, Allan. "The American Revolution, Capitalism, and the Formation of the Yeoman Classes." In *Beyond the American Revolution: Explorations in the History of American Radicalism*, edited by Alfred F. Young, 80–122. DeKalb: Northern Illinois University Press, 1993.

———. *From British Peasants to Colonial American Farmers*. Chapel Hill: University of North Carolina Press, 2000.

———. *Tobacco and Slaves: The Development of Southern Cultures in the Chesapeake, 1680–1800*. Chapel Hill: University of North Carolina Press, 1986.

Kussart, S. "Colonel George Woods, Pittsburgh's First Surveyor." *Western Pennsylvania Historical Magazine* 7 (April 1924): 73–87.

Lambert, Frank. *Inventing the "Great Awakening."* Princeton, NJ: Princeton University Press, 1999.

———. *"Pedlar in Divinity": George Whitefield and the Transatlantic Revivals, 1737–1770*. Princeton, NJ: Princeton University Press, 1994.

Lamoreaux, Naomi R. "Rethinking the Transition to Capitalism in the Early American Northeast." *Journal of American History* 90 (September 2003): 437–61.

Land, Aubrey C. "The Planters of Colonial Maryland." *Maryland Historical Magazine* 67 (Spring 1972): 109–28.

Larson, Rebecca. *Daughters of Light: Quaker Women Preaching and Prophesying in the Colonies and Abroad, 1700–1775*. Chapel Hill: University of North Carolina Press, 2000.

Lawson, Russell M. *Servants and Servitude in Colonial America*. Santa Barbara, CA: Praeger, 2008.

Lazenby, Mary Elinor. *Herman Husband: A Story of His Life*. Washington, DC: Old Neighborhood Press, 1940.

Lee, Jean B. *The Price of Nationhood: The American Revolution in Charles County*. New York: Norton, 1994.

Lee, Wayne E. *Crowds and Soldiers in Revolutionary North Carolina: The Culture of Violence in Riot and War*. Gainesville: University of Florida Press, 2001.

Lefer, David. *The Founding Conservatives: How a Group of Unsung Heroes Saved the American Revolution*. New York: Sentinel, 2013.

Lemon, James T. *The Best Poor Man's Country: A Geographical Study of Early Southeastern Pennsylvania*. Baltimore: Johns Hopkins University Press, 1972.

Levy, Barry. *Quakers and the American Family: British Settlement in the Delaware Valley*. New York: Oxford University Press, 1988.

Leyburn, James G. *The Scotch-Irish: A Social History*. Chapel Hill: University of North Carolina Press, 1989.

Longenecker, Stephen L. *Piety and Tolerance: Pennsylvania German Religion, 1700–1850*. Metuchen, NJ: Scarecrow Press, 1994.

Maganzin, Louis. "Economic Depression in Maryland and Virginia, 1783–1784." Ph.D. dissertation, Georgetown University, 1967.

Maier, Pauline. *From Resistance to Revolution: Colonial Radicals and the Development of American Opposition to Britain, 1765–1776*. New York: Knopf, 1972.

Main, Gloria L. "Maryland and the Chesapeake Economy, 1670–1720." In *Law, Society, and Politics in Early Maryland*, edited by Aubrey C. Land, Lois Green Carr, and Edward C. Papenfuse, 134–52. Baltimore: Johns Hopkins University Press, 1977.

———. *Tobacco Colony: Life in Early Maryland, 1650–1720*. Princeton, NJ: Princeton University Press, 1982.

Main, Jackson Turner. *The Sovereign States, 1775–1783*. New York: Franklin Watts, 1973.

Maloy, J. S. *The Colonial American Origins of Modern Democratic Thought*. Cambridge: Cambridge University Press, 2008.

Marini, Stephen A. "Uncertain Dawn: Millennialism and Political Theology in Revolutionary America." In *Anglo-American Millennialism, from Milton to the Millerites*, edited by Richard Connors and Andrew Colin Gow, 159–76. Leiden: Brill, 2004.

Marrietta, Jack D. *The Reformation of American Quakerism, 1748–1783*. Philadelphia: University of Pennsylvania Press, 1984.

Marsden, George M. *Jonathan Edwards: A Life*. New Haven, CT: Yale University Press, 2003.

Maxson, Charles Hartshorn. *The Great Awakening in the Middle Colonies*. Gloucester, MA: Peter Smith, 1958.

Maze, Scott. *Theodorus Frelinghuysen's Evangelicalism: Catalyst of the First Great Awakening*. Grand Rapids, MI: Reformation Heritage Books, 2011.

McClure, James Patrick. "The Ends of the American Earth: Pittsburgh and the Upper Ohio Valley to 1795." 2 vols. Ph.D. dissertation, University of Michigan, 1983.

———. "'Let Us Be Independent': David Bradford and the Whiskey Rebellion." *Pittsburgh History* 74 (Summer 1991): 76–86.

McConnell, Michael N. *A Country Between: The Upper Ohio Valley and Its Peoples, 1724–1774*. Lincoln: University of Nebraska Press, 1992.

McConville, Brendan. *These Daring Disturbers of the Public Peace: The Struggle for Property and Power in Early New Jersey*. Ithaca, NY: Cornell University Press, 1999.

McCoy, Drew R. *The Elusive Republic: Political Economy in Jeffersonian America*. Chapel Hill: University of North Carolina Press, 1980.

McKenrich, Carl R. "New Munster." *Maryland Historical Magazine* 25 (June 1940): 147–59.

McMahon, Lucia. *Mere Equality: The Paradox of Educated Women in the Early American Republic*. Ithaca, NY: Cornell University Press, 2012.

McMurry, Sally A. *From Sugar Camps to Star Barns: Rural Life and Landscape in a Western Pennsylvania Community*. University Park: Pennsylvania State University Press, 2001.

Meacham, Sarah Hand. *Every Home a Distillery: Alcohol, Gender, and Technology in the Colonial Chesapeake*. Baltimore: Johns Hopkins University Press, 2009.

Menard, Russell R. "Economy and Society in Early Colonial Maryland." Ph.D. dissertation, University of Iowa, 1975.

———. "From Servants to Slaves: The Transformation of the Chesapeake Labor System." *Southern Studies* 16 (Winter 1977): 355–90.

———. "From Servant to Freeholder: Status Mobility and Property Accumulation in Seventeenth-Century Maryland." *William and Mary Quarterly*, 3rd ser., 30 (January 1973): 37–64.

———. "Immigrants and Their Increase: The Process of Population Growth in Early Colonial Maryland." In *Law, Society, and Politics in Early Maryland*, edited by Aubrey C. Land, Lois Green Carr, and Edward C. Papenfuse, 88–110. Baltimore: Johns Hopkins University Press, 1977.

———. *Migrants, Servants, and Slaves: Unfree Labor in Colonial British America.* Aldershot, UK: Ashgate/Variorum, 2001.

———. *Sweet Negotiations: Sugar, Slavery, and Plantation Agriculture in Early Barbados.* Charlottesville: University of Virginia Press, 2014.

———. "The Tobacco Industry in the Chesapeake Colonies, 1617–1730: An Interpretation." *Research in Economic History* 5 (1980): 108–77.

Merrens, Harry Roy. *Colonial North Carolina in the Eighteenth Century: A Study of Historical Geography.* Chapel Hill: University of North Carolina Press, 1964.

Merrill, Michael. "Putting 'Capitalism' in Its Place: A Review on Recent Literature." *William and Mary Quarterly,* 3rd ser., 52 (April 1995): 315–26.

Merrill, Michael, and Sean Wilentz, eds. *The Key of Liberty: The Life and Democratic Writings of William Manning, "A Laborer," 1747–1814.* Cambridge, MA: Harvard University Press, 1993.

Meyers, Debra. "The Civic Lives of White Women in Seventeenth-Century Maryland." *Maryland Historical Magazine* 94 (Fall 1999): 309–27.

———. *Common Whores, Vertuous Women, and Loving Wives: Free Will Christian Women in Colonial Maryland.* Bloomington: Indiana University Press, 2003.

Middlekauff, Robert. *The Glorious Cause: The American Revolution, 1763–1783.* New York: Oxford University Press, 1982.

Middleton, Arthur P. *Tobacco Coast: A Maritime History of the Chesapeake Bay in the Colonial Era.* Baltimore: Johns Hopkins University Press, 1984.

Middleton, Simon, and Billy G. Smith, eds. *Class Matters: Early North America and the Atlantic World.* Philadelphia: University of Pennsylvania Press, 2008.

Miller, Alice E. *Cecil County, Maryland: A Study in Local History.* Elkton, MD: C. and L. Printing, 1949.

Miller, Henry M. "An Archaeological Perspective on the Evolution of Diet in the Colonial Chesapeake, 1620–1745." In *Colonial Chesapeake Society,* edited by Lois Green Carr, Philip D. Morgan, and Jean B. Russo, 176–99. Chapel Hill: University of North Carolina Press, 1988.

Miller, Perry. "From the Covenant to the Revival." In *Religion in American Life,* edited by James Ward Smith and A. Leland Jamison, 140–79. Princeton, NJ: Princeton University Press, 1961.

Mintz, Steven. *Huck's Raft: A History of American Childhood.* Cambridge, MA: Belknap Press of Harvard University Press, 2004.

Mitchell, Robert D. *Commercialism and Frontier: Perspectives on the Early Shenandoah Valley.* Charlottesville: University Press of Virginia, 1977.

Morgan, David, Jr. "The Great Awakening in North Carolina, 1740–1775: The Baptist Phase." *North Carolina Historical Review* 45 (July 1968): 264–83.

Morgan, Edmund S. *American Slavery, American Freedom: The Ordeal of Colonial Virginia.* New York: Norton, 1975.

———. *Virginians at Home: Family Life in the Eighteenth Century.* Charlottesville, VA: Dominion Books, 1963.

Morgan, Edmund S., and Helen M. Morgan. *The Stamp Act Crisis: Prologue to Revolution.* Chapel Hill: University of North Carolina Press, 1995.

Morgan, Kenneth. *Slavery and Servitude in Colonial North America: A Short History.* New York: New York University Press, 2000.

Morgan, Philip D. *Slave Counterpoint: Black Culture in the Eighteenth-Century Chesapeake and Lowcountry.* Chapel Hill: University of North Carolina Press, 1998.

Nadelhaft, Jerome J. *The Disorders of War: The Revolution in South Carolina.* Orono: University of Maine at Orono Press, 1981.

Nagy, Jeffrey William. "'Our Woods Are Full of Mine Hunters': The Fountain Company in Colonial Maryland, 1744–1764." *Maryland Historical Magazine* 106 (Summer 2011): 203–21.

Nash, Frank. "Herman Husbands." In *Biographical History of North Carolina: From Colonial Times to the Present*, edited by Samuel A. Ashe, Stephen B. Weeks, and Charles L. Van Noppen, 2:185–93. Greensboro, NC: Charles L. Van Noppen, 1905.

Nash, Gary B. *The Forgotten Fifth: African Americans in the Age of Revolution.* Cambridge, MA: Harvard University Press, 2006.

———. "Poverty and Politics in Early American History." In *Down and Out in Early America*, edited by Billy G. Smith, 1–40. University Park: Pennsylvania State University Press, 2004.

———. "Slaves and Slaveholders in Colonial Philadelphia." *William and Mary Quarterly*, 3rd ser., 30 (April 1973): 223–56.

———. *The Unknown American Revolution: The Unruly Birth of Democracy and the Struggle to Create America.* New York: Penguin, 2005.

———. *The Urban Crucible: Social Change, Political Consciousness, and the Origins of the American Revolution.* Cambridge: Cambridge University Press, 1979.

Nelson, Craig. *Thomas Paine: Enlightenment, Revolution, and the Birth of Modern Nations.* New York: Penguin, 2007.

Nelson, David Paul. *William Tryon and the Course of Empire: A Life in British Imperial Service.* Chapel Hill: University of North Carolina Press, 1990.

Nelson, John K. *A Blessed Company: Parishes, Parson, and Parishioners in Anglican Virginia, 1690–1776.* Chapel Hill: University of North Carolina Press, 2001.

Newlin, Algie I. *Charity Cook: A Liberated Woman.* Richmond, IN: Friends United Press, 1981.

Noll, Mark A. *America's God: From Jonathan Edwards to Abraham Lincoln.* New York: Oxford University Press, 2005.

———. *Christians in the American Revolution.* Grand Rapids, MI: Christian University Press, 1977.

———. *The Rise of Evangelicalism: The Age of Edwards, Whitefield, and the Wesleys.* Downers Grove, IL: IVP Academic, 2010.

Noll, Mark A., and Luke E. Harlow, eds. *Religion and American Politics: From the Colonial Period to the Present.* New York: Oxford University Press, 2007.

Norton, Mary Beth. *Liberty's Daughters: The Revolutionary Experience of American Women, 1750–1800.* Boston: Little, Brown, 1980.

Norton, Mary Beth, et al. *A People and a Nation: A History of the United States.* Vol. 1. Boston: Houghton Mifflin, 1998.

Novak, William J., and Steven Pincus. "Revolutionary State Formation: The Origins of the Strong American State." In *State Formations: Global Histories and Cultures of Statehood*, edited by John L. Brooke, Julie C. Strauss, and Greg Anderson, 138–55. Cambridge: Cambridge University Press, 2018.

Opfer, Marilyn Holland. "William Husband of Cecil County." *Maryland Genealogical Society Bulletin* 39 (Summer 1998): 419–25.

Ousterhout, Anne. *A State Divided: Opposition in Pennsylvania to the American Revolution*. Westport, CT: Greenwood Press, 1987.

Parent, Anthony S. *Foul Means: The Formation of a Slave Society in Virginia, 1660–1740*. Chapel Hill: University of North Carolina Press, 2003.

Paschal, G. W. *History of the North Carolina Baptists*. 2 vols. Raleigh: General Board North Carolina Baptist State Convention, 1930.

Pearre, Nancy C. "Mining for Copper and Related Minerals in Maryland." *Maryland Historical Magazine* 59 (March 1964): 15–33.

Plank, Geoffrey. *John Woolman's Path to the Peaceable Kingdom: A Quaker in the British Empire*. Philadelphia: University of Pennsylvania Press, 2012.

Plummer, Judith Mitchell. *Andrew and Mary (Husband) Dunbar of Octorara Hundred, Cecil County, Maryland*. Woodbury, CT: Privately published, 1987.

Post, Charles. *The American Road to Capitalism, 1620–1877: Studies in Class-Structure, Economic Development, and Political Conflict*. Leiden: Brill, 2011.

Quarles, Benjamin. *The Negro in the American Revolution*. Chapel Hill: University of North Carolina Press, 1966.

Ramsey, Robert W. *Carolina Cradle: Settlement of the Northwest Carolina Frontier, 1747–1762*. Chapel Hill: University of North Carolina Press, 1964.

———. "James Carter: Founder of Salisbury." *North Carolina Historical Review* 39 (April 1962): 131–39.

Rappaport, George David. *Stability and Change in Revolutionary Pennsylvania: Banking, Politics, and Social Structure*. University Park: Pennsylvania State University Press, 1996.

Rappleye, Charles. *Robert Morris: Financier of the American Revolution*. New York: Simon and Schuster, 2010.

Raymond, Allan. "'To Reach Men's Minds': Almanacs and the American Revolution, 1760–1777." *New England Quarterly* 51, no. 3 (1978): 370–95.

Reavis, William A. "The Maryland Gentry and Social Mobility, 1637–1676." *William and Mary Quarterly*, 3rd ser., 14 (July 1957): 418–28.

Rediker, Marcus. *The Slave Ship: A Human History*. New York: Penguin, 2007.

Richards, Leonard L. *Shays's Rebellion: The American Revolution's Final Battle*. Philadelphia: University of Pennsylvania Press, 2003.

Roark, James, et al. *Understanding the American Promise: A Brief History*. Boston: Bedford/St. Martin's, 2011.

Robbins, Caroline. *The Eighteenth-Century Commonwealthman: Studies in the Transmission, Development, and Circumstances of English Liberal Thought from the Restoration of Charles II until the War with the Thirteen Colonies*. Cambridge, MA: Harvard University Press, 1959.

Rohrer, S. Scott. *Hope's Promise: Religion and Acculturation in the Southern Backcountry*. Tuscaloosa: University of Alabama Press, 2005.

Rothenberg, Winifred Barr. *From Market Places to a Market Economy: The Transformation of Rural Massachusetts, 1750–1850*. Chicago: University of Chicago Press, 1992.

Rupp, Israel. *Early History of Western Pennsylvania*. Pittsburgh: D. W. Kauffman, 1847.

Russo, Jean B., and J. Elliot Russo. *Planting an Empire: The Early Chesapeake in British North America*. Baltimore: Johns Hopkins University Press, 2012.

Rutman, Darrett B., and Anita H. Rutman. "'Of Agues and Fevers': Malaria in the Early Chesapeake." *William and Mary Quarterly*, 3rd ser., 33 (January 1976): 31–60.

Sadlier, Sarah. "Prelude to the American Revolution? The War of the Regulation: A Revolutionary Reaction for Reform." *History Teacher* 46 (November 2012): 97–126.

Salinger, Sharon V. *Taverns and Drinking in Early America*. Baltimore: Johns Hopkins University Press, 2002.

———. *"To Serve Well and Faithfully": Labor and Indentured Servitude in Pennsylvania, 1682–1800*. Cambridge: Cambridge University Press, 1987.

Schama, Simon. *Rough Crossings: Britain, the Slaves, and the American Revolution*. New York: Ecco, 2006.

Schmidt, Leigh Eric. *Holy Fairs: Scotland and the Making of American Revivalism*. Princeton, NJ: Princeton University Press, 1990.

Sellers, Charles G., Jr. "Private Profits and British Colonial Policy: The Speculations of Henry McCulloh." *William and Mary Quarterly*, 3rd ser., 8 (October 1951): 535–51.

Selsam, J. Paul. *The Pennsylvania Constitution of 1776: A Study in Revolutionary Democracy*. New York: Octagon Books, 1971.

Shalhope, Robert E. *Bennington and the Green Mountain Boys: The Emergence of Liberal Democracy in Vermont, 1760–1850*. Baltimore: Johns Hopkins University Press, 1996.

Shankman, Andrew. *Crucible of American Democracy: The Struggle to Fuse Egalitarianism and Capitalism in Jeffersonian Pennsylvania*. Lawrence: University Press of Kansas, 2004.

Sioli, Marco M. "The Democratic Republican Societies at the End of the Eighteenth Century: The Western Pennsylvania Experience." *Pennsylvania History* 60 (July 1993): 288–304.

Skaggs, David C., and Gerald E. Hartdagen. "Sinners and Saints: Anglican Clerical Conduct in Colonial Maryland." *Historical Magazine of the Protestant Episcopal Church* 47 (June 1978): 177–95.

Skemp, Sheila. "America's Mary Wollstonecraft: Judith Sargent Murray's Case for the Equal Rights of Women." In *Revolutionary Founders: Rebels, Radicals, and Reformers in the Making of the Nation*, edited by Alfred F. Young, Gary B. Nash, and Ray Raphael, 253–72. New York: Knopf, 2001.

Slaughter, Thomas P. *The Beautiful Soul of John Woolman, Apostle of Abolition*. New York: Hill and Wang, 2008.

———. *The Whiskey Rebellion: Frontier Epilogue to the American Revolution*. New York: Oxford University Press, 1986.

Smith, Abbot Emerson. "The Indentured Servant and Land Speculation in Seventeenth-Century Maryland." *American Historical Review* 40 (April 1935): 467–72.

Smith, Barbara Clark. *The Freedoms We Lost: Consent and Resistance in Revolutionary America*. New York: New Press, 2010.

Smith, Billy G., ed. *Down and Out in Early America*. University Park: Pennsylvania State University Press, 2004.

———. "Poverty and Economic Marginality in Eighteenth-Century America." *Proceedings of the American Philosophical Society* 132 (March 1988): 85–118.

Smith, Charles. *James Wilson: Founding Father, 1742–1798*. Chapel Hill: University of North Carolina Press, 1956.

Smith, Daniel Blake. "Autonomy and Affection: Parents and Children in Eighteenth-Century Chesapeake Families." In *Growing Up in America: Children in Historical Perspective*, edited by N. Ray Hiner and Joseph M. Hawes, 45–60. Urbana: University of Illinois Press, 1985.

———. *Inside the Great House: Planter Family Life in Eighteenth Century Chesapeake Society*. Ithaca, NY: Cornell University Press, 1986.

Smith, Helene. *The Great Whiskey Rebellion: Rebels with a Cause*. Greensburg, PA: Macdonald/Sward, 1994.

Smith, John Howard. *The First Great Awakening: Redefining Religion in British American, 1729–1775*. Lanham, MD: Fairleigh Dickinson University Press, 2015.

———. "'The Promised Day of the Lord': American Millennialism and Apocalypticism, 1735–1783." In *Anglo-American Millennialism, from Milton to the Millerites*, edited by Richard Connors and Andrew Colin Gow, 115–57. Leiden: Brill, 2004.

Smith, Ryan K. *Robert Morris's Folly: The Architectural and Financial Failures of an American Founder*. New Haven, CT: Yale University Press, 2014.

Smolenski, John. *Friends and Strangers: The Making of a Creole Culture in Colonial Pennsylvania*. Philadelphia: University of Pennsylvania Press, 2010.

Snyder, Terri L. "'To Seeke for Justice': Gender, Servitude, and Household Governance in Early Modern Chesapeake." In *Early Modern Virginia: Reconsidering the Old Dominion*, edited by Douglas Bradburn and John C. Combs, 128–57. Charlottesville: University of Virginia Press, 2011.

Soderlund, Jean R. *Quakers and Slavery: A Divided Spirit*. Princeton, NJ: Princeton University Press, 1985.

Sommerville, Wilson. *The Tuesday Club of Annapolis (1745–1756) as Cultural Performance*. Athens: University of Georgia Press, 1996.

Sparks, John. *The Roots of Appalachian Christianity: The Life and Legacy of Elder Shubal Stearns*. Lexington: University Press of Kentucky, 2001.

Specht, Neva J. "Finding Aid to Lukens Family Papers, 1750–1904." MSS 161, University of Delaware Library, Newark.

Spero, Patrick. "The Americanization of the Pennsylvania Almanac." In *Pennsylvania's Revolution*, edited by William Pencak, 36–55. University Park: Pennsylvania State University, 2010.

———. "The Revolution in Popular Publications: The Almanac and *New England Primer*, 1750–1800." *Early American Studies* 8 (Winter 2010): 41–74.

Spindel, Donna J. "Law and Order: The North Carolina Stamp Act Crisis." *North Carolina Historical Review* 57 (January 1980): 1–16.

Stoeffler, F. Ernest, ed. *Continental Pietism and Early American Christianity*. Grand Rapids, MI: Eerdmans, 1976.

Stout, Harry S. *The Divine Dramatist: George Whitefield and the Rise of Modern Evangelicalism*. Grand Rapids, MI: Eerdmans, 1991.

———. *The New England Soul: Preaching and Religious Culture in Colonial New England*. New York: Oxford University Press, 1986.

Struna, Nancy L. *People of Prowess: Sport, Leisure, and Labor in Early Anglo-America*. Urbana: University of Illinois Press, 1996.

Sturtz, Linda L. *Within Her Power: Propertied Women in Colonial Virginia*. New York: Routledge, 2002.

Sweet, John Wood. *Bodies Politic: Negotiating Race in the American North, 1730–1830*. Philadelphia: University of Pennsylvania Press, 2007.

Sweet, William Warren. *Revivalism in America: Its Origin, Growth, and Decline*. Gloucester, MA: Peter Smith, 1965.

Szatmary, David P. *Shays' Rebellion: The Making of an Agrarian Insurrection*. Amherst: University of Massachusetts Press, 1980.

Tachau, Mary K. Bonsteel. "A New Look at the Whiskey Rebellion." In *The Whiskey Rebellion: Past and Present Perspectives*, edited by Stephen R. Boyd, 97–118. Westport, CT: Greenwood Press, 1985.

Tanis, James. *Dutch Calvinistic Pietism in the Middle Colonies: A Study in the Life and Theology of Theodorus Jacobus Frelinghuysen*. The Hague: Martinus Nijhoff, 1967.

Taylor, Alan. *Liberty Men and Great Proprietors: The Revolutionary Settlement on the Maine Frontier, 1740–1820*. Chapel Hill: University of North Carolina Press, 1990.

Thayer, Theodore. *Pennsylvania Politics and the Growth of Democracy*. Harrisburg: Pennsylvania Historical and Museum Commission, 1953.

Thompson, E. P. "The Moral Economy of the English Crowd in the Eighteenth Century." *Past and Present* 50 (February 1971): 76–136.

Thompson, Michael J. *The Politics of Inequality: A Political History of the Idea of Economic Inequality in America*. New York: Columbia University Press, 2007.

Thorp, Daniel B. "Doing Business in the Backcountry: Retail Trade in Colonial Rowan County, North Carolina." *William and Mary Quarterly*, 3rd ser., 48 (July 1991): 387–408.

———. *The Moravian Community in Colonial North Carolina: Pluralism on the Southern Frontier*. Knoxville: University of Tennessee Press, 1989.

Thwaites, Reuben Gold, and Louise Phelps Kellogg, eds. *Frontier Defense on the Upper Ohio, 1777–1778*. Madison: Wisconsin Historical Society, 1912.

Tolles, Frederick B. *Meeting House and Counting House: The Quaker Merchants of Colonial Philadelphia, 1682–1763*. Chapel Hill: University of North Carolina Press, 1948.

———. *Quakers and the Atlantic Culture*. New York: Macmillan, 1960.

Tracy, Patricia. *Jonathan Edwards, Pastor: Religion and Society in Eighteenth-Century Northampton*. New York: Wipf and Stock, 1980.

Troxler, Carole Watterson. *Farming Dissenters: The Regulator Movement in Piedmont North Carolina*. Raleigh: North Carolina Office of Archives and History, 2011.

Trueblood, Elton. *Robert Barclay*. New York: Harper and Row, 1968.

Tuveson, Ernest Lee. *Redeemer Nation: The Idea of America's Millennial Role*. Chicago: University of Chicago Press, 1968.

Ulrich, Laura Thatcher. *A Midwife's Tale: The Life of Martha Ballard, Based on Her Diary, 1785–1812*. New York: Vintage, 1991.

Upton, Dell. *Holy Things and Profane: Anglican Parish Churches*. Cambridge: Cambridge University Press, 1986.

Ver Steeg, Clarence L. *Robert Morris: Revolutionary Financier*. Philadelphia: University of Pennsylvania Press, 1954.

Vickers, Daniel. "Competency and Competition: Economic Culture in Early America." *William and Mary Quarterly*, 3rd ser., 47 (January 1990): 3–29.

Volwiler, Albert T. *George Croghan and the Westward Movement, 1741–1782*. New York: AMS Press, 1971.

Voorst, Carol Van. *The Anglican Clergy in Maryland, 1692–1776*. New York: Garland, 1989.

Waldstreicher, David. *In the Midst of Perpetual Fetes: The Making of American Nationalism, 1776–1820*. Chapel Hill: University of North Carolina Press, 1997.

Walsh, Lorena S. *Motive of Honor, Pleasure, and Profit: Plantation Management in the Colonial Chesapeake, 1607–1720*. Chapel Hill: University of North Carolina Press, 2010.

———. "Servitude and Opportunity in Charles County, Maryland." In *Law, Society, and Politics in Early Maryland*, edited by Aubrey C. Land, Lois Green Carr, and Edward C. Papenfuse, 111–33. Baltimore: Johns Hopkins University Press, 1977.

———. "'Till Death Us Do Part': Marriage and Family in Seventeenth-Century Maryland." In *The Chesapeake in the Seventeenth Century: Essays on Anglo-American Society*, edited by Thad W. Tate and David L. Ammerman, 126–52. Chapel Hill: University of North Carolina Press, 1979.

Walsh, Lorena C. "The Development of Local Power Structures: Maryland's Lower West Shore in the Early Colonial Period." In *Power and Status: Officeholding in Colonial America*, edited by Bruce C. Daniels, 53–71. Middletown, CT: Wesleyan University Press, 1986.

Walsh, Lorena S., and Russell R. Menard. "Death in the Chesapeake: Two Life Tables for Men in Early Colonial Maryland." *Maryland Historical Magazine* 69 (Summer 1974): 211–27.

Ward, Matthew C. *Breaking the Backcountry: The Seven Years' War in Virginia and Pennsylvania, 1754–1765*. Pittsburgh: University of Pittsburgh Press, 2003.

Ward, W. R. *The Protestant Evangelical Awakening*. Cambridge: Cambridge University Press, 1992.

Wareing, John. *Indentured Migration and the Servant Trade from London to America, 1618–1718: "There Is Great Want of Servants."* New York: Oxford University Press, 2017.

Watson, Alan D. "The Appointment of Sheriffs in Colonial North Carolina: A Reexamination." *North Carolina Historical Review* 53 (October 1976): 385–98.

Watt, W. N. *The Granville District*. Taylorsville, NC: W. N. Watt, 1992.

Weeks, Stephen B. *Southern Quakers and Slavery: A Study in Institutional History*. Baltimore: Johns Hopkins University Press, 1896.

Welch, Pedro L. V. *Slave Society in the City: Bridgetown, Barbados, 1680–1834*. Kingston, Jamaica: Ian Randle, 2003.

Wennersten, John R. *Maryland's Eastern Shore: A Journey in Time and Place*. Centreville, MD: Tidewater, 1992.

White, Julia S. "A Church Quarrel and What Resulted." *Bulletin of Friends' Historical Society of Philadelphia* 5 (May 1914): 90–98.

Whittenburg, James P. "Planters, Merchants, and Lawyers: Social Change and the Origins of the North Carolina Regulation." *William and Mary Quarterly*, 3rd ser., 34 (April 1977): 215–38.

Wilentz, Sean. "America's Lost Egalitarian Tradition." *Daedalus* 131 (Winter 2002): 66–80.

Winiarski, Douglas L. *Darkness Falls on the Land of Light: Experiencing Religious Awakenings in Eighteenth-Century New England*. Chapel Hill: University of North Carolina Press, 2017.

Winner, Lauren F. *A Cheerful and Comfortable Faith: Anglican Religious Practice in Eighteenth-Century Virginia*. New Haven, CT: Yale University Press, 2010.

Wokeck, Marianne S. "Searching for Land: The Role of New Castle, Delaware, 1720s–1770s." In *Ulster to America: The Scots-Irish Migration Experience, 1680–1830*, edited by William R. Hofstra, 25–50. Knoxville: University of Tennessee Press, 2012.

Wood, Gordon S. "Religion and the American Revolution." In *New Directions in American Religious History*, edited by Harry S. Stout and D. G. Hart, 173–205. New York: Oxford University Press, 1997.

Wright, Robert E. *One Nation under Debt: Hamilton, Jefferson, and the History of What We Owe*. New York: McGraw-Hill, 2008.

Young, Alfred F., ed. *The American Revolution: Explorations in the History of American Radicalism*. DeKalb: Northern Illinois University Press, 1976.

———, ed. *Beyond the American Revolution: Explorations in the History of American Radicalism*. DeKalb: Northern Illinois University Press, 1993.

———. *Liberty Tree: Ordinary People and the American Revolution*. New York: New York University Press, 2006.

———. *Masquerade: The Life and Times of Deborah Sampson, Continental Soldier.* New York: Knopf, 2004.

Young, Alfred F., Gary B. Nash, and Ray Raphael, eds. *Revolutionary Founders: Rebels, Radicals, and Reformers in the Making of the Nation.* New York: Knopf, 2001.

Young, Alfred F., and Gregory H. Nobles. *Whose American Revolution Was It? Historians Interpret the Founding.* New York: New York University Press, 2011.

Young, Otis E. "Origins of the American Copper Industry." *Journal of the Early Republic* 3 (Summer 1983): 117–37.

Zagarri, Rosemarie. *Revolutionary Backlash: Women and Politics in the Early American Republic.* Philadelphia: University of Pennsylvania Press, 2007.

Index

Italicized numbers refer to illustrations.

Academy of Philadelphia, 83
Adams, John, 4
African Americans, 4, 113, 185n67; in Barbados, 30; in the Chesapeake, 12; in North Carolina, 33, 155n41. *See also* Husband, Herman: views on; slavery
Alamance, Battle of, 2, 73, 75, 76, 81, 129
alcohol, 14, 45, 119, 122, 150n58. *See also* whiskey tax
Allegany Philosopher, 98–100
Allegheny County, PA, 122, 123, 124, 129
Allegheny Mountains, 76, 79, 102, 111, 129
Allegheny River, 77; map showing, *78*
Allen, Samuel, 161n61
almanacs, 98, *99*
Alsop, George, 8
American Revolution, 2, 5, 73, 80, 82, 83, 85, 91, 104, 122, 123, 131, 139; causes of, 85–87, 136–37; financial problems during, 93–94, 95–97, 106; opposition to, 89; promise of, 3–4, 105, 132, 139, 140, 141, 142; support for, 85–87, 88. *See also* Constitutionalists; Great Awakening; Husband, Herman: views on; postmillennialism; radical Protestantism; radical Whig ideology; republicanism; Republicans; taxation
Anglicanism (Church of England), 2, 20; in Maryland, 15, 18; in North Carolina, 35–36, 45; opposition to, 24, 35–36, 121–22, 135, 136, 152n111. *See also* Great Awakening; Husband, Herman: views on; Orthodox Clergy Act of 1765; radical Protestantism; Vestry Act of 1754; Vestry Act of 1764
Annapolis, MD, 12, 14
Anson County, NC, 43, 53–54, 62
Antifederalists: opposition to Alexander Hamilton's "Report on Public Credit," 118–20; opposition to the second proposed amendment to the U.S. Constitution, 118; opposition to the U.S. Constitution, 114; support for the first proposed amendment to the U.S. Constitution, 116–17. *See also* Bill of Rights; Federalists; Hamilton, Alexander; Husband, Herman; "Report on Public Credit"; U.S. Constitution
Apology for the True Christian Divinity, An (Barclay), 25
Articles of Confederation, 108
artisans: embrace of Great Awakening, 24; opposition to monetary austerity, 107; support for Pennsylvania's 1776 constitution, 88; views on economic equality, 86; views on market economy, 142–43. *See also* capitalism; economic equality; Husband, Herman: views on
Ashe, John, 59, 60
Avery, Waightstill, 71

Badollet, John, 115–16
Baltimore, MD, 12, 14

215

Baltimore County, MD, 14, 29, 31
Baltimore Yearly Meeting, 31
Bank of North America, 105–6, 107, 140
Baptists, 18, 35, 36
Barbados, 29–30, 32
Barclay, Robert, 25
Battle of Alamance, 2, 73, 75, 76, 81, 129
Battles of Lexington and Concord, 87
Bayard, Phoebe, 84
Bedford, PA, 81, 83, 84, 85, 128, 129
Bedford County, PA, 1, 80, 82, 98, 107, 127, 129, 130; during the American Revolution, 85, 86–87, 90–91, 94–95; Antifederalist support in, 114; creation of, 79, 81, 83; economic distress in, 86, 104–5, 140; German Dunker population in, 92–93; opposition to the whiskey tax in, 124–25, 128; settlement of, 79; Woods faction in, 83–85, 89. *See also* American Revolution; Bedford, PA; Husband, Herman; Whiskey Rebellion; Woods, George
Benton, Samuel, 62
Berlin, PA, 124–25, 128, 129
Bethabara, NC, 76
Bethania, NC, 76
Bible, 16, 21, 25–26, 133, 138, 141. *See also* Christianity; Daniel, book of; Ezekiel, book of; Great Awakening; Husband, Herman; New Testament; Old Testament; postmillennialism; radical Protestantism; Revelation, book of
Bill of Rights, 116; debate over first proposed amendment of, 116–17; debate over second proposed amendment of, 118. *See also* Antifederalists; Federalists; U.S. Constitution
Bladen County, NC, 32
Blair, Samuel, 22, 152n90
Bloch, Ruth H., 134
Bloodworth, Timothy, 129
Bohemia Manor, MD, 15
Bohemia River, MD, 12
bond speculators: opposition to, 106, 114, 119–20; policies to protect, 107, 108, 118–19. *See also* Funding Act of 1790; Hamilton, Alexander; Husband, Herman: opposition to

Bonomi, Patricia U., 133
Boston, MA, 84, 86
Boston Tea Party, 86
Bouton, Terry, 137, 185n67
Bowdoin, James, 84
Brackenridge, Hugh, 115, 126
Braddock, Edward, 77
Braddock's Field, 124, 125, 126. *See also* Whiskey Rebellion
Braddock's Road, 76, 79, 128
Bradford, David, 126, 127, 128
Bradford, William, 126
Branson, Ely, 163n109
Branson, Thomas, 159n115
Bridgetown, Barbados, 29–30
Bristol, England, 20
Brothersvalley, PA, 92
Brown, Richard, 90
Brunerstown, PA, 128
Brunswick, NC, 41
Burd, John, 170n99, 172n124
Burnet, Thomas, 102
Bush River Preparative Meeting, 31
Bute County, NC, 71
Butler, John, 161n61
Butler, William, 54–55, 58, 66, 71, 73, 161n61, 163n109

Cable, Abraham, 90
Cacapon River Valley, 36
Caldwell, David, 72, 129
Camden, SC, 38
Campbell, John, 69
Cane Creek, NC, 57, 58, 73
Cane Creek Monthly Meeting, 37–40, 42. *See also* Husband, Herman; Society of Friends (Quakers); Wright, Rachel
Cape Henry, 7
capitalism, 28, 131, 142–43, 184n61, 185n65. *See also* artisans; farmers; Husband, Herman; moral economy
Carlisle, PA, 81, 128
Carter, James, 34
Carteret, John, 2nd Earl of Granville, 32, 34, 35, 36, 42
Caruthers, Eli, 75, 76, 182n191
Carver's Creek Quaker Meeting, 32

216

Index

Catholics, 15, 88
Cathon, William, 46
Cecil County, MD, 13, 15, 32, 74, 75, 76; description of, 12; evangelical movement in, 18–20; Great Awakening in, 22–23; William Husband Sr. moves to, 11–12; iron mining in, 149n57; map of, *19*; Society of Friends (Quakers) in, 24; tobacco and wheat cultivation in, 13–14; George Whitefield's visit to, 21–22. *See also* Great Awakening; Husband, Herman; Husband, William, Jr.; Husband, William, Sr.
Cell, Jonathan, 159n115
Character of the Province of Maryland, A (Alsop), 8
Charles County, MD, 11
Chatham County, NC, 70
Chesapeake Bay, 7, 80
Christianity, 4, 26, 27; as an influence on radicalism, 132–34, 135–36, 137, 141–42. *See also* Bible; Great Awakening; postmillennialism; "radicalism of disappointment"; radical Protestantism; radical Whig ideology
Cisna, Charles, 170n99
Cisna, John, 81
Clymer, George, 122–23, 124
Coercive Acts of 1774, 86
Committee of Correspondence, 86–87
committee of sixty, 127–28. *See also* Husband, Herman; Redstone Old Fort conference; Whiskey Rebellion
Common Sense (Paine), 87, 88
communion season, 19–20, 152n91. *See also* Presbyterianism; Scots-Irish
Connecticut, 36, 111
Connecticut River Valley, 17
Constitutional Convention of 1787, 108. *See also* U.S. Constitution
Constitutionalists, 89, 105, 118; conflict with Republicans, 90–91, 92, 95; fiscal policies of, 93, 95, 106, 107; improved relations with Republicans, 94; views on political dissenters and religious neutrals, 91–92. *See also* American Revolution; Husband, Herman; paper currency; Pennsylvania constitution (1776); Republicans

Continental Almanac, The (Rittenhouse), 98, 99. *See also* almanacs
Continental Congress, 86, 87, 91; fiscal policies of, 96, 105, 106. *See also* Bank of North America; forty-for-one funding measure
Continuation of the Impartial Relation, A (Husband), 65–66
Cox, Harmon, 160n33
Cox, Isaac, 76, 79, 80, 81–82
Cox, Phoebe, 29
Cox, William, 48, 159n115, 160n33
Coxe, Tench, 128
Craven, Peter, 161n64, 163n109
creditors, 45–46, 86, 114; opposition to, 106, 119, 139, 141; policies to protect, 95, 107, 108, 118–19, 140. *See also* Funding Act of 1790; Hamilton, Alexander; Husband, Herman
Cross Creek, NC, 58, 59, 70
cultivation clause, 63
Cumberland County, PA, 81, 83, 84
Currency Act of 1764, 45, 85. *See also* paper currency

dancing, 14, 16, 23, 26
Danger of an Unconverted Ministry, The (Tennent), 22
Daniel, book of, 121–22. *See also* Bible; Old Testament; postmillennialism
Davison, Hugh, 172n124
debt, 44, 140, 142; calls for debt relief, 105–6, 122–23, 138; indebtedness in North Carolina, 44–46; indebtedness in Pennsylvania, 85–86, 105, 106; national debt, 99, 108, 118–19, 122, 142; opposition to debt relief, 95, 107. 108, 120, 140. *See also* American Revolution; farmers; Funding Act of 1790; Husband, Herman
Declaration of Independence, 4, 61, 114
Deep River, NC, 48, 73
Delaware, 15, 18, 19, 111, 120
Delaware Native Americans, 77–78, 94–95. *See also* Native Americans
democracy, 5; constitutional restraints on, 108; economic equality as aspect of, 4, 105, 107, 138, 139, 140, 143; limited by

Index 217

democracy (*continued*)
    Pennsylvania's 1790 constitution, 120; and Pennsylvania's 1776 constitution, 87–88; perceived excess of, 89, 95, 108; threats to, 105. *See also* economic equality; Husband, Herman: views on; political equality; U.S. Constitution
Democratic-Republican societies, 124
Dialogue between an Assembly-Man and a Convention-Man, A (Husband), 120
Dinwiddie, Robert, 77
Dixon, Simon, 57, 58
Dobbs, Arthur, 33, 35, 41
Dossett, Francis, 161n61
Dougherty, Bernard, 85, 168n55, 170n91, 172n124

East Nottingham Monthly Meeting, 31
economic equality: and Pennsylvania's 1776 constitution, 87–88; relationship to political equality, 3–4, 44, 47, 86, 87, 89, 97, 132, 138–39, 140, 141, 143; support for, 3–4, 105–6, 132, 137, 140; as vital to democracy, 4, 105, 107, 138, 139, 140, 143. *See also* democracy; Husband, Herman: views on; political equality
Edenton, NC, 32, 34
Edgecombe County, NC, 71
Edwards, Isaac, 56
Edwards, Jonathan, 17, 134. *See also* Great Awakening
Elk River, MD, 12, 15
English Civil War, 88
English constitution, 46, 48, 52, 57, 65, 86, 121, 135, 138
Enlightenment, the, 131, 133, 134
Eno River, NC, 48, 55
Equiano, Olaudah, 29
Espy, Davis, 168n55, 170n91
Essay toward a Natural History of the Earth and Terrestrial Bodies (Woodward), 102
evangelicals, 2, 17, 18, 19, 23, 24, 26, 27, 36, 40, 45, 49, 116, 133, 134, 136, 141–42. *See also* Great Awakening; New Birth; radical Protestantism; spirit within
Ezekiel, book of, 3, 97–98, 103, 109–10, 115, 117, 120, 141. *See also* Bible; Old Testament; postmillennialism

Fagg's Manor, PA, 22
Fan for Fanning, A (Husband), 50, 131
Fanning, Edmund, 44, 46, 52, 53, 59, 69, 85, 158n94; assault on, 67–68; background of, 43; elected to General Assembly, 68; loses 1769 election, 62, 162n79; opposition in North Carolina to, 43–44, 47, 50, 51, 57, 61, 66, 68, 81; relationship with Herman Husband, 54–55, 59, 60; relationship with North Carolina Regulators, 53, 54–56; relationship with Sandy Creek Association, 47–49, 51; stands trial, 58, 60, 61, 66. *See also* Husband, Herman; North Carolina Regulation; Sandy Creek Association; Tryon, William
farmers: economic distress of, 13, 43, 44–46, 85–86, 104–5, 106, 137, 140; embrace of Great Awakening, 24; as members of the laboring community, 137–38; protest movements of, 43, 47–49, 50–73, 86–87, 105–6, 107, 122–29, 136–37; squatters, 43, 63, 64, 79, 84, 137, 138; support for debt relief, 105–6, 122–23, 138; support for Pennsylvania's 1776 constitution, 88; tenancy, 12, 13, 43, 105, 137, 138, 139, 140; views on economic equality, 2, 3–4, 86, 87, 107, 132, 137–38, 140; views on market economy, 142–43; views on political equality, 86, 87, 132, 140, 141; yeomanry, 11, 47, 93, 137, 138, 139, 140. *See also* capitalism; economic equality; Husband, Herman: views on; North Carolina Regulation; political equality; Whiskey Rebellion
Fayette County, PA, 122, 123, 127, 129
Federalists: opposition to first proposed amendment to the U.S. Constitution, 116–17; political reforms in Pennsylvania of, 118, 120–21; support for U.S. Constitution, 114. *See also* Antifederalists; Bill of Rights; Pennsylvania constitution (1790); U.S. Constitution
Few, James, 73
Few, William, 161n61
Fields, Jeremiah, 67, 163n109
Findley, William, 106, 127
Finley, Samuel, 26
First Congress, 116, 118
Foner, Eric, 142

Forbes's Road, 76, 81, 128
forks of the Ohio, 77, 79
Fort Bedford, PA, 83, 84
Fort Cumberland, MD, 79, 95, 128
Fort Duquesne, PA, 77; map showing, 78
Fort Johnston, NC, 69
Fort Ligonier, PA, 84
Fort Pitt, PA, 78
forty-for-one funding measure, 96–97. *See also* Continental Congress; Husband, Herman: opposition to; paper currency
Fothergill, Samuel, 31
Fountain Company, 37
Fox, George, 24, 30
France, 41, 77–79, 122, 142
Franklin, Benjamin, 62, 162n77
Frederick, MD, 37
Frelinghuysen, Theodorus, 15, 17, 18. *See also* Great Awakening; Pietism
French Revolution, 121, 122
Frohock, John, 61, 62, 71–72, 162n72
Fruit, John, 163n109
Funding Act of 1790, 118–20, 122–23, 141. *See also* bond speculators; creditors; Hamilton, Alexander; Husband, Herman: opposition to; Whiskey Rebellion
Fyke, Malachi, 161n64

Galbraith, Robert, 90, 94
Gallatin, Albert, 115, 126, 176n85
gambling, 14, 16–17, 123
Garretson, John, 15
George II, King, 35
George III, King, 41, 46, 57, 61
Georgia, 20, 102, 111, 140
Germans, 13, 15, 18, 33, 35, 77, 80, 82, 92–93, 101, 115
Gilpin, Samuel, 74, 76, 79, 81, 168n41
Glades, PA, 76, 79, 80, 81, 82, 92, 94, 95, 101, 121, 128
Glouchester, England, 20
Goddard, William, 98
Granville County, NC, 36, 45, 46, 60, 62, 68
Granville District, NC, 32, 33, 63
Great Alamance Creek, NC, 72
Great Awakening, 4; in Cecil County, MD, 18–19, 22; divide within Presbyterian congregations over, 22; as an influence on postmillennialism, 26, 134; in the middle colonies, 18; in New England, 17; as a threat to religious and political hierarchies, 23–24, 27, 35, 133–34, 135–36. *See also* Christianity; Husband, Herman: embrace of; postmillennialism; radical Protestantism; radical Whig ideology; spirit within
Great Wagon Road, 33
Griggs, John, 9, 10
Gross, Solomon, 161n64
Guilford County, NC, 70

Hagerstown, MD, 79, 82
Halifax, NC, 70
Hamilton, Alexander, 119, 121, 126, 143; as author of first "Report on Public Credit," 118–19; crackdown on the Whiskey Rebellion, 127–28, 129; opposition to Hamilton's first "Report on Public Credit," 119–20, 122–23; views on the Whiskey Rebellion, 123–24. *See also* Funding Act of 1790; "Report on Public Credit"; Washington, George; Whiskey Rebellion
Hamilton, Matthew, 161n64, 163n109
Hamilton, Ninian, 161n61, 161n64
Hamilton, Ninian Bell, 55–56, 161n64, 163n109
Hampshire County, VA, 36
Hannastown, PA, 95
Harris, Tyree, 51, 57
Hart, Thomas, 50, 163n114
Hartso, John Philip, 161n61
Harvey, John, 64
Haw River, NC, 33, 51, 72
Henderson, Richard, 60, 66, 67–68
Hendry, George, 160n33
Herman, Augustine, 15
Hern, John, 46
Hill, Wills, 1st Earl of Hillsborough, 61, 73
Hillsborough, NC, 33, 43, 47, 47, 51, 57, 59, 69, 70, 71, 81; April 1768 riot in, 50, 53; court sessions in, 54–55, 58, 60, 61, 66–67; North Carolina militia in, 58, 72; September 1770 riot in, 67–68, 69; William Tryon's visit to, 57. *See also* North Carolina Regulation; Orange County, NC

Index 219

Hiltzheimer, Jacob, 117
History of the Rise, Increase, and Progress of the Christian People Called Quakers (Sewel), 24
Holt, Michael, 163n114
Hooper, William, 61, 162n73, 163n114
Howard, Martin, 60
Howell, Rednap, 55–56, 70–71, 73, 160n33
Hudson's Bay, 102
Hunter, James, 66, 71, 73, 160n33, 161n61, 161n64, 163n109, 164n127
hunting, 14, 16, 45, 76, 79, 80, 81–82
Husband, David, 74
Husband, Emey Allen, 40, 82, 98, 116, 121, 129, 157n83, 167n36, 182n191
Husband, Herman: adolescence of, 14–17, 18–20, 21–22, 23, 24–27; as the Allegany Philosopher, 98–100; arrested, 50, 54, 69, 129; as an attendee of the Parkinson's Ferry conference, 125–27, 130; birth of, 14; calls for political reform, 42, 49, 62, 65, 86–87, 88, 97–98, 109–14, 139, 141; children of, 82, 153n4, 167n36; death of, 1, 130, 182n191; description of, 98–99, 101, 115–16, 176n85; distrust for lawyers, 44, 47, 62, 97, 106, 132–32, 139; distrust for merchants, 47, 93, 96–97, 106, 107, 139; expelled from North Carolina lower house, 69; expelled from Society of Friends (Quakers), 40; flees North Carolina, 73, 75–76; grandfathers of, 7–13, 14, 15–16, 17; landholdings of, 32, 33, 36, 82, 98, 154n27, 155n36, 156n55; as a land speculator, 32–33, 36, 79, 81, 82, 156n55, 168n41; legacy of, 143; local offices held by, 86–87, 90–91, 107, 116; as a member of the committee of sixty, 127; as a merchant, 29–30; moderation of, 52–53, 61, 65, 71, 124–25, 126, 127, 128, 132, 142; moves to North Carolina, 32, 33, 155n34; moves to Pennsylvania, 76, 79–83; and the New Birth, 20, 22, 23, 27, 133; and New Jerusalem, 1, 3, 97–99, 102–4, 109–13, 115, 116, 117, 121, 126, 130, 141; —, Husband's map of, 104; parents of, 13–15, 16, 19, 21, 24; participation in the North Carolina Regulation, 4, 52, 54–55, 56, 58–60, 62, 64–67, 69, 70, 71, 72, 73; —, historical marker commemorating, 2; participation in the Whiskey Rebellion, 124–26, 127–28; as a part-time owner of the Fountain Company, 37; as a politician, 62, 64, 91–94, 116, 117–21, 164n128, 171n101; proposed 1778 paper money scheme, 93–94, 96, 120, 171n115; radicalism of, 3, 131–32; relationship with Edmund Fanning, 54–55, 59, 60; rejection of New Side Presbyterianism, 27; rejection of organized religion, 27, 42, 49, 91, 136; and Sandy Creek Association, 47–49; siblings of, 150n61; stands trial, 54–55, 60, 66–67, 85, 129–30, 161n64; as a supervisor of father's iron-mine works, 29; support of debt relief, 96, 106–7, 119–20, 139, 140; support of Pennsylvania's 1776 constitution, 88; treatment of political dissenters and religious neutrals, 89, 91–93; wives of, 29, 37, 40, 153n4, 157n83; writings of, 39–40, 64–66, 96, 110, 120, 121–22, 175n47, 175n69 (*see also specific works by title*)
—, embrace of: Great Awakening, 18–20, 21–22, 23–24, 27, 133–34; labor theory of value, 139; political activism, 2, 42, 49, 113, 136; postmillennialism, 3, 42, 49, 65–66, 88, 92, 100, 108–9, 112, 121–22, 134–35, 136, 141, 178n122; the spirit within, 24, 25–26, 27, 39–40, 42, 49, 133–34
—, influences on: of liberalism, 138–39, 184n63, 185n65; of Herman Kinkey, 15–16, 17; of Presbyterianism, 23, 24, 26–27; of radical Protestantism, 133–34, 136; of radical Whig ideology, 42, 49, 62, 65, 135–36, 183n27; of republicanism, 138–39, 184n63, 185n65; of Society of Friends (Quakers), 24–27, 28, 29, 31, 42
—, opposition to: bond speculation, 106–7, 119–20, 131, 140, 141; currency speculation, 93, 96–97; forty-for-one funding measure, 96–97; Funding Act of 1790, 119–20, 123, 141; monetary austerity, 96, 106–7, 123, 140, 141; Pennsylvania's 1790 constitution, 120–21; Republicans, 95, 96, 98, 118, 172n138; Society of Friends (Quakers), 37–40, 91–92, 157n79; wide-scale land speculation, 93–94, 112–13, 131, 139, 140; Rachel Wright, 37–40

220   *Index*

—, views on: African Americans, 30, 132, 155n43; American Revolution, 88, 98–100, 131–32, 139; Anglicanism (Church of England), 23, 24, 27, 35–36, 49, 133, 134, 150n68; artisans, 3, 93, 97, 103, 118, 131–32; democracy, 97–98, 108, 131; economic equality, 2–3, 47, 62, 88, 100, 106–7, 112–13, 118, 131–32, 138–39, 140–41, 143; farmers, 2, 30, 34, 36, 47, 49, 62, 65, 92, 93, 96–97, 103, 106–7, 115, 118, 131–32, 138–39, 140, 141; market economy, 142–43, 184n63, 185n65; Native Americans, 113; political equality, 3, 88, 97, 100, 132–33, 138, 140; property, 132, 138–39; slavery, 29–30, 33, 34–35, 132, 155n43; U.S. Constitution, 1, 3, 108–11, 112–14, 114–15, 140, 141; George Washington, 114, 128, 130; women, 132
Husband, Herman, Jr., 82, 153n4, 167n36
Husband, Isaac Tuscape, 82, 167n36
Husband, John (brother of Herman Husband), 82, 150n61
Husband, John (son of Herman Husband), 153n4, 167n36
Husband, Joseph, 91–92, 150n61
Husband, Mary Bowen, 11, 12
Husband, Mary Kinkey, 13, 14, 21
Husband, Mary Pugh, 37, 40, 81, 156n59, 167n36
Husband, William (son of Herman Husband), 167n36
Husband, William, Jr., 12, 28, 29, 32, 149n57; alcohol consumption of, 150n58; attends George Whitefield's field meeting, 21; birth of, 149n47; children of, 150n61; death of, 149n51; marries Mary Kinkey, 13; moves to St. Mary Ann's Parish, MD, 13–14; as a part-time owner of iron-mining works, 14, 149n57; passion for gambling, 14, 16–17; religious beliefs of, 15, 19, 24; as a tobacco farmer and slaveholder, 13, 149n51. See also Anglicanism (Church of England); gambling; Husband, Herman; slavery; tobacco; wheat
Husband, William, Sr., 15, 32; acquires public office, 11; becomes a landowner, 10; becomes a slaveholder, 12; birth of, 146n1 (ch.1); children of, 148n41; death of, 12; as an indentured servant, 8–10; marries Mary Bowen, 11; migrates to Maryland, 7–8; moves to Cecil County, MD, 11–12; value of estate, 149n47. See also Husband, William, Jr.; indentured servitude; slavery; tobacco
Hutrim Hutrim, 98

Impartial Relation, An (Husband), 28, 64–65
indentured servitude, 7–10, 12, 13, 147n16. See also Husband, William, Sr.
inflation, 93, 95–96, 104, 140. See also paper currency

Jackson, Isaac, 161n61, 161n64
Jackson, Jobe, 155n43
James River, VA, 7
Jefferson, Thomas, 117
Johnston, Gabriel, 33
Johnston Riot Act of 1771, 70–71. See also North Carolina Regulation; Tryon, William
Jones, Hugh, 18
Juniata Valley, PA, 77, 79, 83

Kars, Marjoleine, 133
Kent County, MD, 12
Kidd, Thomas S., 133
King George II, 35
King George III, 41, 46, 57, 61
Kinkey, Herman, 13, 14, 15–16, 17, 18. See also Husband, Herman: influences on; Pietism

labor theory of value, 137–39
Lake Erie, 77
Lancaster, PA, 14, 91
Lancaster County, PA, 32, 154n26
Lawson, John, 32
lawyers, 42, 66, 136; in North Carolina, 44; opposition to, 46, 63, 64, 71, 105, 114; in Pennsylvania, 85. See also Husband, Herman; North Carolina Regulation
Lea, John, 58
Lefer, David, 135
Lexington and Concord, Battles of, 87
liberalism, 137, 139, 185n65
liberty poles, 125, 128, 180n170
Lloyd, Thomas, 48, 54–55

Index 221

Logstown, PA, 77
London, England, 8, 20, 43, 77
Lowe, John, 160n33
Lucas, George, 129
Lukens, John, 83, 84

Maddock, Joseph, 47–48, 159n115
Madison, James, 117
Manning, William, 132
Marshall, Christopher, 88
Marshall, James, 125–27
Marshall, John, 47, 159n115, 160n33
Marshall, William, 159n115
Martin, Alexander, 129, 163n114
Maryland, 2, 7, 15, 16, 33, 36, 38, 73, 74, 76, 79, 81, 95, 111, 120, 127, 128; copper mining in, 37; demographic changes in, 11–12, 13; description of, 8–9; forms of entertainment in, 14; indentured servitude in, 9–10; landownership in, 11, 31–32; map of portion of, 19; religion in, 15, 18, 24, 30, 35; reputation of, 8; slavery in, 12, 13, 20; tobacco production in, 9, 13; wheat production in, 14. See also Cecil County, MD; Great Awakening; Husband, Herman; Husband, William, Jr.; Husband, William, Sr.
Massachusetts, 61, 84, 86, 107, 111, 114, 132, 140
Massachusetts Spy, 81
Massett, William, 159n115
Matear, Robert, 72
McCoombe, William, 170n99
McCulloh, Henry, 43, 44
McCulloh, Henry Eustace, 43, 44, 62
McFarlane, James, 124
McGuire, Thomas, 59, 68
McNair, Ralph, 53
McPherson, William, 59
Mecklenburg County, NC, 43, 51, 58
Menneville, Ange de, the Marquis Duquesne, 77
merchants: in London, 43, 47; in Maryland, 9, 14, 29–30; as members of the backcountry elite, 44, 46, 47, 85, 142; in North Carolina, 45–46; in Pennsylvania, 85–86, 105–6. See also Husband, Herman
Messer, Robert, 75–76
Methodists, 20

Mexico, 102
Milford Township, PA, 107
Milner, James, 59, 60, 66–67
Moffitt, William, 48, 160n33, 161n61, 161n64
Monongahela River, 78, 125, 125; map showing, 78
Monongahela Valley, 79
Montgomery County, MD, 37
Moore, Maurice, 69
Moore, James, 73
moral economy, 96, 143, 172n138, 185n65. See also capitalism
Moravians, 76
Morris, Robert, 107, 108. See also Republicans
Murray, James, 65
Murray, Judith Sargent, 132

Nash, Abner, 59, 60, 66–67
Nash, Gary B., 137
Nation, Christopher, 62, 161n64
Native Americans, 9, 57, 58, 77–78, 79, 94–95, 133. See also Delaware Native Americans; Husband, Herman: views on; Seneca Native Americans; Shawnee Native Americans
Neville, John, 123, 124, 125, 126
New Bern, NC, 41, 51, 55, 62, 64, 68, 69, 70, 71, 72
New Birth, 20, 22, 23, 27, 133. See also Christianity; Great Awakening; Husband, Herman; Presbyterianism; radical Protestantism; spirit within
New Castle County, DE, 15, 19
New Hampshire, 111, 114, 138, 140
New Hanover County, NC, 59
New Jerusalem, 1, 3, 96–97, 103, 109–13, 115, 116, 117, 121, 126, 130, 141; Husband's map of, 104. See also Christianity; Daniel, book of; Ezekiel, book of; Husband, Herman; postmillennialism; Revelation, book of
New Jersey, 15, 18, 20, 55, 111, 120, 127, 137
New Side Presbyterians, 22–27, 35. See also Great Awakening; Husband, Herman; Old Side Presbyterians
New Testament, 103. See also Bible; postmillennialism; Revelation, book of
New York, 20, 43, 72, 83, 111, 137

New York University, 115
Noll, Mark A., 136
Northampton, MA, 17
Northampton County, NC, 71
North Carolina, 2, 33, 40, 54, 59, 62, 64, 70, 72, 73, 85, 86, 89, 93, 106, 111, 135; corruption in, 34, 41–43, 46, 51; creation of Sandy Creek Association in, 47–49; description of, 32; emergence of a new elite in, 44; indebtedness in, 44–46; landownership in, 32, 36, 154n31; merchants in, 44, 45–46, 47, 53, 58; and North Carolina Regulation, 50–73; religion in, 31, 35–36, 37–40; settlers in, 33, 35, 36, 42, 44–45; slavery in, 30, 34–35, 155n41; during the Stamp Act crisis, 41–42; taxation in, 32, 35–36, 41, 45, 50–51, 61, 63; wheat production in, 44. *See also* Husband, Herman; North Carolina Regulation; Orange County, NC
North Carolina Gazette, 69
North Carolina Piedmont, 2, 32, 42, 43, 51, 70, 73, 85, 89, 93; settlers in, 33–35, 44–46
North Carolina Regulation, 4, 81, 124, 136, 138, 139, 142; and Battle of Alamance, 2, 73; causes of, 46, 47–49, 50–58, 61–62, 63–64, 65–67; crackdown on North Carolina Regulators, 68–70, 71–73; Edmund Fanning's relationship with North Carolina Regulators, 53, 54–56, 68; historical marker commemorating, 2; and the Johnston Riot Act, 70–71; William Tryon's relationship with North Carolina Regulators, 57–58, 60–61, 70; violence during, 50, 53–54, 67–68, 69. *See also* Fanning, Edmund; Husband, Herman; Johnston Riot Act of 1771; Orange County, NC; Tryon, William
North East, MD, 21
Northwest Territory, 84
Notley, Thomas, 9
Nottingham Lots, MD, 24
Nottingham Presbyterian Church, 22
Nutbush Address (Sims), 46, 62
Nutbush Creek, NC, 36

Ohio Company, 77
Ohio River, 77, 79; map showing, 78

Old Side Presbyterians, 22–23. *See also* Great Awakening; New Side Presbyterians
Old Testament, 3, 103, 109, 113, 121. *See also* Bible; Daniel, book of; Ezekiel, book of; postmillennialism
O'Neill, John, 161n64
Orange County, NC, 2, 37, 38, 47, 61, 71, 72, 73; and county militia, 43, 53, 57; court sessions in, 54–55, 60–61, 66–67; description of, 33; merchants in, 45–46; opposition to corruption in, 47–49, 50–51, 53, 56–58, 62–64, 66, 69, 70; riots in, 50, 67–68; rise of the North Carolina Regulation in, 51–52; settlers in, 36; slavery in, 36, 155n41. *See also* Fanning, Edmund; Hillsborough, NC; Husband, Herman; North Carolina Regulation
Orthodox Clergy Act of 1765, 45. *See also* Anglicanism (Church of England); taxation

Pacific Ocean, 102
Paine, Thomas, 3, 87, 88
paper currency, 9, 46, 51, 142; Continental bills, 95, 96; depreciation of, 93, 95; fiscal conservatives' views on, 95, 105, 108; popular support for continued emission of, 105, 107; shortage of, 45, 46, 51, 63, 85, 97, 104, 105, 106, 140, 174n14; speculation in, 96–97. *See also* Constitutionalists; Currency Act of 1764; forty-for-one funding measure; Husband, Herman; inflation; Republicans
Parkinson's Ferry conference, 124–27, 129, 130. *See also* Husband, Herman; Whiskey Rebellion
Parks, Samuel, 163n109
Payne, William, 161n64
Pembroke College, Oxford, 20
Penn, William, 28
Pennsylvania, 2, 4, 18, 73, 83, 84, 97, 101, 102, 111, 114, 120, 128, 142; during the American Revolution, 86–88, 89–91, 94–95; crackdown on political dissenters and religious neutrals in, 91–92; debate over the Bill of Rights in, 116–17, 118; economic distress in, 85–86, 93, 104–6, 140; economic policies in, 93–94, 95, 106,

Pennsylvania (*continued*)
107; indebtedness in, 85–86, 105, 106; landownership in, 32; map of southwestern, 78; opposition to monetary austerity in, 104–6, 107, 119, 122–23, 124–28; during Pontiac's War, 77–78; religion in, 20, 22; settlement of southwestern Pennsylvania, 78, 79, 81, 82; during the Seven Years' War, 77–78; transportation arteries in, 33, 81; warfare against Native Americans in, 94–95; wheat industry in, 14; during the Whiskey Rebellion, 122–28, 129. *See also* American Revolution; Antifederalists; Bedford County, PA; Constitutionalists; Federalists; Husband, Herman; Republicans; Whiskey Rebellion

Pennsylvania constitution (1776), 87–88, 104, 120, 121; opposition to, 89–90; support for, 89. *See also* American Revolution; Constitutionalists; Pennsylvania constitution (1790); Republicans; Test Act

Pennsylvania constitution (1790), 120–21. *See also* Federalists; Pennsylvania constitution (1776)

Pennsylvania, Delaware, Maryland, and Virginia Almanack (Goddard), 98. *See also* almanacs

Pennsylvania Journal, 81, 86

Pennsylvania Packet, 116–17

Person, Thomas, 62

Peters, Richard, 117, 129

Philadelphia, PA, 1, 3, 14, 81, 83, 84, 85, 88, 107, 130, 137; arrival of prisoners following the Whiskey Rebellion to, 129; captured by British forces, 91; economic inequality in, 140; as host to the Constitutional Convention of 1787, 108; as host to Pennsylvania's 1776 state constitutional convention, 87; as host to Pennsylvania's 1789–90 General Assembly, 116, 118; as host to Pennsylvania's 1790 state constitutional convention, 120–21

Philson, Robert, 125, 128, 129, 130

Pietism, 15–16, 17, 18, 35. *See also* Christianity; Frelinghuysen, Theodorus; Germans; Great Awakening; Kinkey, Herman; Presbyterianism; Scots-Irish

Pile, John, 161n61

Piper, John, 90

Pitt County, NC, 69

Pittsburgh, PA, 103, 105, 115, 122, 123, 124, 125, 127, 128

Pittsburgh Gazette, 124

political equality: and Pennsylvania's 1776 constitution, 87; relationship to economic equality, 3–4, 44, 47, 86, 87, 89, 97, 132, 138–39, 140, 141, 143; support for, 3–4, 89, 132, 140, 143. *See also* democracy; economic equality; Husband, Herman: views on

poll tax, 45, 51, 61, 63. *See also* taxation

Pontiac's War, 78–79

Potomac River, 7

postmillennialism, 26, 103, 134, 153n124; during the American Revolution, 88–89; during the North Carolina Regulation, 65–66. *See also* American Revolution; Bible; Daniel, book of; Ezekiel, book of; Great Awakening; Husband, Herman: embrace of; New Jerusalem; Revelation, book of

Presbyterianism, 24, 35, 72, 129; in Cecil County, MD, 18–20, 22, 24–25; conflict between New Side and Old Side Presbyterians, 22–23. *See also* Christianity; Great Awakening; Husband, Herman: influences on; New Side Presbyterians; Old Side Presbyterians; Scots-Irish

Princeton College, 115

Principio Company, 149n57

Proposals to Amend and Perfect the Policy of the Government of the United States of America (Husband), 74, 96–98

Pryor, John, 62, 162n79

Pugh, James, 81

Pyle, John, 58–59

Quebec Act of 1774, 88

"radicalism of disappointment," 140

radical Protestantism, 47, 49, 65, 131, 133, 136, 141–42. *See also* American Revolution; Great Awakening; Husband, Herman: influences on; New Birth; North Carolina Regulation; radical Whig ideology; spirit within

radical Whig ideology, 41, 46, 48, 134–35, 183n27. *See also* American Revolution; Husband, Herman: influences on; North Carolina Regulation; radical Protestantism; republicanism
Railand, Matthew, 62
Randolph, Edmund, 123–24, 127–28
Randolph County, NC, historical marker in, 2
Raritan Valley, 18
Rawle, William, 129–30
Reagan, Philip, 128–29
Redstone Old Fort conference, 127–28. *See also* Whiskey Rebellion
"Regulator Advertisement, No. 1," 47–48. *See also* Fanning, Edmund; Husband, Herman; Sandy Creek Association
"Report on Public Credit," 118–19. *See also* Funding Act of 1790; Hamilton, Alexander
republicanism, 86, 131, 134–35, 185n65. *See also* Husband, Herman: influences on
Republicans, 89, 92; conflict with Constitutionalists, 90–91, 92, 95; fiscal policies of, 95, 107; improved relations with Constitutionalists, 94. *See also* American Revolution; Constitutionalists; Husband, Herman: opposition to; Morris, Robert; paper currency; Pennsylvania constitution (1776); Woods, George
Revelation, book of, 26, 103, 109, 141. *See also* Bible; New Testament; postmillennialism
Revenue Act of 1791, 122, 177n109. *See also* Funding Act of 1790; taxation; whiskey tax
Rhoads, Henry, 170n91, 172n124
Rhode Island, 111
Rigbie, James, 132n111
Rising Sun, MD, 19
Rittenhouse, David, 98
Rocky River, NC, 56
Ross, James, 126–27
Rowan County, NC, 2, 34, 36, 43, 58, 61, 62, 63, 70, 71, 72
Rush, Benjamin, 129

Sacred Theory of the Earth (Burnet), 102
St. Clair, Arthur, 84–85, 89
St. Malo, France, 41
St. Mary Ann's Church, 23

St. Mary Ann's Parish, MD, 14, 15
St. Mary's City, MD, 8
St. Mary's County, MD, 11, 12
St. Mary's River, MD, 8
St. Stephen's Anglican Church, 15, 18
St. Stephen's Parish, MD, 12, 18
Salisbury, NC, 43, 58, 61, 66, 71, 72
Sally, George Adam, 56, 57, 58
Sandy Creek, NC, 45, 47, 52, 54, 60, 62, 64, 73, 75, 76
Sandy Creek Association, 47–49, 51. *See also* Fanning, Edmund; Husband, Herman; North Carolina Regulation
Sassafras River, 12
Schoepf, Johann, 101–3, 115
School of Manners, The (Garretson), 15
Scots-Irish, 18, 19–20, 33, 77, 82
Second Part of the Naked Truth, The (Husband), 39–40
Seneca Native Americans, 95. *See also* Native Americans
Sermons to Asses (Murray), 65
Seven Years' War, 40, 77–78, 84
Sewel, William, 24
Shawnee Native Americans, 77–78, 94–95. *See also* Native Americans
Sims, George, 46, 62
Sitterell, John, 163n114
skimmington (shaming ritual), 50
slavery, 4; in the Chesapeake, 11, 12, 13; in North Carolina, 33, 34; Society of Friends' (Quakers') opposition to, 30–31; Society of Friends' (Quakers') toleration of, 30. *See also* African Americans; Husband, Herman: views on; Husband, William, Jr.; Husband, William, Sr.; Society of Friends (Quakers)
small-claims court, 61, 64, 70
Smilie, Robert, 116
Smith, Thomas, 83–84, 89, 90, 94, 168n50
Smith, William, 83–84
Society of Friends (Quakers), 15, 32, 48, 49, 50, 58, 135; during the American Revolution, 89, 91–92; business pursuits in the West Indies of, 28–29; in Cecil County, 14, 18, 24; economic ethic of, 28; in North Carolina, 35, 37–40; opposition to slavery, 30–31; in Philadelphia, 85–86, 87; reform

Index   225

Society of Friends (Quakers) (*continued*) movement within, 31; toleration of slavery, 30; and the Rachel Wright affair, 37–40. *See also* American Revolution; Barclay, Robert; Cane Creek Monthly Meeting; Great Awakening; Husband, Herman: influences on; spirit within

Some Remarks on Religion (Husband), 7

Somerset, PA, 80

Sons of Liberty, 41

South Carolina, 38, 111, 137

Sparks, William, 80–81

speculation: in bonds, 106, 107, 117; in land, 8, 40, 77, 79, 81, 82, 83–85; opposition to, 63, 64, 106, 127–38; in paper currency, 96–97. *See also* forty-for-one funding measure; Funding Act of 1790; Husband, Herman: opposition to; McCulloh, Henry; paper currency

Spencer, Samuel, 53–54, 62

spirit within, 24, 25, 27, 39, 40, 42, 49, 133, 134. *See also* evangelicals; Great Awakening; Husband, Herman: embrace of; radical Protestantism; Society of Friends (Quakers)

Springfield, MA, 107

Stamp Act crisis of 1765, 41–42, 59, 135–36. *See also* taxation

Staunton, VA, 89

Stearns, Shubal, 36

Stephens, John, 170n99

Stewart, John, 170n99

Stoddard, Solomon, 17. *See also* Great Awakening

Stuart, Jehu, 37

Stump, John, 168n41

Sugar Creek, NC, 43

Surrey, England, 40

Surry County, NC, 70

Susquehanna River, 77

taxation, 52, 57, 58, 60, 61, 73, 85, 111, 119, 140; in North Carolina, 32, 35, 41, 44–45; opposition in North Carolina to, 50, 51, 53–54, 57, 61, 63, 66; opposition in Pennsylvania to, 85–86, 96, 104–6, 107, 122–27; opposition to tax relief, 107, 108, 120; in Pennsylvania, 85–86, 87, 92, 95; support for progressive taxation, 86, 93–94, 96, 138, 139. *See also* American Revolution; Constitutionalists; Funding Act of 1790; Orthodox Clergy Act of 1765; poll tax; Republicans; Revenue Act of 1791; Stamp Act crisis of 1765; Tea Act of 1773; Townshend Acts of 1767; Tryon's Palace; Vestry Act of 1754; Vestry Act of 1764; whiskey tax

Taylor, Alan, 141–42

Tea Act of 1773, 85. *See also* taxation

Teague, Abraham, 163n109

Tennent, Gilbert, 17, 18, 22, 23, 152n102

Tennent, William, Jr., 17, 18

Tennent, William, Sr., 17, 18, 152n90

Test Act, 91, 92, 94. *See also* Constitutionalists; Republicans

test oath clause, 89, 90. *See also* Constitutionalists; Pennsylvania constitution (1776); Republicans

Thompson, Robert, 72

tobacco, 8, 11, 12, 13, 45; cultivation in the Chesapeake of, 9–10. *See also* Husband, William, Jr.; Husband, William, Sr.; indentured servitude; slavery

Tolland, CT, 36

Tom the Tinker, 124. *See also* Whiskey Rebellion

Tories, 95

Townshend Acts of 1767, 61, 64. *See also* taxation

Tryon, Charles, 40

Tryon, Mary Shirley, 40

Tryon, William, 41, 43, 51, 54, 56, 62, 64, 71, 75–76, 81; background of, 40–41; crackdown on the North Carolina Regulation, 68–70, 71–73; relationship with North Carolina Regulators, 57–58, 60–61, 70; during the Stamp Act crisis, 41–42; support for the Johnston Riot Act, 70. *See also* Husband, Herman; Johnston Riot Act of 1771; North Carolina Regulation; Stamp Act crisis of 1765; Tryon's Palace

Tryon's Palace, 51, 52, 61, 69. *See also* taxation

Turkeyfoot Township, PA, 82

Urmstrom, John, 18

U.S. Constitution, 4, 108; as barrier against democracy, 108; debate over articles of amendment to, 116–17, 118; opposition to, 114; ratification of, 114; support for, 114. *See also* Antifederalists; Bill of Rights; democracy; Federalists; Husband, Herman: views on

Valley of Virginia, 33
Vermont, 137
Vernon, Isaac, 159n115
Vestry Act of 1754, 35–36. *See also* Anglicanism (Church of England); taxation
Vestry Act of 1764, 45. *See also* Anglicanism (Church of England); taxation
Virginia, 64, 73, 75, 76, 77, 89, 91, 111, 127, 128; House of Burgesses, 64

Waddell, Hugh, 72
Wagerline, Philip, 80
Wake, Margaret, 40
Wake County, NC, 70
Washington, George, 1, 77, 84; attempts to negotiate with whiskey rebels, 123–24, 126; crackdown on whiskey rebels, 127–28, 128–29; opposition to his administration, 124. *See also* Hamilton, Alexander; Husband, Herman: views on; Whiskey Rebellion
Washington County, PA, 122, 123, 125, 129
Watson, James, 48–49
Webster, John, 124, 125
Wells, Benjamin, 128–29
Wesley, Charles, 20
Wesley, John, 20
Western Quarterly Meeting (NC), 37, 38, 39
Western Quarterly Meeting (PA), 91
West Indies, 13, 29, 30, 35
Westmoreland County, PA, 84, 95, 122, 123, 124, 129
West Nottingham Presbyterian Church, 19, 22
wheat, 8, 82; cultivation in Maryland of, 13–14; cultivation in North Carolina of, 33, 45. *See also* Husband, William, Jr.
Whiskey Rebellion, 1, 2, 3, 4, 130, 142; in Bedford County, PA, 124–25, 128; causes of, 122–23; divisions within whiskey rebel ranks, 125–26, 127, 142; Alexander Hamilton's opposition to whiskey rebels, 123–24; Parkinson's Ferry conference, 124–27; Redstone Old Fort conference, 127; violence during, 124; George Washington's crackdown on, 127–28, 128–29. *See also* Braddock's Field; Hamilton, Alexander; Husband, Herman; Parkinson's Ferry conference; Redstone Old Fort conference; Revenue Act of 1791; Washington, George; whiskey tax
whiskey tax, 122, 124, 125, 126, 127. *See also* Funding Act of 1790; Revenue Act of 1791; taxation
Whitefield, George, 2, 20–21, 21, 22, 23. *See also* Great Awakening; Husband, Herman
Wilcox, John, 58–59
Williams, John, 67
Williamsburg *Virginia Gazette*, 67–68
Wilmington, NC, 41
Wilson, James (farmer), 116
Wilson, James (lawyer), 114–15
Wisecarver, George, 129
women, 3–4, 132, 133. *See also* Husband, Herman: views on
Wood, Gordon S., 133
Woodmason, Charles, 36
Woods, George, 81, 95, 124, 168n47, 168n55; background of, 83; as leader of the Woods faction, 83–85, 89–90, 94; opposition to, 90, 104–5. *See also* American Revolution; Republicans
Woodward, John, 102
Wright, Charity, 37
Wright, John, 37, 40
Wright, Rachel, 37–40, 47. *See also* Cane Creek Monthly Meeting; Husband, Herman: opposition to; Society of Friends (Quakers)

XIV Sermons on the Characters of Jacob's Fourteen Sons (Husband), 1, 101, *110*; Husband's map of New Jerusalem in, *104*

Yale College, 43
Yearly Meeting of North Carolina, 39
Yeates, Jasper, 126–27
Yorktown, VA, 100

EARLY AMERICAN HISTORIES

Redemption from Tyranny: Herman Husband's American Revolution
    Bruce E. Stewart

Experiencing Empire: Power, People, and Revolution in Early America
    Patrick Griffin, editor

Citizens of Convenience: The Imperial Origins of American Nationhood on the U.S.-Canadian Border
    Lawrence B. A. Hatter

"Esteemed Bookes of Lawe" and the Legal Culture of Early Virginia
    Warren M. Billings and Brent Tarter, editors

Settler Jamaica in the 1750s: A Social Portrait
    Jack P. Greene

Loyal Protestants and Dangerous Papists: Maryland and the Politics of Religion in the English Atlantic, 1630–1690
    Antoinette Sutto

The Road to Black Ned's Forge: A Story of Race, Sex, and Trade on the Colonial American Frontier
    Turk McCleskey

Dunmore's New World: The Extraordinary Life of a Royal Governor in Revolutionary America—with Jacobites, Counterfeiters, Land Schemes, Shipwrecks, Scalping, Indian Politics, Runaway Slaves, and Two Illegal Royal Weddings
    James Corbett David

Creating the British Atlantic: Essays on Transplantation, Adaptation, and Continuity
    Jack P. Greene

The Evil Necessity: British Naval Impressment in the Eighteenth-Century Atlantic World
    Denver Brunsman

Early Modern Virginia: Reconsidering the Old Dominion
    Douglas Bradburn and John C. Coombs, editors